D1602565

THE POLITICAL THEORY
OF
LIBERATION THEOLOGY

THE POLITICAL THEORY OF

LIBERATION THEOLOGY

Toward A Reconvergence Of
Social Values And
Social Science

JOHN R. POTTENGER

State University of New York Press

Published by
State University of New York Press, Albany
© 1989 State University of New York

Printed in the United States of America

For information, address State University of New York
Press, State University Plaza, Albany, N.Y., 12246

Library of Congress Cataloging-in-Publication Data

Pottenger, John R., (date)
The political theory of liberation theology.

    Bibliography: p.
    Includes index.
    1. Liberation theology—Political aspects. I. Title.
BT83.57.P47 1989   261.7   88-34838
ISBN 0-7914-0118-9
ISBN 0-7914-0119-7 (pbk.)

10 9 8 7 6 5 4 3 2 1

To Shelley, Kressent, and Ashley—my end, my meaning, my joy

Table of Contents

Contents

Acknowledgments

THE EVOLUTION OF this book has a relatively long and varied past, but comprehensive and personal reflection on the story would be most appreciated only by the author. Part of that story, however, involves certain associates and colleagues at various institutions who contributed in important ways that public acknowledgment is only fitting. Professor Donald J. Wolf, of Arizona State University, deserves credit for stimulating my inquiry into the subject matter of this book. That inquiry has benefited from the theoretical and philosophical critiques of Professors C. Fred Alford, Charles E. Butterworth, Richard P. Claude, Stephen L. Elkin, Joe A. Oppenhiemer, and Ronald J. Terchek, of the University of Maryland, College Park. In particular, Professor Butterworth yielded invaluable time and incisive discussion that contributed immensely to the sharpening of my own arguments.

In addition, Professors N. Anthony Battaglia, Leroy C. Hardy, Ronald J. Schmidt, Joanna Vecchiarelli Scott, Christian Soe, Barry H. Steiner, and Thomas P. Trombetas, of California State University, Long Beach, provided significant scholarly opportunities, research support, and intellectual encouragement. The University of Alabama, Huntsville, also provided important research support. And other scholars, both known and unknown, deserve mention for their patient reviews of this book and their helpful recommendations, including Professors Paul Lakeland, of Fairfield University, Virginia L. Muller, University of San Diego, and Neal Riemer, of Drew University.

Of course, it is proper that none of the individuals mentioned above be held responsible for errors nor claims made in this book.

Acknowledgments

While I certainly gained much from their input, they may well diverge from my assessments and conclusions. I take full responsibility.

Finally, deep gratitude must be expressed to my wife and daughters who labored alongside me, sharing encounters with trying obstacles as well as experiencing moments of discovery, while offering the emotional strength that makes a scholarly project such as this worthwhile.

Introduction

FOR MANY OBSERVERS of contemporary society, a troubling new development looms on the horizon of acceptable religious thinking, a development that threatens to undermine the traditional understanding of the relationship between religion and politics; for others, a novel approach to religious and political philosophy has arisen that restores a critical and moral dimension to the banality of contemporary politics. Regardless of the varied reactions, a new religious movement guided by a peculiar political theology with a concern for social problems has indeed increasingly garnered worldwide attention in recent years from believers, policy makers, and scholars alike.

Since its emergence nearly two decades ago, *liberation theology* has become a unique and permanent political movement throughout Latin America. From Mexico to Chile, from Nicaragua to Brazil, this movement has been politically effective in merging together traditional, religious values with a commitment to social activism on behalf of "the poor and oppressed." Thinkers in this movement analyze social problems associated with chronic maldistribution of wealth and restrictive and repressive governmental policies. Then they combine these analyses with moral commitments to alleviating the plight of the poor to justify their engagement in a variety of reformist and revolutionary political activities.

Indeed, liberation theology has had frequent successes in influencing the direction of social change as well as on specific policy making in various parts of Latin America. For example, it played a significant role in the Nicaraguan revolution in 1979 and continues to provide a major source of legitimacy for the Sandinista regime. In fact, an

1

Introduction

informed awareness of the role of liberation theology is necessary for a comprehensive understanding of the dynamics of social change today in Central America. And the impact of liberation theology has been felt throughout South America as well. Influenced by the writings of liberation theologians, the existence of over one hundred thousand "Christian base communities" in Brazil alone continues to play an important part in that country's return to democratic politics.

But what is the appeal of this movement? Why has it been so successful? And what are the implications of liberation theology for future politics in Latin America, for theological development generally, and for political and moral philosophy?

Liberation Theology

Liberation theology is both a sociological and philosophical movement. Sociologically, it is a religious movement that deals with social problems generally found in the Third World. Individuals in this movement use their religious convictions as a standard to gauge and critique the effectiveness of economic and other social policies in meeting the basic needs of the citizenry. Furthermore, these individuals generally participate in politics to change perceived conditions of injustice as an ethical act of conscience, given their religious commitments to the poor and suffering. Consequently, this movement involves the clergy, including priests, nuns, and bishops, as well as lay members of the Church, both Protestant and Catholic.

While liberation theology does have a contextual orientation that explains both its origins and its subsequent development, it also has a philosophical dimension that provides a justification for political action and motivation for adherents to engage in politics and thus to change its context. It is in this sense that liberation theology may also be referred to as a "philosophical movement." This phrase captures the broad sweep of liberation theology's concerns—religious values and traditions, theology, social theory, political ethics, economics, technology, and science. A comprehensive philosophical framework—regardless of its origins—is necessary to combine these concerns into one meaningful whole. Philosophically, then, liberation theology provides a novel development in contemporary theology for the emergence of serious scholarly as well as popular reflection upon the meaning of traditional religious themes within the context of industrializing economies and authoritarian political systems. The movement provides serious reflection upon the relationship between God and humanity, salvation history, the Incarnation, morality, and society. It is at once a theological response to contemporary social problems, as well as a result of those problems in the face of religious traditions and values.

But as a philosophical movement, liberation theology offers far more than innovative reflection upon religious traditions. It possesses a political theory that claims to provide a comprehensive alternative to the politics of mainstream religious thought, to redefine the ethical parameters of political activism, including the use of violence, and to close the historic rift between orthodox Marxism and mainstream Christianity. In this way, liberation theology attempts to solve the problem of how the modern era can properly overcome its most debilitating characteristic: the dichotomy between *facts* and *values*.

The *fact-value dichotomy* developed as the path of early modern science began to cross the moral boundaries of discovery set previously by traditional cosmologies. These cosmologies consisted of relatively unified and comprehensive outlooks on religious, political, and economic concerns which had restricted the activities of natural philosophy or science to morally and socially appropriate ends. But a series of historical events, primarily from the fifteenth century through the nineteenth century, hastened the decline of the authoritative dominance over social life exercised by traditional outlooks. One of the social consequences, of the withdrawal of support for a shared moral outlook, was the steady erosion of ethical restraints on scientific investigation and technological development. As moral and theological speculation came increasingly under criticism for lacking empirical evidence to justify various normative claims, belief in scientific progress and the self-evident value of technological change began to fill the void.

The shift from the traditional era to the modern era in Western civilization neared completion as it became fashionably acceptable to define *facts* in terms of the new science with its empirical verification open objectively to all individuals, and then to consign all other claims, including social *values,* to the realm of metaphysics and thus of subjective interpretation only. The consequences have yielded a mixture of benefits and harm, but in many societies the mixture is often skewed violently in favor of a select few members. Various ideological and religious movements have struggled to solve the social problems resulting from the *fact-value dichotomy* of modernity, but with little success. With its religious traditions, its focus on the oppressed poor, and its use of modern social science, the political theory of liberation theology claims to deal successfully with the

3

disjunction between *facts* and *values,* the ultimate epistemological problem of modernity.

The Need for a Critique of the Political Theory of Liberation Theology

In recent years the phenomenon of liberation theology and its impact on Church-state relations, has excited much scholarly commentary from many academic quarters. Several descriptive studies have focused on the contemporary political activities of religious individuals and groups, including those influenced by liberation theology. Scholars interested in the history, dynamics, and impact of religious involvement in Latin American politics have produced important works often containing respectable, if nominal, discussions of the politically important role of liberation theology. The emergence of liberation theology, itself a serious school of religious thought, has encouraged a variety of responses from that sector as well. Both traditional and liberal theologians have produced important critiques of liberation theology's methods and implications for religious reflection and behavior. And a few scholars even ask questions dealing with the more general category of political theology and its relationship to other theoretical questions such as those found in sociology and the philosophy of science.[1]

But virtually no political philosopher nor social theorist has yet thoroughly analyzed the process whereby liberation theology merges considerations of contemporary social theory construction and application with the dynamics and requirements of theological development. Yet, in reading the writings of liberation theologians, the observer senses the existence of a theory of politics that transcends any individual author, although each author appears to complement the other in his contribution to the larger theory. The theory even appears at times to take on a life of its own.

An intense look at the political theory of liberation theology is significant, then, for three reasons. First, debate continues to rage in contemporary social science concerning the limits of behaviorally oriented methodologies with regard to normative questions; theologians of liberation claim to have a methodological framework that allows resolution of the issue. To do so, these thinkers insist on the theological as well as ethical importance of social scientific critiques (such as detailed analyses of the political economies of Latin America). But why does their peculiar approach to theology require the incorporation of social science as a crucial aspect for, and not merely an appendage of, theological development? Can it be justified? Does it work? And does it reveal any critical insights regarding the interface between descriptive assessments and prescriptive formulas?

Second, in their search for an acceptable social science, liberation theologians often incorporate Marxist analytical techniques in their attempt to bridge the gap between values and science. This adaptation raises serious questions as well. Ultimately, can any theology survive *qua theology* with the use of a radical social science approach that relies considerably on sociological analyses, including a sociology of religion? It would seem that Marxist frameworks would negate any potential contributions that religious institutions or theological development might make to the future construction of a just society. How do liberation theologians justify the use of Marxist social analysis?

Finally, as a social movement, liberation theology has, in fact, become a major force for radical change in many Third World countries, such as Nicaragua. How are we to understand the political significance of this movement, especially with regard to its defense of the legitimate use of violence? Furthermore, to what extent does and can liberation theology claim to provide legitimately unique epistemological insights with regard to social theory as well as theology, and to what extent do those insights influence and in turn become influenced by political ethical considerations?

Even beyond these philosophical questions and problems associated with its analytical construction and methodology, the political theory of liberation theology allures the curious observer. Its very presence challenges and entices the concerned individual to reflect upon the moral foundations of an ethical life, especially with regard to politics. Of course, it can do so because liberation theologians are themselves generally well-trained in the scholarly and intellectual methods and teachings of their religious and philosophical traditions and have written extensively for a wide audience. And it is through their writings that they are able to intrigue the fascinated reader, especially with their willingness to adopt alternative philosophical frameworks heretofore considered anathema. But even more, through their writings, liberation theologians elucidate the pathos of the human condition as they reflect upon their own experiences in unique and trying conditions of Third World societies.

The Approach to This Book

In an attempt to answer these normative and theoretical questions, this book presents an exploration of the political theory of liberation theology. It assesses how members of this movement have developed a peculiar methodology that justifies the inclusion of modern social science, especially Marxist frameworks, as a necessary element for responsible theological development. In this regard, it also demonstrates how they perceive the political and economic conditions of Latin America. It considers their political ethics, especially with regard to the use of violence, as well as the impact of liberation theology on individual and organized political behavior, from the phenomenal growth of "Christian base communities" to active engagement in politics at every level of society, including, at times, significant influence in the formulation of governmental policy.

This book attempts to set forth, as accurately as possible, the methodology used by liberation theologians for social theorizing, and to present the political theoretical arguments they endorse as they understand them. It does so by analyzing their theological discourse to extract the political theory that is embedded within that discourse and not readily apparent. Consequently, this investigation relies primarily on the selected writings of liberation theologians themselves who grasp various aspects of the political theoretical implications of their arguments.[2] In addition to the logical assessments of the political theoretical arguments of the writers, this book utilizes critical suggestions from other quarters as to the possibilities and limits of liberation theology generally. To this end, the first five chapters deal with the necessary elements of liberation theology's comprehensive theory of politics.

Chapter 1, "The Context of Liberation Theology," presents a discussion of the religious, political, and intellectual conditions that encouraged the development of this movement in Latin America. Recent official Catholic church pronouncements on social issues set the stage for the development of measured theological responses to problems of poverty and oppression in Latin America. But liberation theologians want to look beneath the symptoms of social injustice and discover the root causes. A discussion ensues on the failure of modernity to preserve a normative edge to scientific, technological, and economic development and examines how this failure further encourages attempts to restore a critical moral dimension to contemporary political economies. Given their normative assessments, liberation theologians have felt the need to develop an alternative methodological approach to biblical interpretation, theological development, and moral philosophizing. An explication of the methodological process in liberation theology follows in chapter 2.

Inasmuch as liberation theology is a political theology, then, it must deal with both theoretical and practical politics. In chapter 2, "Toward a Methodology for Liberation," critical evaluation focuses on liberation theologians' argument for the adoption of a methodology that requires the use of a social science to assist them in evaluating current social conditions. Consequently, they argue, an assessment of current social conditions will help them develop a theology in response to conditions of social injustice to serve as a moral guide for political activism. However, in criticisms of some mainstream or "academic" approaches to doing theology, they maintain that the methodological approach to theological development must be devoid of absolute certitudes so as not to impede philosophically, and later politically, the development of accurate criticisms of social conditions.

The methodology of liberation theology often takes the form of a *hermeneutic circle*. This circle emphasizes a continual critical assessment of status quo-oriented theologies and political ideologies that claim to justify the existence and continuation of poverty and oppression. The circle also emphasizes political action, or *praxis,* in connection with critical assessments to change the unacceptable social conditions. Hence, liberation theologians have merged an emphasis on *evangelization* with hermeneutics to develop a morally and socially responsible theology. To this end, the hermeneutic circle requires the use of social scientific critiques of society. With regard to the selection of a social science as required by this methodology, liberation theologians have generally opted for the incorporation of Marxist social analysis. But the merger of any aspect of Marxism with Christianity raises serious questions of both the theoretical compatibility as well as acceptable consequences of such a merger.

Chapter 3, "The Marxist-Christian Tension," invites careful and cautious considerations of the theoretical problems of a Marxist-Christian alliance vis-à-vis liberation theology. The choice of Marxist social analysis to serve as the appropriate social scientific component of their theology is significant. Liberation theologians argue that the use of such an approach allows for both descriptive assessments of social conditions as well as demands for social change. Furthermore, they point out that Marxism, too, utilizes a dialectic that corresponds directly to the dialectic of the hermeneutic circle. Yet conservative critics have advanced strong counterarguments that a basic problem of theory construction must be resolved when attempting to unite select parts from traditionally incompatible frameworks. The consequences of such unification may in fact end with the destruction of one side by the other. They argue that the destruction of the theological enterprise will result if Marxist sociology forces any reflection upon religious activity to accept the absolutely social basis of its origins.

Nonetheless, in terms of reuniting social values (traditional Christian norms) with social science (selective Marxist analysis), liberation theologians argue that they have worked out a legitimate compromise. Furthermore, they maintain, this compromise provides an initial step in developing a genuine, morally responsible, and comprehensive political theory. This theory upholds the integrity of its traditional religious values alongside modern social science and thus provides the foundation for restoring the critical dimension to modern science, economics, and politics. And it does so with the utilization of its peculiar methodology that holds basic religious moral concerns in tension with social science's analytical techniques, both of which are pulling in opposite directions. With an appropriate and effective set of analytical tools, political thinkers in liberation theology then proceed to search for the causes and dynamics of social injustice in Latin America.

Chapter 4, "Assessing Latin American Political Economies," presents and evaluates two perceptions of social reality in Latin America as found in liberation theology: an analysis of the world economy using "dependency theories," and an analysis of the "national security state" in Latin America. These assessments are crucial for the development of political ethics in liberation theology. They indicate that one of the sources of moral evil in the world is, in fact, systemic or structural. And as a result of their assessments of social conditions, liberation theologians find moral justification for various forms of political action to change "sinful social structures," including the use of revolutionary violence.

Now, the primary emphasis on theological development in this particular movement, as will be seen from chapter 2, is that "theology comes second." That is, the religious individual develops a particular theological understanding of reality, including justification for various forms of political behavior, as a result of life experiences coupled with specific moral commitments. Given a commitment to certain Christian values (chapters 1 and 2) and a particular approach to assessing the morality and dynamics of social conditions (chapters 3 and 4), the political theory of liberation theology claims it has argued the need for social change and discovered the origins of social injustice. Now it is in a position to lay the moral foundation for the ethics of particular forms of political behavior.

Chapter 5, "The Ethics of Reform and Revolution," assesses the primary moral arguments for political activism, examining justifications for both reformist politics and social revolution. This chapter pays careful attention to the political significance of "Christian base communities." These "communities" combine the dynamics of neighborhood associations with the purpose of Bible study groups. This combination of politics and faith can have far-reaching social consequences. The moral problem of violence for the religious individual is also carefully analyzed. Liberation theology does not rule out absolutely violent revolution for the transformation of society. By the conclusion of this chapter, the exploration in this book will have traversed the intellectual terrain from the initial idea of the importance of the study of politics to its conceptual development, analysis, and implementation. The book then concludes with an essay probing the potential contributions of the political theory of liberation theology to moral philosophy.

Chapter 6, "Ethics and Social Theory," pays special attention to problems of theory construction and epistemology. In particular, how well has the political theory of liberation theology bridged the gap between facts and values? Has it adequately restored the moral critical dimension to contemporary science, economics, and politics? A key factor in this attempt, of course, has been the incorporation of Marxist social analysis. Yet a problem remains for liberation theology with regard to the sociology of religion of orthodox Marxism. Can components of one philosophy (in this case from Marxism) be separated from their original framework and placed within the framework of another, perhaps alien, philosophy (in this case from theology) and survive? It is at this point that the insights of the Frankfurt School of *critical theory* may well provide the theoretical components necessary for liberation theology to defend its claim as a legitimate and unique approach to bridging the gap in the current dichotomy between social values and social science that has been the legacy of modernity, a legacy that has allowed values and science to drift apart. In this regard, more serious encounters between critical theory and liberation theology may well be worthwhile.

Chapter 1

The Context of Liberation Theology

NOT SO LONG ago in a small town in Brazil, a pastoral worker conducted a Bible study session with a group of peasants. While discussing with them the meaning of a passage from the Book of Acts depicting an event where an angel frees some apostles from prison, he asked: "Who was the angel?" A woman responded:

> Oh, I know. When Bishop Dom Pedro Casaldáliga was attacked in his house and the police surrounded it with machine guns, no one could get in or out and no one knew what was going on exactly. So this little girl sneaked in without being seen, got a little message from Pedro, ran to the airport, and hitched a ride to Goiana where the bishops were meeting. They got the message, set up a big fuss, and Dom Pedro was set free. So that little girl was the angel of the Lord. And it's really the same sort of thing.[1]

Initially such a response may strike us as evidence that the woman misunderstood the question. After all, the pastoral worker simply asked for clarification on an aspect of historical narrative from ancient Scripture. However, after further reflection upon the woman's response we may perceive alternative ways of understanding the intent of the question—from a simple straightforward, literal reading of the text as the pastoral worker presumably intended, to a recognition of the biblical passage as a symbolic representation with normative content of recurring historical events as suggested by the woman. In other words, there is an unresolved hermeneutical issue here of how to read and interpret Scripture.

And this particular occurrence in Brazil was not an isolated incident, nor the response atypical; it is itself symbolic of a growing phenomenon among Bible study groups throughout Latin America. So just what is the significance of this vignette?

The Religious Context

The search for meaning in everyday events by looking to the past is certainly not unique to Brazil nor to the twentieth century. That a relationship exists between the documents of the foundations of religion and the cultural values of the prevailing society—between *text* and *context*—has long been of interest to theologians, social philosophers, and sociologists alike. It is the conditions surrounding the event just depicted, however, that has set in motion a relatively novel if not unique movement. This is a philosophical movement that has moved beyond identification with religious values only to developing political dimensions whose ramifications threaten the legitimacy of the foundations of Latin American society itself. To grasp the significance of this story we need to look at another, earlier event whose long-term significance was also not immediately recognized.

Medellín, 1968

The world often perceives events only in terms of their immediate political impact; for example, in 1968, the abruptness and brutality of the Soviet-led invasion of Czechoslovakia, the Nigerian civil war, the political assassinations in the United States, and the worldwide student demonstrations and protests commanded immediate public attention. Yet the public attention induced by these dramatic events was short-lived; the actors and commentators moved on to other issues. As with other momentous historical events, the long-term significance was typically left to dwindle in obscurity with few traces left other than journalistic descriptions as monuments to their spent energy.

As years go, 1968 was little different in Latin America than 1967 before it, or 1969 after. The economy was at its usual state of sluggish performance. For example, the average Real Domestic Gross Product (RDGP) in Latin America was $1,520 per capita, ranging from El

11

Salvador with a per capita RDGP of $945, to Venezuela with a per capita RDGP of $3,495. By comparison, the United States had a per capita RDGP of $6,634.[2] Politically, Latin American governments generally came in the form of moderate to excessive military regimes; few nominally democratic processes were in existence. Perhaps Colombia adequately typifies the social and economic conditions of the time. Colombia's RDGP was $1,234 per capita, 81 percent of the average for Latin America, and 19 percent of the average for the United States. And its government consisted of an uneasy coalition between liberals and conservatives with a tense military establishment waiting in the wings.

But in contrast to the front-page news events of other parts of the world, it was this relatively inauspicious time and "normal" conditions in Latin America that set the stage for the little noticed, but soon to burgeon, development of a philosophical movement with religious foundations. This movement would develop political aspirations that would grow and spread throughout Latin America and become a potent political force two decades later.

In 1968, Medellín, Colombia, a city of over one million residents exhibiting the social characteristics typical of other urban areas throughout Latin America, played host to the Second General Conference of Latin American Bishops (*Consejo Episcopal Latinoamericano,* CELAM) that had been called to address immediate social problems from a religious perspective. A group of increasingly influential and socially concerned Latin American theologians who attended the conference hoped to advise the bishops and influence the proceedings. These theologians, convinced that highly touted government policies of political "modernization" and economic "development" were not proving to be the panacea for the political and economic ills of the continent, had reassessed their religious values and commitments with regard to moral questions of political oppression and poverty. They came to Medellín to find ways to use their position and status in society as a source of moral support for radical theological development to act ultimately as leverage to influence governmental policy making. But in addition to their intellectual training in theology, philosophy, and the social sciences, recent political events in Latin America also had a profound effect on their thinking.

Most notably, the triumph of the Cuban Revolution in 1959 had inspired other attempts by revolutionary groups throughout Latin America to realize Fidel Castro's vision of an alternative political economic system to those generally found in the Western Hemisphere.

Furthermore, in the early 1960s, radical critiques of liberal democracy and capitalism became commonplace as highly visible intellectuals applied them extensively to all aspects of Western culture. Radical economists and social theorists moved beyond analyses of economics and politics, and included assessments of virtually all aspects of human activity and thought, from technology to theology. Consequently, along with the development of political theories of revolution in many Western countries, theologies of revolution also emerged, especially in countries with pervasive religious sensitivities in the culture, such as in Latin America. By the late 1960s, however, the narrowness of the applicability of revolutionary thought, and the general failure of revolutionary movements in Latin America, forced theorists and theologians alike to reassess their positions and to search for a broader selection of approaches to problems of social injustice. Specifically, the recognition that liberation from oppression might come from reformist as well as revolutionary activity again gained credence by the early 1970s.

More significantly, though, the goals of critical social scientific studies and critical theological development had much in common, since both had the same ethical concerns about the social consequences of modern industrialization. Many social activists and thinkers would often forge political as well as intellectual alliances of an interdisciplinary nature. As these alliances grew and disparate disciplines influenced each other, a peculiar combination yielded at least one potentially powerful, new force in Latin American politics: a social scientifically sophisticated, activist clergy with the development of a "popular church" (*la iglesia popular*) to challenge the political and ecclesiastical status quo of the continent.

Many radical Christian thinkers were attempting to fashion theological positions that addressed contemporary problems of social injustice by addressing the ethical problems of govenmental social policy as well as individual political activism. For example, one theologian, Juan Luis Segundo, suggested in an early article that the use of violence against unjust practices by the government might find moral justification, even beyond that found in traditional theories of the just war.[3] Another theologian, José Porfirio Miranda, noticed much commonality between scriptural critiques of the relationship between individual wealth and political power, and Karl Marx's own critiques of industrialized societies exhibiting similar behavior and phenomena.[4] And shortly after the CELAM meeting another theologian, Gustavo Gutiérrez, completed the development of a path-breaking theological treatise that would ultimately provide the perspectives and impetus for, as well as the label of, the emergence of the new social movement: *A Theology of Liberation.*[5] Hence, these and other religious thinkers were not only attempting to fashion personal responses to problems of the day, but were attempting to enlist the formal support of the Church in their drive to social reform. It was not a coincidence, then, that these and other individuals found themselves at the CELAM meeting in Medellín, Colombia, in 1968.

At this meeting, the bishops of Latin America came together for the express purpose of considering the meaning of the religious reforms and considerations of the Second Vatican Council (1962–65) with regard to the modern world, and how best to apply them to the social conditions in Latin America. With several official proclamations, the Council had formally opened the Catholic church to various themes of modernity, including popular, if limited, participation in the liturgy, engagement in social activism on behalf of the poor, and the use of contemporary social science to enhance religious effectiveness.

For example, in *Gaudium et Spes* the Council recognized that the role of the Church ought not to be perceived strictly as outside of politics but as an integral part of humanity and history with a serious commitment to the cause of the poor.[6] While it suggested that the Church did not always have the solutions to all socioeconomic problems, it maintained that "the lawfulness of private ownership is not opposed to the various forms of public ownership," and reaffirmed the long-standing argument that private property may be expropriated justly if it is being misused.[7] Furthermore, the Council repudiated the position of atheists who fight against religion and its power of spiritual liberation. But it also chastised Christians as partly responsible for the growth of atheism in the world, and urged them to engage in dialogue with atheists, stressing the importance of believers and non-believers working together to improve social conditions.[8] It even confirmed the right of revolution under certain conditions.[9]

After days of lengthy and energetic debates, the conference at Medellín produced a set of documents that represented the consensus of opinion by Latin American bishops and their theological advisors on the problems of social injustice from a religious perspective. The Medellín Documents, however, would prove to have widespread influence on theological development throughout Latin America among both Catholic and Protestant thinkers. Specifically, the documents gave formal and prestigious acknowledgment to the development of the concept of "prophetic denunciation" found in liberation theology.[10] For heretofore concerned with the causes of political and economic "development," the bishops now took up the increasingly popular concern for "liberation" in a sociopolitical, as well as a theological, sense.[11] And the general themes of prophetic denunciation and liberation given by the bishops at Medellín would provide the impetus for the continual development of new theological frameworks that would connect the reinterpretation of biblical passages and their symbolic meanings to the development of a just society.

While liberation theology, then, was not the creation of the CELAM meeting in Medellín, the expression of liberation themes and concerns in the final documents of the proceedings took liberation theology a great distance in its quest for theological legitimacy, social acceptance, and political impact. A look at the major themes emanating from Medellín demonstrates the significance and potential of liberation theology as a serious political movement.

Medellín Documents

Influenced by earlier papal encyclicals as well as the Second Vatican Council, the Medellín Documents deal with a variety of issues with social and economic themes.[12] These themes can be classified into three broad categories: the recognition of the dangers of foreign imperialism that result in economic dependence as the root causes of poverty, the meaning of a commitment to solidarity with the poor, and the biblical grounds for the development of the concept of "liberation," as applied to contemporary social problems.[13]

With regard to the first category focusing on imperialism, the bishops argued that the political economies of Latin America had generated vast social inequalities in terms of both economic well-being and political power. Furthermore, they maintained, these "excessive inequalities systematically prevent the satisfaction of the legitimate aspirations of the ignored sectors, and breed increasing frustrations."[14] Thus, they saw poverty in itself as an evil, since it prevented individual access to material possessions necessary to live a decent Christian life. According to the bishops, "The prophets denounce [poverty] as contrary to the will of the Lord and most of the time as the fruit of the injustice and sin of men."[15] They argued that such inequalities are not primarily a function of natural causes, but result directly from human selfishness. And it is this selfishness that

15

has subjected the vast majority of the population to the slavery of hunger, ignorance, hatred, and oppression.[16]

The bishops further argued that the connection between foreign and local interests has created institutions of human organizations and practices that actually promote social and economic exploitation. This situation itself has taken on a life of its own, a condition of "institutionalized violence" as a result of its "structural deficiency of industry and agriculture, of national and international economy, of cultural and political life . . . thus violating fundamental rights."[17] The bishops condemned as unjust and sinful the prevailing arrangement of most Latin American political and economic institutions.[18]

Furthermore, as pointed out in earlier encyclicals of the Church, the bishops maintained that the mass suffering of Latin America arises from a profound misunderstanding by the business community of the ethics of private property and the proper handling of capital. They argued that the right of ownership and the morally proper ends of economic activity should not be seen as activity primarily designed to benefit a few. More properly understood, according to the bishops,

[a] business is an authentically human economy, does not identify itself with the owners of capital, because it is fundamentally a community of persons and a unit of work, which is in need of capital to produce goods. A person or a group of persons cannot be the property of an individual, of a society, or of the state.[19]

In fact, critical of the two major approaches to industrialization found throughout the world, they stated that generic systems of liberal capitalism and contemporary communism both "militate against the dignity of the human person," since the former focuses on the normative primacy of capital, while the latter focuses on totalitarian state power. The bishops urged Latin American societies to find an alternative economic system that upholds the importance of individual human dignity.

With regard to their second category dealing with a commitment to solidarity with the poor, the bishops' assessment of social conditions in Latin America led them to realize that the traditional Christian teachings of a dualism of spiritual concerns distinct from temporal concerns must now be avoided in the search for salvation.[20] This early theological position of "ontological dualism," however spiritually appealing, has had the practical effect of diverting Church teachings and practices away from attention on this life, to a focus on the Hereafter. The bishops accepted an alternative reading of Scripture that indicates that the Church, to fulfill its moral calling, must become more involved in temporal affairs of society, and the preferential option of the temporal Church must be on the side of the poor. And with regard to poverty, the Church must denounce the lack of material goods and the sin that begets it as unjust; it must preach as well as live in spiritual poverty; and it must itself be bound to material poverty. "The poverty of the Church is, in effect, a constant factor in the history of salvation."[21] Hence, the bishops concluded that the Church must direct its energies to find solutions to the problems of the poor.

And with regard to the final category dealing with the concept of liberation, the bishops put forth the notion that liberation, in the biblical sense, in fact refers to both physical and spiritual salvation.[22] While retaining traditional teachings on the importance of spiritual liberation from individual sin, the bishops added equal emphasis to the requirement of temporal liberation from "sinful social structures"; and to change the basic social structures in Latin America, "we believe that change has political reform as its pre-requisite."[23] But to be liberated physically from political and economic oppression, freedom and rights must first be understood. This meant that the Church must become involved in assisting the political education of its members to increase citizen participation in politics. The Church must use its moral position and resources, they argued, to help increase awareness, especially among the poor, with regard to the nature of present social conditions, "so that they might come to know their rights and how to make use of them."

Heavily influenced by the pedagogical methodology of the Brazilian educator Paulo Freire, the bishops placed great emphasis on educating the illiterate in a way that would increase their awareness or consciousness—"conscientization" (*conscientização*)—about the political dimension of their social conditions, including the origins and consequences of particular political relationships.[24] Furthermore, the bishops encouraged attempts to convert the poor away from "the individualistic [ethical] mentality into another one of social awareness and concern for the common good."[25]

With the Church actively involved in the liberative process, the bishops were confident that a new Latin American continent would result with "new and reformed [social] structures" and "new men" who know how to be free.[26] With this goal in mind, the bishops

17

denounced the Latin American arms race as a threat to freedom; and, in the face of numerous military regimes, they defended human rights as necessary for freedom. They also encouraged the development of grass-roots organizations as a vehicle for political activity among the poor to effect their liberation.[27] And as a result of this encouragement—to develop "Christian base communities" (as *comunidades eclesiais de base*, CEBs)—the greatest social impact from Medellín has been felt on recent political developments in Latin America.[28]

In these "communities," neighbors gather to discuss how traditional biblical themes and other religious teachings relate to current social problems of economics and politics. Out of this discussion emerges a normative foundation for the development of an ethical standard from which to analyze critically economic policies and political conditions. But it is this peculiar approach to the interpretation of Christian values vis-à-vis problems of social injustice, as opposed to the traditional focus on problems of social instability, that has led to the development of alternative understandings of religious thought and, consequently, to new theologies; and these in turn have had their own subtle but decisive influence on aspects of the institutional Church. According to the political commentator Penny Lernoux, "The emphasis of the Medellín Documents on Christian rather than political values was fundamental to the Church's declaration of independence from the state." [29] With this theoretical separation from the state, in an ideal situation the Church could now exercise its prophetic duty by standing outside of the social structures that gave ideological support to the destructive activities of the state and denouncing as unjust various institutions, policies, and practices.[30] Furthermore, under these conditions, the bishops' quest for peace and justice could become more than a call for the cessation of violence; it could become a call for the development of a genuine sense of community as well.[31] According to the bishops,

a community becomes a reality in time and is subject to a movement that implies constant change in structures, transformation of attitudes, and conversion of hearts. . . . An authentic peace implies struggle, creative abilities and permanent conquest. . . . Peace is not found, it is built. The Christian man is the artisan of peace.[32]

With the evidence of similar attempts throughout history before them, the bishops recognized that any attempt to build a new community and eventually a new society at the behest of the marginal members of the present society, would encounter opposition from entrenched sectors of the state. The current structures of institutionalized violence that they desired to transform would not hesitate, when threatened, to turn on the Church and committed Christians as well.[33] Aware of the potential for a widening cycle of violence, the bishops warned those in power not to risk provoking violent responses by taking advantage of the peaceful, reformed-oriented activities of the Church.[34]

Inasmuch as this commitment to solidarity with, and liberation of, the poor increases the potential for greater social violence, the bishops were forced to confront the moral problem of violence by elaborating on its meaning and its proper role in the liberative process. They challenged as incomplete, Pope Paul VI's concept of violence in his own introductory comments at Medellín. While recognizing the unjust character of Latin American society, the pope stopped short of endorsing violent revolutionary change and ruled out individual violence as an appropriate tool for social reform. The bishops argued, however, that many forms of violence exist, not only by the individual or groups, but by "the day-to-day operations of unequal, unjust, and oppressive social structures."[35] Furthermore, they maintained that, while preferring peace to violence, "the Christian man is peaceful and not ashamed of it. [But] he is not simply a pacifist, for he can fight."[36] And citing Paul's own earlier encyclical, *Populorum Progressio* (1967), the bishops reminded him that he had also admitted the possibility that under certain conditions violent revolution can indeed be justified.[37] With this authoritative support, the bishops confidently warned those holding political and economic power of the latent possibility for violent, revolutionary change. "One should not abuse the patience of a people that for years has borne a situation that would not be acceptable to any one with any degree of awareness of human rights." [38]

Unlike the immediate political impact of other events of 1968, the CELAM conference at Medellín with its broadly disseminated official documents contributed in a crucial way to the encouragement and long-range development of alternative, even radical, political theologies. Of particular importance for the maturation of liberation theology and specifically the development of its own political theory, then, were the liberation theologians' own elaboration on the following specific Medellín themes: the centrality of socioeconomic conditions in religious life and the necessity for critical social evaluation;

the reinterpretation of traditional religious concerns and values and their application in light of these social critiques; and the commitment to active participation in politics to realize conditions of social justice.

After Medellín

As they interpreted the Scriptures and their own Christian intellectual tradition and with the formal encouragement of the CELAM proceedings at Medellín, liberation theologians confidently argued that the poor and oppressed of this world need not wait until the next for improvements in their spiritual conditions. They maintained that religious and scriptural accounts of God's dealings with humanity argue that justice must be sought in temporal conditions as well. Such teachings, they concluded, encourage the religiously sensitive individual to become active in the political life of the community to give deeper meaning to Christian values.

With the support of CELAM at Medellín, the development of a "new awareness" of social problems from a religious perspective began to grow in popularity throughout the Church. Many religious thinkers struggled with the problem of discerning proper ethical attitudes toward contemporary problems of social injustice in Latin America—but the focus was not on attitudes alone. They also recast their moral commitments in a way that encouraged them to be involved in political activities that seek to effect often dramatic social change. As a result of this commitment to social change, they were faced with three fundamental problems: how to relate the Church to the modern world, both politically and theologically; how to explain the relationship between religious faith and political ideology; and how to assess morally the human costs involved for such "Christian discipleship." [39] And it was the debate dealing with the human costs that raised the most profound objections within, as well as outside, the religious community to radical political activism. For in the transformation of political, economic, and other social structures, all concerned individuals understood that the consequences of social change may have a direct impact on the lives of millions of inhabitants. And the ethical questions associated with the cost of social change in Latin America could not be ignored. Of most concern to participants in this debate was the question of violent revolution.

According to the political scientist Daniel Levine, the bishops' formal recognition of the central role played by institutionalized violence in Latin American society "opened the way to justifying counterviolence—violent acts intended to undo the inherent, institutionalized violence of the established order, replacing the old order with a more just society." [40] He further elaborates on the consequences of the thinking at Medellín by noting that the Latin American political economies characterized by injustice, oppression, and institutionalized violence "were [perceived as] sinful because they imposed social conditions making a fully moral and decent life impossible." Hence, the bishops concluded that religious grace—that is, freedom from sin—involves a commitment to change the sinful social structures, "by revolution if necessary."

The perception of poverty as a structural problem and not simply a problem of lack of individual motivation, of course, has far-reaching consequences. For one, individual charity may not be adequate to resolve the misery of poverty or the injustice that caused it. As Levine puts it, "Rather, the structures which cause poverty must be challenged—and this is a matter of power and political action." [41] As a result of their renewed interest in the origins of poverty and their identification with the poor, many religious thinkers began to justify their involvement in revolutionary struggle as they took a new look at the problem of the moral legitimacy of violence.[42]

The early 1970s saw the short-lived development of "theologies of revolution" as well as actual participation by members of the clergy in violent political behavior.[43] This led to a reaction by more conservative religious thinkers against those individuals who criticized from radical perspectives any government policies of economic and political development.[44] Yet this reaction against theologies of revolution had the effect of broadening the subject matter of theological discussions and thus encouraging new developments in Latin American political theology in general. The nominally disparate concerns of social issues and religious values became integrated into the more complex frameworks of theologies of liberation as opposed to the more narrow focus on revolution of the earlier radical theologies. Many religious thinkers were able to maintain their general criticisms of current economic policies and institutions, and not be necessarily committed to violent politics.[45]

The religious context dealing with the themes of poverty, institutionalized violence, and liberation, contributed substantially to setting the foundation for the development of a genuine theory of politics. Of course, any theoretical or philosophical approach to politics must attempt to integrate a variety of pertinent themes into a relatively consistent and meaningful whole. Liberation theology does indeed attempt to maintain a theoretical whole with regard to politics—but perhaps at considerable "theological cost" with regard to its implications for religion. An awareness of the potential costs to religion forced early radical thinkers to select a particular theological concept as a basis for including politics in their philosophizing. To this end, they attempted to refine further the concept of "prophetic denunciation," as just discussed, to provide legitimate religious grounding for their political theory.

With support for prophetic denunciation found in abstract official Church documents, radical theologians began to charge that the institutional Church was not interested in real fundamental change, nor did it possess the sophisticated theological and sociological tools to justify and bring about fundamental change. These criticisms were widespread among the lower clergy and among other religious thinkers. According to the theologian J. Andrew Kirk, liberation theology was born as a movement of protest against the institutional Church's conservatism and alliance with the status quo, against prevailing social and political conditions in Latin America, and against many expressions of mainstream theology taught in academic centers in North America and Europe.[46] A closer look at the intellectual and social consequences of the third form of protest against certain tendencies of mainstream theology is of particular interest with regard to assessing the political theory of liberation theology. For liberation theology becomes an alternative theological enterprise by accepting aspects of the methodology of mainstream, academic theology while denouncing its subservience to the status quo in society and the Church. In this way, it will be seen, it attempts to maintain its credibility as a proponent of serious theological reflection, while justifying its engagement in social criticism and political activism. And it is through engagement in social criticism and political activism—that is, the enterprise of political theory—that liberation theology may offer potential contributions for dismantling the modern dichotomy between facts and values.

So before proceeding to an analysis of the methodological approach to liberation theology and its distinction from mainstream theology as a first step toward the development of a theory of politics, we have set the stage for alternative theological developments in Latin America by looking only at the religious context for such development. Inasmuch as this book attempts to set forth and evaluate the political theory of liberation theology, a closer look at the political theoretical context that influences the development of this political theology is necessary.

The Political Theoretical Context

The importance of the community, of course, places any theological development in the same arena of concern as political theory. The development of political society with its emphasis on community, necessarily raises questions concerning how the community is understood to function (descriptive concerns); what goals are appropriate for it to pursue, achieve, or maximize (normative concerns); and, given the nature of the community and its purposes, how best to achieve its objectives (prescriptive concerns). The domain of political philosophy, then, appears to overlap if not subsume that of political theology.[47]

Because Latin American liberation theology comprises a significant philosophical movement actively involved in the quest for a just community, of crucial importance is the viability of its social theory and its related justification for various forms of political action. Following the basic questions to be answered by political theory, there are three concerns that any philosophical movement that claims to be concerned with social issues, including liberation theology, must take into account: the normative underpinnings that give meaning and value to human existence; the explanations that describe extant social conditions; and the moral restrictions that delineate and define acceptable political behavior.[48] But in essence, liberation theologians claim that their efforts represent an attempt to restore a critical, normative edge to assessments of the modern legacies of positivist-oriented social science as it influences economic and other public policies as found in Latin America.

Generally speaking, contemporary societies of the industrialized world and those attempting to copy them have been implementing basic governmental processes and assumptions founded on claims proposed during the age of the Enlightenment at the advent of the modern era. These claims include the recognition of universal reason, the privatization of ethics, the advocacy of consumerism and democracy, and the elevation of the pursuit of self-interest, either individually or collectively, as a proper vocation. These claims had the historic effect of challenging the traditional status quo of the Middle Ages with regard to the legitimacy of the state, Church, and local community. And this in turn undermined the consensus on the universal standard of morality that ought to apply to governmental as well as to individual decision making. Of significance were the far-reaching effects occasioned by the release of the heretofore pent-up individual drive to satisfy insatiable desires.

To appreciate fully the critical role of liberation theology as it assesses the moral failings of political economic regimes in Latin America and its claim to make an original contribution to contemporary political theory, a brief tracing of the historical loss of normative criticism in Western social thought is in order.

The Modern Understanding of the Individual and the Community

The established wisdom of traditionalism of the classical and medieval eras, was based on authoritative writings of venerable philosophers and theologians from Plato, Aristotle, and Cicero, to Alfarabi, Avicenna, and Aquinas. These thinkers taught the importance of submerging the rambunctious ego to rationality, of the individual to the community—not completely, but enough so that a stable tension between the two existed in such a way that the individual would become virtuous over a lifetime, thereby attaining true happiness and helping the community, and thus others, at the same time.[49]

For example, distinctions had been made between property rights and subsistence rights, with community rights defined as derivative of these two. Greater moral and political emphases were placed on the latter. This tense but stable arrangement between the two meant that while some notion of private property and unequal distribution of wealth was tolerated, individual pursuits were to be constrained by such moral maxims as: "No one should go without basic necessities of life." The wealthy, for example, were morally obligated to provide the basic necessities for the lame and needy. Hence, a particular relationship existed between the concepts of "duty" and "rights." According to the social theorists Frances Fox Piven and Richard A. Cloward,

> While some were rich and most were poor, the rich had a responsibility to ensure the subsistence of the poor that tempered their authority, and the poor had a right to subsistence that mitigated the burden of their duties to the rich.[50]

"Tempering authority" through accepted concepts of moral obligation provided the constraints necessary to avoid the arbitrary and

24

malicious exercise of personal and political power. Such a general social philosophy provided the foundations for an organic community of both socially responsible as well as individually deserving citizens, however unequal and perhaps inequitable the distribution of wealth and the exercise of political authority.

But it was the advent of the Protestant Reformation and its emphasis on individual salvation that provided the foundation for the liberal values of individual rights, including free speech, free association, and private property.[51] Furthermore, with the legitimacy of absolutist theology undermined by developments in natural philosophy (science) as well as the Protestant Reformation, the movement for freedom only from learning and teaching about Church and state explanations of the physical universe quickly spread to other areas under the control and influence of the conservative traditionalists, including politics and economics.

Symbolic in the shift in thinking about the role of the individual in society that was ushered in with the modern era, were the writings of Niccolò Machiavelli, Thomas Hobbes, and John Locke. Machiavelli, for example, seemed to argue that men were naturally flawed, imperfect, and selfish. He recommended that public policies should reflect the possibilities and limits of human nature and thus be themselves limited to attempts to achieve the public good by playing interest against interest; for any attempt to create a virtuous citizenry would be doomed to failure.[52]

Hobbes and Locke also helped to create alternative symbolic images of nature, humanity, and society, as a challenge to traditional conceptions. Their writings would accordingly be used to drive further the wedge between the individual and the traditional community. The individual, they maintained, should be liberated from aristocratic politics and mercantilist economics. The individual, naturally flawed, is egoistic, selfish, and a rational maximizer. Natural resources are scarce, resulting in competition; and the individual, says Hobbes, fears death, not only of starvation when he has nothing, but of his neighbor when he has something.[53] With the proliferation of these views, it soon became generally acceptable to perceive each individual as free, with natural rights, to seek and aggrandize power, through the domination of nature and his neighbors. Only the individual can decide what is ethically appropriate, it was thought, given the intellectual equality of humankind, and hence what is good must be what gives pleasure, evil pain. Reason itself, then, was accepted wholly as an instrument in the service of passion, not the pursuit of

25

virtue. And with science—that is, mathematics, geometry, and as-tronomy—newly liberated from the ethical constraints of theology, the individual became morally free to invent and use any new device to increase his material condition.

Several symbolic images, literary devices, and concepts, such as "the state of nature," "natural right," and "social contract," gained popular credence, acceptability, and legitimacy. These terms were used extensively by many writers of the day to depict a harsh world populated by generally isolated individuals who were guided pri-marily by an ethic of radical individualism. Pursuing their self-interest and often with limited resources available, these competitive in-dividuals were portrayed as in continual conflict with each other and thus in need of a larger stabilizing force to bring social order out of chaos. Locke, too, utilized these images and argued that, to avoid a world of rapacious marauders and the inevitable power struggles that occur among men, a government is necessary to main-tain social stability and to provide a safe environment for each in-dividual's pursuit of selfish interests—to protect life, liberty, and property.[54]

In the same way that thinkers from Nicholas Copernicus to Isaac Newton had broken the tension between mathematics and the natural sciences and theology,[55] so the influential writings of such modern thinkers as Machiavelli, Hobbes, and Locke broke the tension be-tween the egoistic individual and the traditional community. Further-more, these modern writers often patterned their new models of the dynamics of society after those of the physical world devised by René Descartes, Newton, and others.[56] The control and manipulation of symbols and values by the venerated theologians and statist poli-ticians were overthrown as the bourgeois revolutions of the seven-teenth century—quickly on the heels of, and in conjunction with, the Scientific Revolution—swept away the domination of traditionalism. In the relatively short time span of four hundred years, the tradi-tional, monolithic theological community was rapidly reduced to a state of pluralism; and so, too, the traditional and religious commu-nity's theory about the naturalness and necessity of society was sup-planted by the stark explanation that the human condition is one of radical individualism, hyperpluralism, and agnosticism. Hobbes and Locke, however, argued that a new understanding of community with government is needed once again, but this time as a necessary evil to protect radical individualism. Yet along what lines would the state be restructured?

A general consensus on the political theoretical foundation of the classical liberal state finally emerged. The new state would be understood as an artificial community dependent upon the individual members of society. Each member contracts with every other member to obey the rules and laws of the community as long as life, liberty, and property are recognized as inherent rights to limit and be protected by government. Furthermore, the use of power by the government as well as the formulation of laws would proceed according to decisions based on the consent of a majority of those in the community. These limitations on government should provide for maximum freedom of the individual balanced with the protection by government of those harmed by any individual who ignores the contract. Thus, the new liberal state is to provide for the safety, convenience, and prosperity of its members.[57] In this way, the state of classical and medieval thought—the state that maintained a tension between the needs of the community and the inordinate passions of the individual—was destroyed by classical liberalism in conjunction with the Scientific Revolution, and then reconstituted based on the primacy of the individual and his contractual agreements with others. Consequently, the modern state is now restructured, based on tension between individual and individual as each pursues his destructive path only to the point of the next individual's right to do the same.[58] In the modern liberal state, the government and the community are artificial creations of real and natural individuals to safeguard their autonomy. Virtue is now wholly a private matter, and justice exists only to protect an individual's liberty.

Market Economy as Market Society

Defenders of the liberal state were quick to provide moral justification for their new community. The tension that bound the community together was based on each individual's limited but diverse exercise of personal liberty. In a peculiar way, social institutions were necessary to encourage yet restrain that liberty.

The importance of liberty becomes apparent as it is recognized that any arrangement, including economic arrangements, entered into freely by one individual with another is just, as long as there is no fraud, deceit, or theft. The engagement in economic activity is itself an enterprise whose nature and goals are to be dictated only by the individuals involved. Ideally, there should be no state control and goals for the common good as under traditional conservatism. Adam Smith argued that the common good will be served as each individual engages in economic activity with only his own interest in mind, as though an "invisible hand" were exploiting and allocating resources efficiently.[59] Thus, once the liberal state has been reconstituted along lines respecting individual freedom and autonomy, a market economy of freely participating actors is the next requirement.

A market economy, then, assumes that individual participants or consumers are free to make choices, and that adequate, if not perfect, information exists for rational and efficient decision making. The existence of consumer uncertainty in the marketplace motivates producers to compete for consumer attention and thus to provide goods and services of reasonable quality at an affordable price.[60] This price, the efficiency price, is by definition just, since both buyer and seller, consumer and producer, agree—voluntarily. And furthermore, resources are used efficiently; there should be no wastage. In a market economy and a market society, the results of agreements voluntarily entered into and freely agreed upon are just. Of course, redistribution of wealth is never justified except as perhaps to rectify past injustices in the ownership and legal transmission of ownership of property.[61] And there are no natural obligations that exist for one individual to help another exercise his rights. One is only morally required *not* to interfere with the rights of others. The only artificial obligations are those defined by contract when two or more parties freely agree to abide by its terms. These the state must enforce. (Again, the classical liberals argued that the state itself is merely the result of a contractual agreement among individuals who freely come together for mutual advantage and individual benefit).

Market Economy and the Industrial Revolution

One of the consequences of the Scientific Revolution, in conjunction with the bourgeois or liberal revolutions and their freeing of the economy, was the accelerated pace of technological improvement and innovation. From farming, coinage, and weaving, to warfare, food preservation, and maritime navigation, broad areas of human endeavor experienced a revaluation and revitalization in their methods of production and operation.[62] With the abandonment of moral and theological restrictions on science and technology of an earlier era, new inventions and innovations, especially with regard to the economy, initiated an Industrial Revolution.[63]

With developments in mathematical theory applied to solving problems in scientific observations, these observations were themselves often perceived as having greater value than simple curiosity about nature and its perceived anomalies. If one could understand the dynamics of natural processes, one should, conceivably, be able to predict nature's activities. With sufficient information, one could then ultimately control nature, or at least parts of it. And with the rational superiority of man over nature, the domination of nature by man, could, if it were complete enough, for the first time allow man to determine his own destiny on this planet, instead of being subject to the unpredictable, if not capricious, and destructive forces of nature. Thus, it was argued, nature could be tamed and utilized to provide benefits for those who understood her secrets.

The Industrial Revolution brought about an explosion in human creativity as science and technology pushed back the frontiers of nature's secrets. New inventions—applied technology—coupled with improved and innovative business practices permitted the newly liberated ego of individual self-interest to extend the range of the pursuits of profits, wealth, social prestige, and political power, with few limits and obstacles. But with unequal starting points economically, a few became exceedingly wealthy. And in the euphoria of dominating nature with its perceived unlimited resources, the Vanderbilts, the Carnegies, the Rockefellers, and others, became paradigmatic examples, if not idols, to those who also longed for the fulfillment of dreams for a way of life of personal freedom that presumably only material acquisitions could provide.[64]

Indeed, in the epitome of the liberal state, the United States, the Industrial Revolution, coupled with the advent of the Civil War, required rapid development of steel-producing capabilities and other heavy industries for military procurement. This in turn resulted in the irreversible transformation of the American economy and society, from a primarily rural and agricultural economy, to one of urbanization and manufacturing. The material success of industrialization had the effect of providing the basis for a new social or public philosophy: capitalism.[65] The defense of capitalism as the most appropriate way to organize a political economy would be parroted by politicians and invoked by entrepreneurs at the slightest criticism or hint of public regulation. Not only in the boardrooms, but in legislative bodies and courtrooms, the virtue of private property, the private ownership of the means of production, would be preached—even supplanting the original cause of liberty itself. And the social echoes of these sermons would be felt throughout the world as local enterprises grew and developed into multinational corporations spreading the new gospel of wealth.

Within the ranks of social thinkers of the new public philosophy, however, voices of warning were also heard; the dream of materialism was not to be fulfilled for all. The apostles of egoism warned that not all could be accommodated materially and satisfactorily in even the wealthiest of nations:[66] Smith had warned of the beneficial if limiting effects of the division of labor and specialization; Thomas Malthus had also warned that the rising tide of affluence (arithmetical) would never catch up with the ever-increasing expansion of the national population (geometrical); David Ricardo also argued that the increase in population with industrialization playing catch-up would drive wages down and depress even more the living conditions of the working poor; and Henry George warned of a similar effect on real estate prices and rents. Even John Stuart Mill argued that unequal starting points would always result in the unequal distribution of wealth, and that this would have a distorting effect on politics.[67]

Liberalism in Latin America

Much of the adverse social consequences of post-Second World War development in Latin America can be attributed to an underlying but decisive attitude toward the concept of property rights just described. The introduction of Protestantism, Enlightenment thinking, and modernization, had the effect of breaking the commercial monopoly of Spain and the religious monopoly of Catholicism. In fact, the introduction of liberalism into Latin America can be tied to the successful independence movements of the nineteenth century.[68]

In those parts of the world where the Protestant Reformation had comparatively little or no effect, the revolutionary effects of liberalism on politics and economics were likewise slow to germinate.[69] In Latin America, until the late nineteenth century, Catholic social teaching, while generally supporting the political and economic status quo, continued to emphasize the moral obligation and social duty of the powerful and wealthy to the weak and destitute.[70] Church doctrine emphasized that the subsistence needs of the poor be given priority over private property rights. In essence, while they could dominate politics and maintain virtual total social control over the peasantry, the wealthy were also expected to provide sufficient means and conditions by which the peasantry could earn a living. Thus, a skewed distribution of political power and economic wealth in favor of a minority could be morally appropriate in an area abundant with natural resources.

Many Third World countries, however, have pursued particular policies of economic development in response to demands by the industrialized countries of the West for raw materials and cheap labor in the recession that followed the Second World War. As a result of their link with the world economy dominated by industrialized nations, they anticipated the return of benefits to improve the standard of living. In Latin America, Western "developmentalism" (*desarrollismo*)—the increasing of domestic industrial and agricultural production by introducing greater amounts of foreign capital—was initially greeted as the best means by which to achieve prosperity. However, later critics have pointed out that the succeeding four decades yielded only insignificant improvement with regard to Latin American social conditions.[71]

The drive for economic development by Latin American governments has led many policy makers to disregard subsistence rights in favor of property rights. This has occurred, in large part, as a result of the demands of foreign business interests who wanted guarantees of sizable returns on their investments in consonance with the recognition of prevailing investment patterns and property rights of the industrialized countries of the West. Unforeseen, at least by a majority of Latin Americans, was the subtle but ultimately decisive shift in attitudes toward property rights on the part of the wealthy bourgeoisie and landowning classes who succeeded in reversing the subordination of property rights to subsistence rights. This attitudinal shift opened the way for the transformation of the foundations of community from the earlier notion of a basic tension between the individual's ego and the common good, to the modern premise of a tension between the diverse and often contradictory goals of each individual. And with this transformation came the introduction of liberal economic policies. Today modified market economies now characterize most of the economic arrangements in Latin America. Yet curiously, far from traditional laissez-faire conditions of classical liberalism, state monopolies and large corporate enterprises, primarily foreign, dominate the economic activities and the profits of Latin America.[72]

As the wealthy have become more concerned, then, with personal profits and less with social obligation, and with the state primarily concerned with satisfying the demands of the local elite and international interests, peasants have been more easily removed from the land they have worked but to which they held no legal title or claim; furthermore, they have been provided little or no relief.[73] Unemployment has soared as subsistence farming has decreased with the appropriation of land by certain wealthy families and foreign business enterprises and the introduction of mechanized techniques.[74] Sprawling slums in the major cities of Latin America continue to grow rapidly as rural peasants, driven off the land, are forced to seek work and enter the labor market of the more industrialized areas. However, with high rates of illiteracy, virtually no appropriate job experience, few jobs available, and inadequate social welfare programs, the growing slums provide not only breeding grounds for crime, disease, and starvation, but a potential base for those disaffected with government-supported development policies. And just the potential for such a base is often perceived by political elites as a challenge to the very system that legitimates, protects, and perpetuates the conditions of poverty. Hence, the frequent introduction of oppressive measures by military and political authorities to maintain stability and order has become commonplace.

The extensive and often systematic use of oppressive measures by authoritarian regimes in recent years has provoked heated debate and political responses from several quarters throughout Latin American society, including the Catholic church. Many well-respected and powerful ecclesiastical officials have denounced the abuses of human rights in their own as well as neighboring countries and worked to bring about their eradication.[75] For example, the military coup that came to power in Brazil (1964) with its often violent disregard for the rights of leaders and members of opposition groups, brought swift moral resistance from such figures as Dom Hélder Câmara, Bishop of Recife, and Paulo Cardinal Arns, Archbishop of São Paulo. Ultimately, the Church can be credited with contributing in a major way to the transition from military rule to civilian control by 1982. But it was the increasingly violent deprivation of human rights by authoritarian regimes as well as the growing poverty throughout Latin America that provided the focus for discussion and official positions by CELAM at Medellín.

Toward Restoring the Moral Critique: Liberation Theology

How are we to comprehend the response at the beginning of this chapter from the woman who unexpectedly interpreted a passage of Scripture in a very contemporary and political way? What kind of methodology did she use that influenced her to see the essence of traditional religious values threatened under current social conditions, and to do so in a highly critical fashion?

As discussed earlier, destitute social conditions provide the setting for the emergence of moral critiques of economic and political development policies that appear to deny any definition of individual rights to the very citizens who presumably are to benefit from that development. But the presence of these critiques is particularly relevant in destitute societies with a strong religious dimension to their culture. The assessment of social conditions from a specific religious framework ultimately points to the larger question of how to reinstate moral constraints on scientific, technological, and economic developments—ultimately, that is, on how to overcome the fact-value distinction of the modern era.

It is in response to destitute social conditions that radical theologians have begun to voice moral outrage.[76] Their religious sensibilities have been violated and they feel some ethical response is necessary for matters of conscience. They have come to see that the primary flaw in the modern era was the failure on the part of scientific, technological, and economic development strategies to include a critical, normative aspect to their work above that of individualist ethics. This failure, they believe, has allowed development in these areas to run apace with virtually no consideration for the moral implications of its "success." The project, then, for liberation theology is to restore the critical dimension to human organization and social policies by pointing out where such questions should be raised and what they should address. Furthermore, they want to restore to society a sense of community that respects human dignity and rights.

The essence of liberation theology's project, then, is to bring moral critique to bear on the structure of the present "community" of the political economies of Latin America while attempting to provide direction for the development of a new, if not truer, sense of community. Yet Scriptures, papal encyclicals, and other Church documents, say little about how to provide sophisticated evaluations of contemporary social conditions and how these analyses should relate to proper ethical behavior.

Before the moral critique can be restored to modern politics, a methodological approach to theological development that requires the inclusion of modern social science must be set forth. But what kind of theological methodology is appropriate for liberation theology?

Chapter 2

Toward a Methodology for Liberation

Introduction

As the social philosopher Isaiah Berlin reminds us, when he paraphrases the German poet Heinrich Heine, "Philosophical concepts nurtured in the stillness of a professor's study could destroy a civilization."[1] But for this to happen, now to paraphrase Plato, the interests of political power and those of moral philosophy must coincide. Whether for destructive or constructive ends, the mixture of ideas and power has always been volatile. History is replete with political and economic elites who have maintained their social positions through the manipulation of intellectually inspired but commonly held beliefs to justify various political activities and particular economic arrangements. And not unexpectedly, the development and acceptance of particular theologies that give meaning to common beliefs, have often been used to the advantage of those in power, regardless of theological merit. What is it, then, about the dynamic of a particular theoretical or theological impetus that gives it a certain direction as well as potential for co-optation by others?

One of the characteristics of Western religious thought has been its relatively easy adaptability by various elites in providing ideological support for a variety of political regimes. Historically, such adaptation has been most successful as a result of the manner in which religious beliefs have been systematized to explain the supernatural realm as well as nature itself, including the social world. This development of a comprehensive, systematic theology is then often used by those holding political power to justify their particular regime; and, of course, the regime in turn usually gives legitimacy to the religious institutions that hold to that particular theological version of social reality. Hence, a static social system often arises, impervious to both theological and political challenges.

Despite denials from those presumably engaged in esoteric theological development, the importation of aspects of various philosophical systems into "pristine" religious thought cannot be avoided entirely. The origins of biblical Scriptures extend several thousand years into the past, usually reflecting the exigencies of disparate cultures. Copies of original literature as well as some authentic documents, written under a variety of political, economic, social, and environmental conditions, often contain conflicting accounts of God's dealings with humanity. With regard to Christianity, throughout Western history various philosophical systems have been modified by religious thinkers and introduced into Christian thinking to give coherent, consistent, and otherwise rational meaning to scriptural theological accounts.[2] Furthermore, these systems have evolved over time and given way to others as ideas concerning reality have shifted.

Yet problems persist. Perhaps it is unavoidable that Christian theologians have and must continue to use "secular" and imperfect philosophical tools to better understand the diverse and often incompatible intentions of ancient authors of scripture. But the effects that various tools have had in the history of ideas and the relationship of ideas themselves to politics must not be underestimated.

Functionally, the generally accepted separate, disciplinary categories of "religion" and "politics" may merely reflect differences in degree, not kind. Depending on one's perspective, religious institutions may only serve or be part of a separate social function. Conversely, particular political activities may simply be manifestations of deeper religious moral concerns. Even so, specific differences are frequently acknowledged, claiming to reveal a dichotomy between the realm of theology and social theory that restricts the former to attempts to reflect upon and explain the concept of God and related beliefs and traditions, and the latter to attempts to explain the nature of power and the structure of society and related policies; such disciplinary distinctions are generally advocated by theologians and social scientists alike. Yet as suggested in chapter 1, theologians of liberation

35

steadfastly claim that a necessary relationship exists between the two realms, that primary theological concerns in modern times actually require social theoretical explanations that blur, if not erase completely, barriers between the two realms. This relationship, they claim, becomes more apparent once the primary focus of theology shifts away from dogma and emphasizes more methodology.

The purpose of this chapter is to evaluate the basis for the strong relationship between theological methodology and modern social science recognized by Latin American liberation theology. To begin, an assessment by liberation theologians of the basic approach to theological development by contemporary mainstream or "academic" theology will reveal the essence of liberation theology's peculiar methodology, which is the key to understanding this new, social movement. Then an explication of this methodology will in turn reveal the demand for, and hence the necessary inclusion of, social science as an integral part of liberation theology.

Critique of Academic Theology

Until recent decades, the prevailing approach to serious theological studies in the Christian world was often referred to as "modern" or "liberal theology." That is, with the methodological approach of theological liberalism replacing that of scholastic theology at the end of the nineteenth century, liberal theologians supplanted appeals to dogma with analytical tools and criticisms in their attempt to discover the true meaning or essence of Christianity.[3] This approach of critical analysis became the basis for most biblical studies in higher education in North America and Western Europe.

But of late, many scholars point to an "ethical crisis" confronting Western liberalism generally, including modern theology. According to the theologian David Tracy, the modern Christian theologian is faced with a conflict of commitments: primarily, a commitment to "the morality of scientific knowledge" and a commitment to "the morality of traditional beliefs."[4] The former commitment grew out of the Enlightenment commitment to "the values of free and open inquiry, autonomous judgment, critical investigation of all claims to scientific, historical, philosophical, and religious truth."[5] The latter commitment evolved from long-standing and time-honored traditional religious beliefs and customs. But it is this demand for rational explanations of religious beliefs that has forced the liberal theologians, committed to both reason and faith, into a crisis.[6]

Furthermore, Tracy suggests, the moral crisis of the liberal theologian has taken on an added twist as the West moves from the Enlightenment or modern era to post-Enlightenment or postmodernity in its attitudes toward the shape of culture and civilization.[7] That is, contemporary critiques of modernity, particularly those of the Frankfurt School of critical theory, have argued with much rigor that the Enlightenment project of open and free inquiry has itself become a restrictive ideology. Modernity has appropriated the language, arguments, and findings of modern administration, science, and technology to promote and continue the illusion of rationality, while masking otherwise morally unacceptable arrangements and exercise of power throughout society. Consequently, the contemporary theologian is faced with both a personal moral crisis, given his commitment to scientific knowledge and traditional beliefs, and an intellectual crisis, given the postmodernist critiques of modernity, including scientific morality.

It is in response to the shortcomings of liberal theology, especially its inability to confront the crisis of modernity, that liberation theology emerges. Alongside its criticisms of liberal theology, liberation theology attempts to construct an alternative model for theological development. Tracy refers to this attempt as a "neo-orthodox" model of theology that does not revert to the premodernity "orthodox" model.[8]

Yet liberation theology's own approach to theological development has evolved out of the critical intellectual climate maintained by liberal theology, or what liberation theologians refer to as "academic theology." In fact, most liberation theologians in Latin America have had advanced training in liberal or academic theology as well as in other disciplines from major European universities. The example of Gustavo Gutiérrez is not atypical. Gutiérrez, the most well-known of liberation theologians and its primary progenitor, works and writes primarily in Lima, Peru. He studied medicine, philosophy, and theology in Peru and Chile before completing his graduate education in Europe with various degrees in philosophy, psychology, and theology from such institutions as the University of Louvain in Belgium, and the Gregorian University in Rome. In 1971, Gutiérrez published his ground-breaking work, *A Theology of Liberation*, which set the agenda for the explosive development of radical theology throughout Latin America.[9]

But as pointed out in the last chapter, liberation theology has also arisen out of a sense of protest, including protest against contemporary liberal or academic theology.[10] Liberation theologians claim that their own theological predecessors, in the adaptation of their intellectual techniques, have stopped unnecessarily short of the promise of their approach. Because of their distorted understanding of intellectual integrity, they have failed to fully criticize the entire domain of Christian thought and practice by refusing to move beyond biblical criticism to ecclesiastical and social criticism. Consequently, this failure has led to the present moral and political impotence of academic theologians in an unjust world. So to avoid this situation and to be able to address moral problems in society, liberation theology expands certain crucial methods developed in academic theology, primarily the latter's emphasis on "critical analysis."

In various ways, then, liberation theology claims to address the problem of mainstream theology's inability to deal with social injustice. To see how this argument comes together, an overview of the general criticism will emerge first as we assemble in a composite fashion the critical insights of several theologians of liberation who deal directly with this issue, including those of José Comblin, Gutiérrez, José Míguez Bonino, Raúl Vidales, Ignacio Ellacuría, and Juan Luis Segundo.

Comblin's discussion of the nature of academic theology serves best as the general basis for critical appraisal of academic theology by the other theologians of liberation.[11] Comblin focuses on three distinctive elements of academic theology: *university* as a place and privileged social position, *history* as a method, and *criticism* as a project. While in sympathy with the intent of their intellectual approach, theologians of liberation find the particular way these three elements are implemented by academic theologians as obstacles to a morally appropriate and thoroughgoing critical approach to theological development.

University

According to Comblin, mainstream or academic theologians tend to regard the university as the proper place to carry out their theological enterprise of discovering the essence of Christianity. They claim that the typical university or academic setting provides a haven for scholarly research, a haven necessary to protect them from the distractions of struggles and conflicting interests found elsewhere. Thus, in this position of supposed objectivity and impartiality, their work can proceed unhindered and with utmost integrity. However, Comblin maintains that claims for the presence of such objectivity are highly questionable. Historically, the university has never occupied a social position detached from the rest of society; in fact, the integrity of its position is "conditioned by the sociological context of its presence."[12]

So from this perspective the reverse seems to be true with regard to the academic theologians' claims of objectivity and impartiality. According to Comblin, there are two principal limitations to the discovery of religious truth that already exist in the university: "separateness of its place and the false purity of its privilege." With regard to "place," any place other than the university will provide a more conducive atmosphere for comprehending Christian truth. The study of a subject can best be undertaken by engagement with the life of the subject; "sharing in action is a necessary precondition to discovering the reality of anything."[13] But by distancing themselves from situations similar to those subjects and social conditions of the past as discussed in the original documents, academic theologians cannot fully grasp the moral intent of the original authors, which is their stated goal. Consequently, the university setting at best offers "formal" knowledge, but not "real" knowledge about the essence and intent of Christianity.

Furthermore, the university's "purity" is undermined by its ties to other specific interests in society; in a situation of competing interests, there can be no objective neutrality in politics. Comblin argues that all human beings, including academic theologians, live in a world of various class distinctions and to some extent are influenced and even conditioned by those distinctions. In the West, and especially in Latin America, the political interests of the university are generally linked to those of the bourgeoisie, the economic class that tends to occupy nearly all positions of political authority in the modern nation-state. Consequently, the university's existence and interests generally serve ruling-class interests.

With regard to the social status of academic theologians, Ellacuría also challenges its effectiveness with regard to political issues of social injustice. He argues that the importance of philosophic inquiry must not be limited solely to objective scholarly research and reporting; "in the last analysis, philosophy is an intellectual treatment of real problems or, if you prefer, of the reality of real-life problems."[14] The intellectual pursuits of philosophical activity cannot be entirely separated from other aspects of daily life; "philosophical concepts must be historical and total, effective and real." There is an activist component to all philosophical inquiry, including that of theology. Regardless of intellectual ability, the ultimate objective of theological inquiry itself is "to comprehend and transform reality from a Christian point of view."[15] He places strong emphasis on "transformation" as the key to evaluating the appropriateness of any theology. Any theological faculty or university that stresses solely detached, intellectual education, fails to understand the proper role of the study of theology itself. Such an approach "is a bourgeois conception of what a theology department and a university are supposed to be."[16] To the extent that such intellectual conditions are indeed legitimate in typical universities, they are of secondary importance. The proper aim of the university in society "should be to be a critical and creative consciousness effectively at work in the service of the community." For Ellacuría, such pursuits include "science and scholarly knowledge"—but in conjunction with the transformation of society.

Comblin also sees a valuable role for aspects of academic theology with regard to analytical problems in methodology, hermeneutics, auxiliary sciences, and language study. But, in terms of contemporary ethical issues, he finds that it lacks adequate understanding of the nature of social injustice and, consequently, it lacks any effective moral guidance for living the Christian message of salvation.[17] In its university setting, then, academic theology's proclivity toward abstraction and "objectivity" preclude arriving at a competent understanding of God's word that has been revealed to, and through, the poor, ignorant, and weak. And, says Comblin, "only the poor are able to feel what salvation, hope, justice, or justification are [sic]."[18]

History

With regard to "history as a method," scientific explanations of doctrine and practices in academic theology refer to interpretative problems in the history of Christianity's emergence and subsequent development. By focusing criticism on original documents, academic theologians typically compare original intentions of ancient authors to historical stages in the development of Christianity and point out contradictions and inconsistencies. By disclosing errors of interpretation in earlier scholarship, they claim that one can come closer to, if not reveal, the original intent of Christianity. "In this way," says Comblin, "the history of an entity takes the place of the ancient idea of essence or nature."[19] Historical criticism, then, even reveals the relativity of contemporary orthodoxy itself, since the interpretation of Christian dogma at any point in time can be shown to be influenced substantially by certain cultural conditions.

Academic theologians, unfortunately, emphasize the importance of the historical criticism of documents over other potentially fruitful methods and sources of grasping the essential meaning of "God, Christ, and Christianity." Comblin further maintains that "the absolute objectivity of the historical method is a myth."[20] Historians, in fact, are unable to stand outside of history and investigate it objectively; consequently, there is only the illusion of objectivity in the use of their critical methods.

Criticism

With regard to "criticism as a project," academic theology accepts the importance of reason over prejudice. That is, as Comblin explains, "through various methods of criticism, human reason discloses the truth that has remained covered by innumerable prejudices."[21] Yet even this admission by academic theologians of the importance of critical reasoning in theological development, historically has not always enjoyed acceptance.

Gutiérrez discusses how the intellectual enterprise of theology has only intermittently incorporated a critical feature. He explains that the broad development of Christian theology has historically passed through two phases; in the first phase, Christian theology developed as a "theology of wisdom," in the second phase, as a "theology of rational knowledge."[22] In the theology of wisdom, the early Christian church focused primarily on developing a theology as a guide to the spiritual life, a theology reflecting upon the Bible as a source and symbol of spirituality. Primarily through meditation on the Bible, personal spiritual growth was thought possible.

> This theology was above all monastic and therefore characterized by a spiritual life removed from worldly concerns; it offered a model for every Christian desirous of advancing along the narrow path of sanctity and seeking a life of spiritual perfection.[23]

Using Platonic and neo-Platonic categories, this theology formulated a metaphysics that assisted it in stressing "the existence of a higher world and the transcendence of an Absolute from which anything came and to which everything returned." Consequently, with regard to social issues, early Christians considered earthly life of little value in and of itself, contingent on the next for any meaning.

41

Gutiérrez notes that a form of this spiritual emphasis found in early Christian theology continues to the present. In principle, he also continues to support the inclusion of wisdom in theological development, but finds that overemphasis on abstract values to the exclusion of rational thinking detracts from living a just life.

After the twelfth century, continues Gutiérrez, "theology begins to establish itself as a science."[24] Thomas Aquinas, implementing Aristotelian categories in his religious arguments, attempted to give Christian theology a more all-encompassing systematic description of the relationship between God and man. Gutiérrez uses the approach of Aquinas as an example of rationality being implemented for theological clarification, a much lacking but necessary, scientific component in current theological development that tends to emphasize "wisdom" to the near exclusion of "rationality."

Critics of Gutiérrez's assessment have pointed out, however, that Aquinas used rationally logical arguments for improved comprehension of revealed, abstract truths.[25] Since Gutiérrez's own theological approach finds no comfort in epistemological absolutes, it would seem that discussion of Aquinas's concerns are out of place here. Yet this criticism tends to overlook Gutiérrez's broader inquiry into the benefits of rational exposition and his finding in their favor. He refers to Aquinas only to support his own plea for the necessity of developing a rational, theological response to other concerns, in addition to the development of logical argumentation with regard to revealed truths. The methodologies of Aquinas and Gutiérrez, if not purposes, appear to hold similar significance.

While contemporary notions of scientific thinking and theological development differ in many respects from those of Aristotle and Aquinas, Gutiérrez points out that the importance of linking faith and reason continues to endure in contemporary theology. He maintains, however, that the problem has now become one of linking the spiritual and rational traditions in Christian thought in a way that proclaims the Christian message of salvation in a socially effective manner.

With regard to the laudable use of rationality, then, academic theology incorporates various forms of critical analyses that have evolved over the centuries. Theologians in this tradition apply methods of criticism to scriptural texts to ascertain the essence of Christianity as understood and intended by early writers. In this way, claims Comblin, Christianity itself is taken as a historical subject to be analyzed critically for the truth that lies buried beneath centuries of extraneous embellishment. More importantly, the modern Church itself has learned that through the use of findings resulting from critical analysis, it can "reach the level of a rational religion. In other words, critical theology offers the churches certification of rationality."[26]

Many contemporary theologians, however, while finding the emphasis on criticism by academic theologians as inherently appropriate as a methodology, fault their colleagues for not applying it widely enough.[27] Academic theologians, they maintain, have been generally effective at demonstrating the value of criticizing most individual ideologies and various social institutions with regard to liberating truth from the bind of superstition and prejudice. But as Comblin explains, their criticisms generally have been advanced in the name of freedoms for the intellectual and upper classes. For example, academic theologians have written in defense of "freedom of conscience and expression, freedom of religion and philosophy, freedom from any irrationality in religion, politics, economy, and social life"—all with an eye toward the individual.[28] Yet, complains Comblin, they have neglected to focus their criticism on the broader implications of the causes for the massive existence of inadequate material conditions of life; in particular they have not defended the struggle of the common worker for freedom, thus ignoring any moral commitment to the liberation of the oppressed classes. Hence, the social criticisms of academic theology, while important as far as they have gone, have failed to analyze the comprehensive, irrational factors in social relations and social structures crucial to understanding the normative importance of the Christian message itself; they lack a sensibility to collective problems of social injustice.[29]

Yet despite liberation theologians' criticisms of academic theologians' general lack of a knowledge of, and concern for, social justice, it would seem unlikely that the poor or anyone else, knows precisely what justice is, as opposed to what justice generally is not. Comblin castigates academic theologians' attempts to bridge the gap between descriptive and prescriptive religious beliefs because of their assumption of the existence of historically verifiable, propositional certitudes. Yet he, too, indicates the acceptance of a similar assumption in his own criticism with his reliance on the poor as the only proper arbiter of moral behavior. If certitudes have a questionable defense in academic theology, then Comblin's own absolute assertion concerning the poor as the central concern of God's revelation must be suspect as well.

Still, any interpretative scholarship requires a particular view from which history can be read and understood. The adoption of a particular view, then, becomes crucial, albeit subjective. Whose view should be chosen, that of the academic theologian, the ruling classes, the poor? Comblin maintains that history must be understood as a process of mediation itself for everyone, not just for a privileged few. Yet this would seem to contradict his own assessment that the poor have the best insight into the nature of justice and therefore must be the primary source of theological development.

But the perceived limitations of academic theology are not merely self-serving for liberation theology. That is, there exist deeper reasons as to why academic theologians pursue certain questions and ignore others. The following section will attempt to explain more fully the criticism by theologians of liberation of the implementation of critical analysis by academic theologians, and hence how they would rectify this shortcoming and push on toward social activism.

Limits and Grounding

The Problem of Certitudes

While liberation theology embraces the emphasis on critical analysis as found in academic theology, its reasons for doing so provide the distinctive difference between the two approaches to theological development. Academic theology, in its search for the true meaning of Christianity, assumes that absolute truth exists and that it can be apprehended propositionally in terms of revealed certitudes. It then attempts to derive set theological categories of personal belief and social behavior to give meaning and consistency to Christian doctrines (based on the discovered truths that have resulted from critical, historical analyses) and to create dogma by which one can act morally in the world. However, any set of categories necessarily may be too restrictive in its application to unanticipated social conditions. That is, depending on the range of the certitudes, real-world applications likewise will be limited. And from liberation theology's perspective, this is precisely the problem for academic theology; for given the broad range of human concerns and dynamic changes, a determination of the range of revealed certitudes from rigid interpretations of Scripture, will of necessity be more narrowly focused than is desirable. Consequently, the religious individual will only find partial if any guidance to the growing stresses on living the moral life; many deeper moral implications of various aspects of social life may well be ignored.

But this condition of limited applicability in academic theology arises from the a priori claim of the existence of infinite universal principles. Yet these principles have been inductively created from finite and particular experiences. For any experience involving a relationship between God and man would seem necessarily to involve on the part of man, finite capacities to intuit and explicate the infinite. Thus, a certain amount of error and incompleteness of reporting must be presumed present in relating such experiences. Given finite experiences and error-prone explanations as the basis for set categories, academic theology is unable to deal adequately with unexpected contingencies. And the practical result of such inadequacies is that the unexpected contingencies will not be dealt with. Hence, not only must rigid theological categories be avoided as a practical matter, according to theologians of liberation, but they must be avoided to understand properly the nature of the relationship between God and man. They argue that the methodology of academic theology is not only inadequate in terms of its overall applicability, but is inherently unsound in its basic assumptions, and thus that the entire intellectual enterprise of academic theology is morally as well as intellectually flawed.

Phenomenological and Exegetical Analyses

Segundo, for one, has attempted to explain the flawed nature of academic theologians' enterprise by utilizing phenomenological and exegetical analyses that provide examples of problems encountered with their basic approach. His phenomenological analysis begins with the basic question often asked by those who criticize the use of theology to justify participation in politics: "How can the Church know the [social] context of her actions since obviously this type of knowledge cannot be deduced entirely from revelations?"[30] That is, recognizing the limitations of a theological system structured upon and built around inflexible certitudes, how can the Church speak out on contemporary social concerns—for example, favor one economic arrangement over another—if there is no basis in divine revelation to explain empirically the nature of contemporary social conditions? Should the Church risk speaking out on the appropriateness of various economic arrangements, only to be proven wrong in its analysis by experts from the secular sciences? This question, Segundo points out, contains a particular conservative and insupportable bias.

45

It assumes that divine revelation can provide "us with deductive conclusions about that which is eternally Christian in human conduct," yet it is incapable of deriving from universal principles explanations of specific social contexts.[31] Furthermore, it assumes that those explanations are necessary to fully explain human conduct. Recognizing this limitation or constraint on the development of theology, then, academic theologians are able to conclude that theology may appropriately explicate meanings found in divine revelation, but may not provide analytical descriptions of various social phenomena originating in specific historical contexts. Segundo finds their assumption and conclusion ethically unacceptable, given his own understanding of the broader biblical theme of moral commitment to liberation; consequently, he countercharges that the original question concerning Church involvement in politics with its errant assumption posed by academic theologians is itself inappropriate.

To strengthen his position, Segundo points to the world of modern science as an analogy where real-life situations are not perceived in a way that "the problems of man" can be subjected to an independent and objective "plane of knowledge" and then applied to specific historical contexts. In fact, the opposite is the case. Science does not, and indeed cannot, provide a priori options to solve all potential contingencies and conflicts; it can only assist in implementing options to achieve solutions chosen in the midst of conflict. "Once a human being has made some general options, science or scholarship can point out some set of instruments that dovetail with his option."[32] Thus science, claims Segundo, serves an instrumental function in achieving certain objectives; it cannot say whether those objectives are reasonable or moral in themselves.

Segundo maintains that the analogy of science and its secondary role with regard to descriptive and prescriptive conditions of human experience, applies as well to theology. In accepting a particular theology, a prior selection of a contextually conditioned option must first be recognized. As with the example of science, the theological system should then be used to attain the goals set by the option previously chosen. Only in this way can the adoption of a theology itself have any meaning, a meaning clearly dependent on the relation between the theological system and real-life conditions. According to Segundo:

> In other words, theology is not chosen for theological reasons. Quite the
> contrary is the case. The only real problem is trying to decide whether it

puts a person in a better position to make a choice and to change the world politically.[33]

Thus for Segundo, the value of theology is its instrumental role for any particular, individual commitment. And as Gutiérrez more succinctly puts it, "theology follows; it is the second step."[34]

Given this understanding of the proper attitude toward theological development, then, the apparent problem of commenting on social concerns in a way that can be deduced from theological certitudes is a moot point, since theological development does not begin with theological certitudes, but rather follows a prior commitment to a particular value, such as liberating the poor and the oppressed. That the modern era has inverted this more accurate and realistic approach to theological development merely indicates, claims Segundo, "that unreality has taken over the methods of academic theology."[35]

With regard to his exegetical analysis as a demonstration of the inadequacies of academic theology in the face of social injustice, Segundo demonstrates the difference between academic theology and liberation theology by contrasting Jesus' approach to theology with that of the Pharisees. Trained in a particular theological tradition, the Pharisees asked of Jesus essentially the same question just quoted; to paraphrase, how can the community of the synagogue understand, judge, and account for present social conditions when any accurate understanding of the conditions themselves cannot be deduced from revelation?[36] Since such accounts cannot be deduced from universal revelation and since the risk is too great wherein such accounts, if undertaken, may be shown wrong by experts in other fields, the Pharisees maintained that matters of a purely religious nature must be kept separate from those of a political nature. By explicating various dialogues between the two antagonistic camps, as related in the New Testament, Segundo attempts to demonstrate that Jesus clearly rejects this approach of the Pharisees.

For example, Segundo deals with one of the disputes between Jesus and the Pharisees regarding the propriety of Sabbath-day activities. When asked by Jesus whether it was permitted to heal or kill on the Sabbath (Mark 3:1–5), the Pharisees were unable to answer. Because the nature of Jesus' own activities and questions did not fit their set theological categories, they were unable to deduce a proper response. According to Segundo, "[Jesus] is something new about which past revelation has nothing specific to say; from it nothing certain can be deduced about him."[37] Furthermore, the Pharisees dared

47

not form any judgment concerning the significance of Jesus' presence nor his questions at the risk of later being falsified. In fact, claims Segundo, the very question Jesus asked of the Pharisees indicates that "one cannot begin [theological development] with certitudes from revelation."[38] The Pharisees had anticipated a more abstract and less realistic question that fit their systematic theological approach. "Jesus' question points up a level that is prior to any and all theological questions, a level where human beings make their most critical and decisive options: i.e., the heart." Segundo contends that the Pharisees had long since entirely bypassed this real-world, human element.[39] Again, for liberation theologians, theological development begins with the human situation, after the initial moral commitment; it does not precede it.

Furthermore, Segundo interprets Jesus' actions as revealing the political dimension of faith. This is demonstrated not only in his own activities, but in Jesus' preference for "signs in history," as opposed to "signs from heaven." Jesus indicates that the typical emphasis on signs from heaven (revealed certitudes) as proof of divine origins as opposed to the fulfillment of scriptural predictions and historical events (socially conditioned interpretations), limits the Pharisees' own theological development. According to Segundo,

> [Jesus] tries to show them that they must leave room and openness in their theology for the relative, provisional, uncertain nature of criteria that human beings actually use to direct their lives in history when they are open to what is going on around them.[40]

One should read "the signs of the times," not look for a sign from heaven.

The inherent weaknesses, then, of a theological system constructed upon premises of absolute certitudes limit the application of the religious individual's moral judgments. Instead, every historical judgment should rely on "an upright human heart," explains Segundo. And furthermore, such "uprightness and openness of heart" can only be fully expressed in politics. Not only is the original question by academic theologians concerning the deduction of statements on specific and concrete historical conditions from abstract, universal certitudes of no intellectual importance, but any theology that seeks to liberate others cannot do so effectively with such an approach. "Why? Because that is precisely the kind of approach that is ruled out by Jesus";[41] that is, Scriptures provide examples that demonstrate otherwise. Thus, phenomenologically and exegetically, Segundo attempts to reveal the methodological weakness of academic theology with regard to contemporary social issues and in turn the moral weakness of its ethical foundation with regard to modern politics. For Segundo, "the only real problem is how will theology open itself up to the human realm in all its dimensions, and formulate questions for revelation on the basis of options taken in that realm."[42]

Process Thinking

The shortcomings of deductive theological systems stem from their inability to deal effectively with changing historical conditions. This results from systemic reliance on narrowly defined certitudes that order reality in such a fashion that the ethics of temporal social conditions cannot be addressed completely. If this is the case, then, any alternative approach to theological development must proceed along lines that do not begin with abstract universal certitudes. Indeed, a different approach to understanding the Scriptures themselves must be devised. Yet the value of certitudes is precisely their ability to provide a grounding for a variety of moral categories that then set limits on behavior. With limits, of course, judgments can be made on the moral appropriateness or inappropriateness of a particular act. But limits on appropriate behavior can only be known if something else can be contrasted with it; that is, something *outside* the limits of proper behavior. If "religion," with its theological interpretation, is to be understood as the realm or source of moral orientation, and "politics," with its arena for human interaction, is to be understood as the world of conflict over the proper interpretation of moral behavior, then academic theology's assumed distinction between religion and politics may, in fact, be sound. If so, then, the utilitarian weakness of academic theologians may not be their proclivity to separate religion from politics absolutely as liberation theologians complain; it may well be a question of where to draw the line between religion and politics, and where to set the limits on the role of religion in politics.

Furthermore, if indeed a properly developed theology is as closely linked to social conditions as Segundo suggests, its subjective application to social issues immediately encounters difficulties. Subjective interpretations may be charged with either moral relativism or smuggling absolutist theology in under the guise of prior commitments to particular social values that in practice are really another set of

49

certitudes. To avoid such problems, an element of objectivity must be found upon which faith and theologies can be grounded, an element that still precludes abstract certitudes. A promising alternative to reliance on ahistorical and absolutistic certitudes may be reliance on an understanding of historical *process*. That is, it recognizes that a particular transcendent but contextual process guides an individual's approach to comprehending the religious and political aspects of the world and acting morally within it. For example, process may be detected in the development of history as God deals with humanity in a significant yet changing or evolving fashion.

In any event, the exact nature of this historical process and its impact on human freedom may vary in interpretation of Christian eschatology as witnessed by various philosophical thinkers from Augustine to John B. Cobb, Jr., and David Ray Griffin.[43] Furthermore, some theological frameworks may not find the use of certitudes and process incompatible. But crucial to the enterprise of developing a theology based on a process rather than on a particular identifiable set of certitudes, such as liberation theology, is the problem of identifying the nature of truth itself to provide the limits to judge the morality of individual acts as well as social policies.

Truth and Justice

But exactly what truth is becomes rather vague for theologians of liberation. For example, according to Míguez Bonino, "God's Word" in the Old Testament should not be understood

> as a conceptual communication but as a creative event, a history-making pronouncement. Its truth does not consist in some correspondence to an idea but in its efficacy to carrying out God's promise or fulfilling his judgment.[44]

He suggests that emphasis be placed on grasping the significance of proper acts over abstract words; that is, not an "ethical inference but an obedient participation" is required of those who obey God. A further merging of identity seems to occur here as truth is associated less with certain knowledge and more with moral activity or justice itself. According to Míguez Bonino, this association of truth with justice forms the moral basis for, and justification of, political activity in liberation theology.

As discussed earlier, the ethical dimension of liberation theology, expressed in its commitment to liberating the poor and oppressed, has arisen from its search for justice in this life. A crucial relationship exists between belief in God and social justice. If the goal of most Christians is to know God, one of the likeliest places to understand the meaning of God is in the Scriptures. Hence, it would seem reasonable that a study of the Scriptures should assist in knowing God. But how should one approach the study of Scripture?

Another liberation theologian, José Porfirio Miranda, provides an example of typical biblical exegesis in liberation theology as he scrutinizes passages in an attempt to comprehend the meaning of various references to God or *Yahweh.* Citing a number of passages from Old Testament prophets—including Jeremiah, Amos, Hosea, Isaiah, and Micah—as well as from the Pentateuch, his exegesis reveals that in essence "to know Yahweh is to achieve justice for the poor."[45] For example, Jeremiah states, "He defended the cause of the poor and the needy; is not this what it means to know me? It is Yahweh who speaks" (22:16). Conversely, in reading the Scriptures, Miranda finds that "the direct cause of the internecine destruction of the people is the lack of knowledge of Yahweh, that is, simply speaking, the prevailing injustice."[46]

Furthermore, Miranda explains that the moral concepts of "justice" and "right" comprise essential elements of a knowledge of God. The prophets continually assert that they have nothing new to reveal of the knowledge of God, that knowing God is not a strictly cognitive activity between God and man but, on the contrary, is the living of a just life by man that seeks justice for others. This is so because God is the Other; actions toward others is action toward the Other, that is, toward God. For example, Miranda looks at another passage—". . . since what I want is compassion, not sacrifice; knowledge of God, not holocausts" (Hosea 6:6)—which refers to the "compassion" which believers must have for God. Although translated from Hebrew into other languages in later centuries as "love" or "fidelity," Miranda argues that in fact, in the original Hebrew, the word *ḥesed* comes closer in meaning to being understood as "compassion."[47] This passage from Hosea is also referred to frequently in the New Testament (for example, Matthew 9:13 and 12:7) and is crucial to understanding other New Testament teachings. The New Testament writers understood *ḥesed* as "interhuman compassion" in the same way as the Septuagint, which continually places *ḥesed* "together with justice (*sᵉdaḳah*) and/or right (*mišpat*)."[48]

This is a compassion strictly related to a sense of justice. In the passages we have cited we see that it is a compassion-for-the-poor-and-oppressed, which can be identified with the indignation felt before the violation of the rights of the weak.[49]

The point that Miranda attempts to defend, then, is that to know God does not mean simply to have abstract knowledge or solitary awareness of another existent and Supreme Being. God cannot be objectified; he can only be known in "the immediate command of conscience, . . . in the cry of the poor and the weak who seek justice."[50] Hence, God's transcendence places knowledge of him in the Other *qua* human being not *qua* Supreme Being. Thus, "direct" knowledge of God is impossible, states Miranda; only in the "indirect" act of justice and compassion for others can God be known.

Similarly, for Míguez Bonino, religious faith is based not on a "gnosis" (transcendent knowledge) but on a "way" (a method). The concept of truth is understood through action, doing proper actions through obedience to God. "Correct knowledge is contingent on right doing. Or rather, the knowledge is disclosed in the doing"[51]—that is, greater emphasis is placed upon *orthopraxis* or proper action, rather than upon *orthodoxy* or correct beliefs. No neutral knowledge exists; "the sociology of knowledge makes abundantly clear that we think always out of a definite context of relations and action, out of a given praxis." We must, he says, become more aware of the influences on our understanding of truth that we derive from the social environment. Hence, justice is not an ideal concept revealed by an omniscient and abstract God; but comprehension of God himself is revealed in the activity of searching for justice with the oppressed.

Perhaps Gutiérrez offers a statement that best summarizes the general understanding among liberation theologians of the relationship between truth and justice and how to talk about it.

Such witness [of Third World poverty] compels us to find a way to talk about God. We need a language rooted in the unjust poverty that surrounds the vast majorities, but also nurtured by the faith and hope of a people struggling for its liberation. We need a language that is both contemplative and prophetic: contemplative because it ponders a God who is love; prophetic because it talks about a liberator God who rejects the situation of injustice in which the poor live, and also the structural causes of that situation. . . . It is the fact that the poor see their struggle for liberation as a way of "cleaving to God."[52]

Liberation Theology as a Process Theology of Society

As we can now see, theologians of liberation emphasize the importance of a methodology that encourages reflection upon theological as well as social questions. According to Gutiérrez, "Our reflection follows a circular dynamic seen many times in church history: moving from the word of the Lord to experience and from experience to the word of the Lord."[53] And, furthermore, they consider the dynamics or process of evolutionary change as the basis for a proper methodology for theological development as opposed to the typical methodology that establishes absolute certitudes to provide the element upon which a transcendental objectivity may be founded.

We should recall that the theme of this chapter focuses on the question of how theologians of liberation link theology to sociology; or better, how one merges discussion of the nature of God with discussion of the very nature of politics in a socially liberating fashion. Theologians of liberation attempt to demonstrate that, given the enterprise of academic theologians, the link between God and politics cannot be adequately apprehended in a way that a religious individual could strive for social justice. Were they to do so, their theologies would appear radically different with corresponding social consequences. Yet that such an attempt must be made is evident to theologians of liberation from their critical interpretation of the basic thrust of Christian values, as discussed earlier in chapter 1. And with regard to moral orientation and values, they maintain that the study of Scripture must be central to any Christian theology. In their rejection of typical, "academic" approaches, then, how do liberation theologians incorporate their own approach to biblical studies?

What now follows is an analysis of the methodological framework of liberation theology which seeks to unite moral values and social action. But more specifically, this analysis will demonstrate the point at which liberation theologians claim the necessity of including social science for any comprehensive theological development. Perhaps Vidales best explains the three concepts generally accepted as necessary elements of the methodological process essential to the enterprise of radical theological development in Latin America: *praxis, hermeneutics,* and *evangelization*.[54] For our purposes, the first two concepts will suffice to reveal the relationship between theology and social science in liberation theology; the last concept will be discussed more appropriately in chapter 5.

53

Praxis

Academic theologians attempt to discover the abstract categories of truth necessary for their theologies, and, of course, they claim these categories are, or at least ought to be, free from human "contamination" and "corruption" of finite, limited perspectives. As we have seen, liberation theologians find such approaches socially meaningless even if intellectually possible in the real world. Conversely, then, if abstract and absolute certitudes do not exist, one is hardpressed to maintain theologically any form of "ontological dualism." That is, instead of maintaining two worlds, one of transcendence and the other of immanence, it would appear for liberation theologians that there can be only one world or realm of existence that manifests both transcendent and immanent characteristics. This notion is at the heart of their concept of praxis.

As noted earlier, liberation theologians hold to religious beliefs and corresponding theologies in light of actual social conditions, not according to some abstract, intellectually deficient, and socially ineffectual pattern. With regard to "praxis as the starting point," according to Vidales, contemporary "concrete experience" forces one to reflect upon the nature of how religious faith is to confront lived reality. Consequently, one must shun the temptation in any theological development to posit a dualism of separate realms, such as between the natural and supernatural, the temporal and spiritual; for theological development can only begin when Scripture is understood and lived under real-life conditions. Instead of incorporating a dualism of two separate realms of existence, states Vidales, one would be better off assuming a single historical realm or category, a category consisting of the dialectical relationship "between the word of God and Christian experience."[55] In its critique of human relations and conditions, Scripture provides a "critical and subversive dimension" as its teachings are applied to everyday life, to the religious system, and to society; but this can only be appreciated if ontological dualisms are avoided. And liberation theologians reject dualisms in terms of both their social consequences and epistemological grounding.

With regard to social consequences, liberation theologians argue that mainstream theologians and established ecclesiastical authorities have promulgated a type of religious dogma that has generally placed the hierarchy of the Church in a position of ideologically supporting the status quo of society.[56] Rather than acting as an agent of social change, the Church, with its teachings and practices, typically acts to pacify the demands of the socially deprived and dispossessed by stressing the importance of civil obedience with its reward of individual salvation and justice in the next life rather than in this life. Consequently, economic and political practices have generally benefited the elite few over, and at the expense of, the wretched masses. Conversely, liberation theologians point out that the history of the Church, with few exceptions, has not shown it to be one where ecclesiastical authorities antagonize or confront secular authorities and challenge them with regard to inhumane and unjust social practices and policies.

Epistemologically, liberation theologians also find serious weaknesses. Modern biblical exegesis demonstrates for them the inconclusive if ineffable nature of God's relation to humanity. At times, God is involved directly in human affairs, at other times aloof; at times advocating violence, other times patience, long suffering, even a martyr's death in the face of the unjust exercise of political power. By contrast, what emerges from serious scriptural studies for many liberation theologians is the crucial role of the "prophetic tradition" of preaching a God who advocates the importance of human dignity and rights, who criticizes the negative effects of man-made social institutions, and who possesses limited ability to deal with earthly concerns. And while this God emphasizes salvation, the attainment of salvation is historically bound and worked out; moreover, as Ellacuría notes, a process of "salvation in history" incorporates and gives meaning to the traditional understanding of "salvation history."[57] Consequently, argues Vidales, all dualisms must be avoided and faith itself must be recognized as "the meeting point of salvation and history."[58]

Present social conditions of political violence, economic exploitation, and interference by international interests in Latin America, according to Vidales, have forced many individuals to reconsider the meaning of Scripture in light of oppressive conditions; but such reconsideration ought not be without direction. For Vidales, any adequate response to social injustice must "serve to animate and mobilize peoples' energies for the construction of a more just and fraternal society." To this end, a liberation praxis may develop "in the light of the new [rational and critical] scientific line of reasoning." And this is a real possibility since political liberation is properly understood as an aspect of eschatological liberation. Thus, the lack of dualistic theological categories now provides the pretext for committed Christians "to plunge into the complex and conflict-ridden world of the poor."[59]

The committed Christian becomes a "new person," claims Vidales, by replacing his old moral identification with the world of oppression with a new moral identification with the world of the oppressed, and is thereby motivated to seek to transform the world. With this moral conversion, the religious individual attempts to recapture many of the spiritual dimensions of traditional Christianity that have too often been ignored: "the biblical dimension, the historical dimension, and the dimension of personal commitment and involvement."[60] Furthermore, reflection upon social conditions and scriptural accounts of God working through history forces liberation theology to broaden the scope of its complex, theoretical application by delving into other disciplinary areas—for example, geographical and social—for theological development, thus making it a theology to serve all human beings, not just those in Latin America. And since liberation theology is open to all of human history as a result of its critical function, Vidales maintains that praxis as critical reflection, applies to "all systems that seek to become absolute."[61] As such, all absolute systems are understood as exploitative, including absolutist religious systems.

Does this mean that the radical Christian in his role as subversive must call for nothing less than permanent revolution in all dimensions of life? That this seems to be the case is suggested by the next stage in Vidales's methodological process: a new *hermeneutics* for providing "a different understanding of the faith."

Hermeneutics

The application of some notion of hermeneutics has become popular recently in a variety of disciplines. For religious studies, the theologian J. Andrew Kirk defines hermeneutics as

> the task of transposing the biblical message from one situation to another: an attempt to understand how the Word of God, which was written and lived out some 2,000 or more years ago, can command obedience in today's context.[62]

The essence of liberation theology which distinguishes it from other theologies is the critical function that hermeneutics serves. The critical use of hermeneutics allows for a moral as well as interpretative inspection of both theological claims and religious practices. Given liberation theology's commitment to revolutionary involvement in society as a result of its commitment to human liberation, Vidales maintains that "theory and practice are now seen to be indissolubly united as embodiments of one and the same reality."[63] But even as a theology of liberation develops, its hermeneutical approach must be turned on itself. For as with any theology, it, too, may be co-opted— for example, formal institutions adopting similar language—by the Church and other groups and thereby used to perpetuate injustice.[64] Thus, claims Vidales, it must afford criticism of all social conditions, including that of its own making; "it maintains a critical outlook in order to offer provocation, in order to keep prodding us on toward the final consummation."[65]

But a critical function that criticizes its own source of existence may in fact afford no basis whatsoever for legitimate criticism. Again, this is the problem of relativism. Vidales seems to recognize this problem by maintaining that liberation theology in its critical function must continually refer back to the Scriptures as its "ultimate grounding." This means that, while Scripture is "the soul of theology," liberation theology must attempt "to recover the historical dimension of God's message, to move that message away from all abstract universalism, ahistoricism, and atemporal conceptualizations."[66]

As noted earlier, history and its meaning comprise crucial interests for theologians of liberation. The Christian message of salvation originally emerged in a specific historical context and thus is itself directly related to all of human history. Hence, according to Vidales, the historical dimension must be salvaged to maintain "its prophetic character and functions, its subversive undertones, and its provocative Christian originality: only thus can we preserve the only field wherein God's message retains its validity for reflection."[67]

Perhaps the critical function of hermeneutics can now be appreciated. Vidales observes that liberation theologians can now move between "the original Bible containing God's word and the other 'Bible' known as history." Consequently, a hermeneutics of liberation is developing in liberation theology that attempts to relate the historical reality of God's incarnation and message with the historical reality of contemporary conditions of poverty and oppression. Furthermore, Vidales argues,

we need a hermeneutics that will pay heed to the voice of the sciences, not only the sciences that help us better to understand the world of the Bible but also the sciences that help us better to understand the present-day world.[68]

Scriptures are not to be read as books of abstract doctrines, but "as a creative and provocative witness to our mission in the world."[69] To the extent that the Scriptures have a temporal dimension, such a dimension finds meaning in the present; to the extent that the Scriptures have a transcendental dimension, such a dimension finds its meaning in the future. And it is the dynamic relationship between the two, according to Vidales, that the new hermeneutic must attempt to reveal. Such a hermeneutic will analyze all aspects of Latin American life, including political, economic, and other social dimensions.

> It will tend to be critical rather than dogmatic, process-minded rather than formalistic, social rather than personalist, populist rather than elitist.[70]

Vidales now clarifies the relationship of praxis to hermeneutics. Praxis occupies a specific place in liberation hermeneutics with its emphasis on history. To make a commitment to liberate the poor from poverty and oppression is to undertake a historical activity. As a liberation praxis, it is a praxis of love for others as well as fidelity to God. Vidales indicates that "God himself chose to become history, and his love is made manifest in history; and the privileged manifestation of that love is to be found in the praxis of total liberation."[71] In liberation praxis, liberation theology "sees the convergence of God's word and human history."

Furthermore, Vidales maintains that a unity of "faith" and "reason" occurs in liberation hermeneutics. For faith to be the origins of theology, it must be understood. And to be understood by a human being, faith must be positive; it must manifest itself as a human act. Liberation praxis, then, as a human act, "is the exercise of faith as a mixture of promise and fulfillment and as an openness to full consummation in the future."[72] Promise and fulfillment, as the dynamic elements of faith manifested in liberation praxis, also "constitute the primordial field or locus of liberation hermeneutics."

Ethical problems associated with concrete experiences provide the initial concerns in liberation theology. From there, a process of "abstraction" begins with the formulation of theoretical categories to assist in developing systematic hypotheses of social reality. According to Vidales, the critical function of praxis forces the methodological process "to structure and systematize the whole."[73] Yet it is not obvious from his explanation just what a systematized whole would look like nor to what extent it would apply. However, it appears that it must be of such a nature that contradictions between the *is* of reality and the *ought* of theology can be pointed out and denounced. As suggested in chapter 1, this endeavor becomes the essence of liberation theology's attempt to restore the moral critical dimension to the politics and science of the modern era. Thus, theology must incorporate two functions: that of occupying a particular role of service to society, and that of a provider of a general critical position of commitment to liberation.

At this point, we may wonder suspiciously if liberation theology has not arrived at the same place as academic theology, despite the former's disavowal of absolutist theological models and rejection of abstract certitudes and propositional truths. After all, with its unyielding concern for the poor and oppressed as the object of theological reflection and its development of a liberation praxis and hermeneutics as the foundation for a more broadly based theology, has not liberation theology merely shifted the focus of its politics from the status quo to the disenfranchised with no other discernible qualitative intellectual shift? To deal with this problem, theologians of liberation attempt to unify the themes just discussed into a coherent yet dynamic whole that appears to be qualitatively different, both intellectually as well as socially, from academic theology.

The Hermeneutic Circle

Building primarily upon the two theoretical concepts of praxis and hermeneutics, Segundo wants the following question answered: How are we to relate religious meanings of the past via praxis and hermeneutics to present living conditions? Segundo's "hermeneutic circle" provides an example of the analytical framework that any methodology of liberation must incorporate in some fashion to accomplish this task successfully and yet to avoid the sterile grip of an intransigent theological system. He defines the hermeneutic circle as "the continuing change in our interpretation of the Bible which is dictated by the continuing change in our present-day reality, both individual and societal."[74] A characterization of Segundo's circle now follows and will act as a general summary of liberation theology's peculiar methodology.

The circle consists of four stages or steps that each individual must take to insure the integrity of proper theological development and thus the efficacy of religious faith and practice in contemporary society. In the first step, the concerned individual makes a profound commitment or "act of will" to change that which is morally

59

repugnant. The individual's moral reaction to injustice and the impetus and direction of the will are usually influenced by a variety of life experiences and other general socialization processes, including religious orientation. According to Segundo, the individual's experiences may encompass a lifetime of poverty and political oppression as well as activities that involve helping the poor. The individual's religious orientation also may have undergone a transformation in the conceptual understanding of the Scriptures. For example, the individual is initially faced with a variety of bewildering positions if he were to absolutize any number of particular biblical passages. But upon careful reconsideration, it then becomes clear that the only constant set of biblical themes consists of injunctions against the rich and admonitions to help the poor, the needy, the lame, the widows, the orphans, and those in prison.[75] Now with a strong moral commitment to liberate the poor and oppressed, the individual must evaluate contemporary social conditions for adequate solutions. At this point, he arrives at the second step of Segundo's circle: the development of "ideological suspicion."

Given the normative commitment to helping the poor and oppressed, the religious individual now becomes suspicious of official explanations and ideologies that attempt to justify existing political institutions, social policies, and economic conditions that perpetuate human suffering. But any proper analysis of current social conditions requires a sophisticated understanding of contemporary politics and economics, such as the complex dynamics of pluralism, monopoly capitalism, the mass media, and the social impact of modern theology. Thus, modern social theoretical explanations take on extreme importance. Of course, these explanations are not intended to displace the Bible and its focus on the moral implications of God-man relationships; however, they are understood as necessary to augment biblical teachings and to help the individual committed to human liberation to better guide his actions. Consequently, the religious individual finds the need to implement social scientific analyses from various disciplines, including social theory and philosophy, psychology, sociology, and economics. And with the increased use of responsible social analyses, the individual gains critical insight into the various roles of all actors in society, including the role of the Church. Consequently, he becomes more suspicious of traditional usages of scripture by the Church that attempt to justify the status quo in society. Thus, the religious individual has arrived at the third step of Segundo's circle: the development of "exegetical suspicion."

The use of social analysis to satisfy ideological suspicions of the "political world" inspires the religious individual to apply the same critical techniques to the "religious world." Critical theological investigations now reveal the incompleteness as well as the ideological role of traditional interpretations of Scripture. They reveal how these interpretations, by ignoring sociological factors, often unwittingly lend moral support to the perpetuation of social injustices. This realization motivates the enlightened, religious individual—now enlightened spiritually and intellectually as well as politically—to create a "new hermeneutic," as the fourth step of the circle.

By reinterpreting the meaning of Scripture in light of his praxis of religious commitment to human liberation and understanding of contemporary social problems, the religious individual can now proceed to develop a religiously more meaningful, socially more relevant, and politically more adequate theological response to contemporary social problems. And with this new understanding of Scripture as well as social conditions, the commitment to liberation can be more effectively pursued as the concerned individual approaches once more the first step of the circle. Thus the hermeneutic circle, really a spiral, continues its critical dynamic as social conditions and the individual's comprehension continue to evolve.

Conclusion

Important assumptions and implications of this circle can now be discerned as we reconsider the essence of the methodology of liberation theology. Most apparent is the initial acceptance that no propositional truths exist in Scripture with regard to ethical behavior; there exists only a process of God seeking justice for humanity in a variety of ways, including encouraging mortals to do the same.

Furthermore, given that the social context is the beginning point for theological development, the religious individual's experiences with social injustice precede his commitment to human liberation. On the other hand, theological development itself follows this commitment; it ought not precede it. That is, the individual does not begin with theological certitudes and deduce from them how to act responsibly in a troubled world; he begins with the world and, given a set of religious or moral values, then develops a theology to deal with it.

And finally, given the nonpropositional character of God's dealings with man, the religious individual must analyze carefully, specific social problems before deciding on an appropriate, ethical response.

That is why liberation theology as a philosophical as well as a sociological movement is so vigorous. (And that is why an assessment of this movement and its methodology is crucial to any understanding of social change in Latin America: It ties the two intellectual concerns of theology and social theory together.) With this methodology, individual ethical responses to social injustice will vary as a rather wide variety of responses may be considered morally legitimate. Activities will often include petitioning government officials, organizing peasant cooperatives, advising rural and urban workers' unions, and instituting "Christian base communities."[76] But in liberation theology, the range of morally legitimate political activities does not end with a list of legally acceptable political activities. With regard to extralegal behavior, the morally committed individual may appropriately consider such social engagements as passive resistance, nonviolent strikes, boycotts, guerrilla warfare, and violent revolution.

Yet before we evaluate the political ethics of liberation theology,[77] the crucial role social science plays as the bridge between theological methodology and political behavior must be clarified. Of particular interest for political philosophy at this point in the study is the second step of Segundo's hermeneutic circle: "ideological suspicion." Again, this step requires the concerned individual to comprehend the nature of contemporary economic conditions, political institutions and structures, even international relations, and to integrate this understanding with religious values in a way that provides analytical leverage to explain poverty and oppression—and thus to be able to act more assuredly in an ethically appropriate manner. Analytical descriptions and explanations of such socially relevant activities as the intricate mechanisms of international capital and finance, the complexity of modern social relationships and their connection to the various economic arrangements for production and distribution, the nature of import-export credits and deficits, and the International Monetary Fund, are not found in ancient Scripture. Consequently, liberation theologians argue that other sources and analytical techniques are necessary for guidance—in particular, many of those from the social sciences. But which social science? What are the requirements for an acceptable social scientific approach, especially acceptable for a theological methodology that has as its goal social liberation?

In response to these and other concerns dealing with the appropriate interface between theological development and the social sciences, the use of Marxist theoretical explanations and empirical data play a crucial role in liberation theology. But why Marxist social science? And what are the implications for such a joint venture? We turn now to the critique of the Marxist-Christian tension of liberation theology.

Chapter 3

The Marxist-Christian Tension

Introduction

During the past two decades Latin American liberation theology has grown in both scholarly treatment of religious themes and political influence in society. With the reforms of the Second Vatican Council from 1962-65, the proceedings of the Second General Conference of Latin American Bishops at Medellín in 1968, and the publication of Gustavo Gutiérrez's seminal work in 1971,[1] radical theologians and religious social activists have taken the cue to involve their theologies and their lives with the problems of poverty and oppression in their societies. Influenced by alternative theological approaches and readings of Scripture, scholars and activists both have often forced confrontations with ecclesiastical and secular authorities as they challenge the moral legitimacy of Church behavior and state policy.

With confrontation, the political importance of liberation theology becomes apparent once its capacity for critical social theory is appreciated. For an adequate social theory that explains contemporary society, including the origins and nature of its social problems, can provide clearer directions to the religious individual as how to behave efficaciously as well as ethically. And, as we have seen, given the initial commitment to human liberation, the religious individual finds moral force, even obligation, to select political paths of change. Yet, the selection of a particular option necessarily involves the special expenditure of much intellectual and emotional energy to sort out and overcome theological issues and obstacles.

As we saw in the previous chapter, liberation theology could be argued as consisting more of methodology than theology. That is, liberation theology's contribution to contemporary religious and social thinking may well be its proposal of an alternative approach to doing theology as opposed to offering alternative systematic, theological insights resulting from established approaches to theological development. And it is this alternative approach with its assumptions and their consequences that ultimately separates the critics from the proponents in the debate over the use of Marxist social analysis by radical Christian thinkers.

Liberation theology, furthermore, has the onerous task of criticizing religious orthodoxy while simultaneously propagating alternative interpretations of the Christian message. This is not simply a theological issue of coherency, but a political problem of survival as well. For alongside the criticisms must come viable alternatives for any modification of orthodoxy to be considered reasonable and legitimate; otherwise, defenders of the status quo will usually be successful in mounting a counterattack on any would-be challengers by simply pointing out that, despite the deficiencies of their positions, there is no reasonable alternative. In addition, it should be kept in mind that liberation theologians are committed to the existing Church. They want to conserve the traditional values and concerns that have given substance and shape to Christianity through the centuries; they are not disposed toward, nor desirous of, promoting schisms and apostasy, but of promoting a strong sense of community within existing institutions. Nevertheless, with its scathing critique of contemporary social conditions and institutions, including the role of religious institutions, liberation theology currently finds itself in the position of challenger facing powerful defenders of orthodoxy in the political world of religious scholarship.

While this situation is not surprising, given the general nature of theoretical argumentation and political conflict, the primary concern of the critics of liberation theology may be rather unexpected. Rather than focus discussion on the necessary metaphysical and epistemological assumptions for proper theological reflection to discount liberation theology's appeal, critics instead have accorded greater energy to highlighting the *political theoretical* dimension of liberation theologians' writings, primarily by bringing attention to the role Marxism often plays.

Liberation theologians, as indicated earlier, find the use of social science essential to theological development and pastoral activity. Yet with a variety of sociological perspectives from which to choose, most incorporate some aspect of Marxist-oriented social science. The question as to why this would be the case has intrigued many political scientists. Michael Dodson, for one, has suggested that the ubiquity of Latin American intellectuals who utilize various Marxist frameworks for social analysis has had a contagious effect on all those who would understand and explain Latin American social conditions.[2] While there may be a cross-disciplinary, "bandwagon" effect with regard to avant-garde methodologies and their popularity, this still does not adequately explain their adoption by Christian theologians who are also academically trained in theology and committed to a religious faith—a faith that has traditionally been defined as antithetical to communism in general and to Marxism in particular.[3]

Again, as discussed in the previous chapter, crucial to developing a new hermeneutic in liberation theology is a theoretical understanding of social conditions that will assist efforts at social change. Notice the importance of social theory in general, as well as a particular social theory for theological reflection at this level of "ideological suspicion" in the hermeneutic circle. The normative intent of the social theory to be selected must be compatible with the moral commitment and goals of the radical theologian. Furthermore, the methodological approach to social scientific analysis must be compatible with the methodological approach to theological development. It is in consideration of these two points of normative and methodological intent that serious interest by liberation theologians in Marxist social analysis becomes apparent.

Normative Intent

First, with regard to the ethical or normative dimension, the strength of their common interests and social goals more than their metaphysical dissimilarities attracts liberation theologians to Marxism. As with Marxism's concern for social justice and its use of theoretical insights as an additional tool for effecting human liberation, the biblical prophetic tradition, as interpreted by liberation theologians, also emphasizes the importance of committing oneself to the struggle for social justice. This apparent identification of interests between the two traditions is not a novel observation originating with liberation theologians. The emphasis on social justice found both in Marxist literature and in the prophetic tradition of Scripture, has long proven to be a ground of common interest for the establishment of Marxist-Christian dialogues in the twentieth century.[4] Moving beyond dialogue to analysis, Latin American liberation theologians argue for the necessity of a social science that will both evaluate extant social conditions and provide moral leverage for those committed to active participation in alleviating the suffering of the poor and oppressed; they claim that Marxism provides the "energy" for both.[5]

Focusing on the structure of society to explain problems of social injustice, both Marxists and liberation theologians are critical of capitalism for its incapacity to maintain an atmosphere of social concern.[6] And because the problems of social injustice are perceived as structural in origin, liberation theologians find the prevailing philosophical foundation of liberalism with its lack of a theory of justice unsatisfactory to deal with social problems.[7] They argue that other contemporary social theories with their attendant bourgeois values also serve only to provide legitimacy for the political and economic status quo. Only Marxist class analysis appears to them to afford a comprehensive, analytical theory adequate to explain the root causes of poverty and political oppression in a way that simultaneously and self-consciously encourages their eradication.

The overlap in biblical and Marxist normative criticisms of social injustice have been dealt with from intriguing angles by liberation theologians. For example, José Porfirio Miranda points out that both the Bible and the writings of Karl Marx extol the benefits of communism.[8] According to his exegesis, the Scriptures portray Old Testament prophets as well as Jesus in the New Testament excoriating their own societies for lack of sensitivity to issues of social justice. The normative message from God to man via the Scriptures reveals that the Kingdom of God, a kingdom of perfect justice, is meant to be built on earth in mortal life; that private property and equality of wealth is denounced in favor of communism as the only divinely justified form of economic arrangement; and that only a classless society can meet any standard of social justice.[9] Moreover, Miranda maintains that the normative values of Marx himself find their origin in early Christian humanism.[10]

Regardless of the proper chronological order, the "hope" of both the prophetic and Marxist traditions is for a future society of peace, liberty, and justice, a society free from the exploitation of man by man.[11] In their attempt to transform the present social arrangement from that of the past, both generally hold out the possibility of a utopian society in the future. Furthermore, this vision of perfect social justice and peace sets the foundation for their advocacy of socialist economic arrangements and democratic politics.[12] According to Gutiérrez, liberation theologians reveal the "will to build a socialist society, more just, free, and human, and not a society of superficial and false reconciliation and equality."[13]

Yet despite the general interest in their profession of common concern—that is, the critique of capitalism and the advocacy of socialism—ultimately the verification of normative beliefs in liberation theology and Marxism are themselves acts of faith. Of equal if not greater interest for political philosophy, if only because of the open and more accessible question of logical consistency, is the more tendentious claim of the compatibility between their theoretical frameworks.

Methodological Intent

With regard to the methodological dimension, liberation theologians tend to avoid any structural predisposition in their philosophical discourse that relies on propositional certitudes. As mentioned earlier, this suggests that they have a proclivity toward theorizing in a way that takes change into account—even the changing nature of theorizing itself. In fact, they accept change as the essence of reality, including the historical evolution of society, the establishment of religious institutions, and the development of theology itself; hence there is widespread use of "dialectical thinking" in liberation theology. In this way, liberation theologians maintain that an appreciation for the dynamics of political society must be in tandem with efforts toward social change; and, of course, the development of theology with an appropriate social science will then be able to remain in flux.

The relationship between the dialectical thinking found in liberation theology and the dialectical thinking found in Marxism may be the most binding relationship between the two and hence the reason for the adoption of Marxist social science by radical Christians. It is at this point that we can identify the connection between theological development and social science—with Marxism as the preferred social science—as required by the second step of the hermeneutic circle. A closer look at dialectical thinking is in order.

Dialectical Thinking

The Spanish theologian Alfredo Fierro attributes the rise of political theology in general[14] and liberation theology in particular, and the subsequent incorporation of Marxism, to a particular moment in the history of Western thought. According to Fierro,

> It is sheer fantasy to think that the rise of political theology right now is due simply to a reconsideration of the basic sources of the Christian faith. That reconsideration is real enough, and it is the most immediate root of present-day political theology. But why did it arise precisely at this time? If its origin and deepest roots are to be found exclusively in the gospel and tradition, why did it take two thousand years to manifest itself?[15]

Fierro finds the answer to this question in a recent shift in ethical thinking, "from existential and humanist sensibilities to political awareness."[16] And it is in this shift that the turn to "dialectical thinking" emerges.[17]

In an earlier shift, the establishment of moral thought and the grounding of political ethics had moved away from transcendental, natural law theories, to practical, individualist, and utilitarian solutions to moral questions and social problems.[18] The anomalies and inadequacies of medieval cosmologies provided an opening for the development and acceptability of the enlightened and democratic approaches of the modern era. But today, this exchange of transcendentalism for existentialism has not been as successful as hoped for. The failure of existentialist thought includes its inability to understand fully the dynamics of social relationships, the origins of social injustice, and the necessity for political action. It is existentialism's inherent inability to provide adequate guidance for solutions to social problems that has prompted renewed attention to theories that claim both practical insights for individual moral considerations and comprehensive remedies for problems of injustice.

Furthermore, says Fierro, a number of events have occurred that contributed to the demise of existentialist and humanist attitudes. These include the failure of liberal democracies to address adequately social problems and the emergence of liberation movements against colonialism and imperialism in much of the Third World, as well as among oppressed minorities in both developed and developing countries.

All these facts have helped to rule out the possibility of a neutral, apolitical, and purely humanist attitude such as that which prevailed among theologians prior to 1965. . . . They could no longer go on with existentialist disquisitions; they were constrained to undertake political reflection.[19]

This political reflection, then, is closely bound up with historical conditions that call forth reflection in the first place. Yet religious values inherently give moral force to such reflection. Hence, the recognition of the influence of values in changing the world invoke a dialectical relationship between morally unacceptable social conditions and political action to change those conditions. Even so, it has not been only the crises of various world events that have caused new developments in theology. Fierro suggests that change has also come about "indirectly through the mediation of certain theoretical and interpretative instruments provided by the human sciences in their new organization and approach."[20]

Much of contemporary social science has indeed undergone rapid evolutionary change, from that of a behavioral and positivistic approach to a more dialectical and transcendental approach.[21] The advent of modern philosophical thought concerning dialectical reasoning has had enormous impact in setting the foundations for reuniting facts and values, a unification of material conditions and objective interpretations with transcendental values and normative assessments.[22] Fierro feels that the penetration of dialectical reasoning and historical materialism into Western learning is of utmost significance. He notes that this shift from existentialist and humanist attitudes to a dialectical and historical materialist outlook can be found in all aspects of Western culture, such as modern philosophy and education and in the theater and the literary world.[23] Even the existentialist philosopher Jean-Paul Sartre finally recognized the limits of existentialism and proclaimed, "I consider Marxism as the unsurpassable philosophy of our times, and I regard the ideology of existence as an enclave within Marxism itself."[24]

Fierro argues that new concepts of the scientific approach, especially in the human sciences, "have now come to be viewed from what is essentially a practical, critical, political, and dialectical standpoint."[25] Marxism, broadly defined, has given primary philosophical coherency to contemporary expressions of dialectical reasoning and historical materialism in the new human sciences. In turn, given their own increasing focus on social conditions and their dialectical approach, political theologians now possess a means to comprehend and interpret social reality better as the result of implementing Marxist social analysis. For Fierro, the, the analytical gap between social reality and theological development as well as the traditional gap between the disciplines of politics and theology becomes narrower as the need for the adoption of social science by radical Christians increases and as the philosophical compatibility with Marxist social science also becomes more apparent.[26] Now, Marxists and Christians, historically at odds with each other politically, are able to find common ground to justify even stronger intellectual reconciliation than attempts in the past had afforded.

Moreover, there are two additional presuppositions concerning Marxist dialectical thinking that further hastens the merger between radical Christian and Marxist movements, according to Fierro.[27] First, it is recognized that the scientific observer is implicated in the very social process under scrutiny; that is, he cannot wholly and objectively extricate himself from involvement and participation in the very process he is attempting to assess. Secondly, and following from this recognition, it is also realized that "real" knowledge resulting from scientific discovery does not result from pure contemplation, but from "the practical handling of things." Hence, the understanding of scientific knowledge as itself a component of social dynamics, may serve a revolutionary function as a method of social criticism. In this way, argues Fierro, "The peculiar and proper feature of knowledge, science, and theory is its delineation of historical alternatives to the present state of affairs."[28] Thus, properly understood and conducted, social studies perform a critical function in any philosophical system by revealing the normative disparity between *reality* and *appearance,* the distinction between *is* and *ought* of facts and values.[29]

Now, given that the objective of social analysis and the analysis itself are inextricably linked, of importance to dialectical thinking, then, is the importance of *totalities.*[30] That is, such thinking "considers facts and events as elements of a historically defined reality from which they cannot be isolated." Although the totality of history cannot be fully grasped, various aspects are open to comprehension and in this way "relative" totalities can be investigated and explicated. Fierro maintains that, while there exist many approaches to understanding totalities, the Marxist account becomes important when totalities are seen as built upon a material base involving production processes and a peculiar set of social relations spawned by those processes. And as discussed earlier, liberation theologians highlight a prophetic tradition that reveals God's concern for the totality of man's existence, including the material aspect.

So in its requirement of incorporating modern social science in order to pursue effectively the religious commitment to human liberation, liberation theology claims to provide the initial intellectual conditions for the incorporation of Marxist analytical categories and actively utilizes Marxist social analysis. And to this end of fulfilling the requirements of the second step of the hermeneutic circle, a crucial aspect of the political theory of Latin American liberation theology is the use of dialectical thinking. Again, dialectical thinking bridges the traditional gap between Christianity and Marxism so that the use of Marxist social science itself can bridge the gap between religious values and political action.

Marxist studies of society, however, have typically included critical observations of the social role played by religious institutions and have argued that religious thought and practices offer no assistance to the attainment of social justice. Such analyses provide their own set of theoretical problems of observation and utilization for radical Christians. And in this regard, of the several theoretical obstacles to an effective Marxist-Christian alliance, perhaps the most serious is the issue of the sociology of religion.

Indeed, liberation theology provokes consternation as a result of its attempt to unite the two philosophical traditions of Marxism and Christianity, traditions that have historically opposed each other. The Marxist tradition, while providing analyses of social conditions, includes explanations of the social origins of knowledge itself. In particular, acceptance of its sociology of knowledge has posed a threat to belief in the existence of spiritual concerns by questioning religious claims to transcendental truths. Alternatively, the Christian tradition has taught values of moral judgment whose spiritual truths transcend social conditions in their origins and emphasize the greater importance of the Hereafter to this life. Consequently, Christianity's traditional lack of enthusiasm for social theories, especially those that potentially threaten the spiritual legitimacy of religion, has provided powerful discouragement for dialogue with secular social science in general, and with Marxism in particular.

With these concerns in mind and given their commitment to social justice, liberation theologians have attempted to find an appropriate critical approach to understanding and changing society while not destroying religion simultaneously. They claim to have succeeded in achieving this objective by creating a theological context via the hermenuetic circle that maintains a peculiar epistemological tension. The tension permits attempts to utilize Marxist social analysis while preserving the traditional and transcendental values of Christianity. But this can exist only as long as there occurs a separation of social analysis from ideology in any appropriation of Marxism.

Nevertheless, can any religious institution and set of practices escape the scrutiny of Marxist analysis when rigorously and comprehensively applied to all aspects of society? Given a socially and materialistically rooted explanation of religious beliefs and practices, how can transcendental theology and religion itself survive? Furthermore, the ultimate end of the Gospel—eternal salvation—explicated by most theologies, including liberation theology, remains for Christian social teachings and social practices. So in fact, can the Marxist-Christian tension in liberation theology be maintained? Can each side find some room for accommodating the other without the destruction of either? For conservative Christian thinkers, accommodation is not possible and any attempt to achieve it will destroy the essence if not the existence of religion. For liberation theologians, the tension is possible but only under certain epistemological conditions.

A look at the reactions by those who assume and argue that Marxist social critiques and fundamental religious beliefs are incompatible, will further explicate the intricate approach to liberation theology's use of Marxism.

Conservative Criticisms

Because neither Christianity nor Marxism is compatible with the other, conservative critics maintain that liberation theologians who want to incorporate Marxist social science have placed themselves in a dilemma. Any attempt to merge the two traditions will ultimately provoke a crisis forcing the abandonment of one for the other. Among other similar treatments on liberation theology and Marxism, the most recent and perhaps best-known, formal criticism from a high-level ecclesiastical office is the Catholic publication of *Instructions about some Aspects of "Liberation Theology,"* the first of two related documents originating from the Sacred Congregation for the Doctrine of the Faith and written under the direction of Joseph Cardinal Ratzinger.[31] The argument in this document and other related criticisms succinctly reveals one of the primary concerns of the conservative critics: the unacceptable consequences for religion, as a result of any theology utilizing any aspect of Marxism.

Unacceptable Consequences

Ratzinger maintains that theologians who incorporate Marxist analyses of socioeconomic problems have not been careful in their adoptions; they have made uncritical assumptions about Marxism that cannot be supported. Specifically, liberation theologians presume that Marxist social analytical techniques alone can be implemented as tools for explaining social conditions, without accepting the rest of the "philosophical-ideological structure" of Marxism. However unwitting this presumption, it is mistaken, claims Ratzinger, and such an adoption by theologians leads to morally unacceptable outcomes. A separation of analytical techniques from normative structure is simply impossible.[32]

While he does recognize the diversity of treatments and conclusions among even the most sympathetic interpreters of Karl Marx's writings, Ratzinger claims that all explications of Marxism agree on the presence of "a certain number of fundamental theses that are incompatible with the Christian understanding of man and society."[33] He singles out the Marxist ideological emphasis on class struggle, and its attendant characteristics of violence, materialism, and atheism, as one of the fundamental theses. Ratzinger laments the ignorance of, or avoidance by, theologians of liberation of the moral, practical, and historical significance of this concept.[34]

In his criticism of Marxism, Ratzinger first notes that, despite its importance as a fundamental law of history in Marxist theory, the assumption of class struggle can command no empirical evidence for its support. Thus, given their origins in an incomplete and flawed perception of industrialization from the nineteenth century, Marx's assessments of socioeconomic conditions simply do not apply to modern conditions.[35] Not only have industrialized societies become more complex and intricate during the past century, but the social sciences have, too, become more differentiated. He points out that contemporary social science disciplines, with their pluralism of methodologies, have been unable to form a consensus on the proper interpretive framework for social analysis itself.

More troubling for Ratzinger, however, are the devastating *consequences* that the acceptance of this absolutist claim from Marxism has had, and will continue to have, for theology and religion. According to Marxist social science, the dynamic of class struggle as "the motor of history" defines all other parameters of social development, including cultural values. As a result, the nature and content of truth itself takes on a class bias. A "class truth," then, about social reality becomes the standard for measuring claims about any aspect of that reality, including social norms and personal ethics. This claim and its acceptance by theologians who utilize Marxist social science denigrates the traditional standing and transcendental moral claims of Christian theology. By contrast, Ratzinger quickly reaffirms the traditional view that theology itself is, and ought to remain, the only source of virtue for sustaining any standard of moral behavior.[36]

Furthermore, Ratzinger points out that Marxist ideology and analysis rely on economic class as the primary source of change, truth, and social organization. This reliance has had the effect of directing and focusing the study of human evolution, ideas, and institutions strictly on material processes. And this narrow understanding in turn has led to the conclusion that the other dimensions of society, including religion with its practices and teachings, lack autonomy.[37] If all truth and the meaning of all practices are class-based and the material processes of the economy determine other social activities, including those of religion, at what point, then, does God break into human history and affect man's destiny? For Ratzinger, the ultimate and inescapable outcome of accepting the Marxist fundamental law of class struggle is the admission that only atheism can be rationally justified with regard to questions of the existence of God; "Let's remember that atheism and the denial of the human person, of his liberty and rights, are found at the center of Marxism."[38]

Finally, Ratzinger maintains that the acceptance of Marxist social analysis with its fundamental law of class struggle places radical theologians in the position of more than simply condoning the use of violence in unjust situations. For Marxism requires that violence itself be recognized as a *necessary* aspect of reality, thus beyond any judgment as to its moral character. With this recognition, the radical theologian is obliged to participate in violent activities and consequently must choose sides as to whom he will love. Yet this is antithetical to the essence of Christian teachings of God's universal love for his creation.[39] Therefore, argues Ratzinger, "the transcendental character of the distinction between good and evil, the basis of morality, is implicitly denied from the class struggle point of view."[40]

As we can see, Ratzinger denies the possibility that any "Marxist social science and analysis" can be separated from "Marxist ideology and *praxis* (political behavior)." He argues that claims concerning class struggle are *ideological* assertions primarily and not simply *empirical* claims about the real world. And he complains that the sad history of political movements and institutions guided by, and operating under the label of, Marxism with these ideological assertions is inextricably linked to any social scientific analysis so inspired; and the future will be no different from the past. Accordingly, theologians of liberation are committing a grave error in assuming that a separation of the two is possible.

Still, something seems to be lacking in Ratzinger's discussion. What exactly is the central barrier that prevents any kind of Marxist-Christian dialogue, alliance, or merger? Is it merely the *consequences* of accepting one argument over another? If so, then ends-oriented, utilitarian calculations of acceptability will have supplanted means-oriented, absolutist positions of moral obligation—a denial of Ratzinger's own theological outlook. Or are there certain initial *assumptions* that prevent the amalgamation of two, presumably different, philosophical frameworks, and, if so, what are they? The latter issue is the more likely concern. We get a little closer to the answer by looking at two sources of criticism of liberation theology from Latin America, sources that apparently influenced Ratzinger's thinking.

A Priori Problems

In an earlier criticism of liberation theology, Bishop Alfonso López Trujillo also argues against the claim that Marxist social analysis can be separated from Marxist ideology. As indicated by the title of his work, *Liberation or Revolution?*, López Trujillo worries that the morally appropriate concern for human liberation from social as well as spiritual oppression is being reduced in liberation theology to a matter strictly of social revolution—that is, of Marxist class struggle.[41] He points out that the Medellín Conference documents of 1968, as well as the criticisms of liberation theologians, such as those of Gutiérrez who influenced the proceedings at Medellín, utilize findings from Marxist analyses of socioeconomic conditions and attempt to apply these findings to their pastoral work.[42] As a result, however, the pastoral work often degenerates into political work as radicalized priests participate in mobilizing parishioners to confront political authorities to effect social change. Frequently, the confrontations are violent, and this puts the priests on the side of revolutionary movements. Given his commitment to a Christianity that deals primarily with the spiritual salvation of the soul, López Trujillo is unable to accept the "theological baptism" of revolutionary violence.[43]

Perceiving spiritual devastation as a result of the politicization of the Gospel, López Trujillo argues that the cause for this outcome can be found in the integral connection between Marxist social analysis and Marxist ideology and political behavior, so often ignored by radical theologians. He cites Marx, Lenin, Mao and other like-minded writers who, using materialist-based social analyses, emphasized the importance of understanding history solely as the outcome of changes in methods of economic production. They wrote that economic transformations in conjunction with revolutionary violence directly affect "the legal, ethical, political, religious and other kinds of relationships in the superstructure."[44] But more importantly, religious beliefs and practices are themselves reduced in Marxist social theory to mere epiphenomena determined by the changes in economic arrangements, and thus take on a political ideological role in maintaining the legitimacy of those arrangements.

López Trujillo, of course, finds this assessment of society and religion problematic. The use of such analysis reduces the status of religion to merely a social tool of either oppression according to orthodox Marxists, or liberation according to radical theologians, depending on its relationship to the class struggle under way. In either case, as echoed later by Ratzinger, López Trujillo warns that the acceptance of class struggle, a nonnegotiable demand of Marxist social science, will have devastating consequences for theology: for in the consummation of the struggle, true religion will be consumed.

But unlike Ratzinger, López Trujillo considers the problem of class struggle as only one consequence of the larger issue dealing with the potential merger between different philosophical frameworks. Although he never fully reveals them, certain conditions are necessary for a successful merger. Certainly the capricious borrowing of one aspect of a philosophical system by another system with no consideration for the theoretical integrity of, and consequences for, each is unacceptable to him. And he finds this to be the case with regard to the liberation theologians' use of Marxist social analysis while supposedly rejecting Marxist philosophy and ideology. For López Trujillo, the scientific rationale of Marxism—however enlightening it may be for analyzing capitalist economies—cannot be separated from the doctrinal contents of Marxist philosophy.[45] Since these doctrines will lead eventually to the annihilation of religion and since the acceptance of one aspect of Marxism necessarily implies and requires the acceptance of all, the real problem, then, has to do with the doctrinal or moral *basis* of Marxism.

Marxist philosophy is structured around certain analytical catego- ries that are not objectively neutral in their application. While all philosophical systems naturally have categories, maintains López Trujillo, Marxist categories are closed to metaphysical considerations of the transcendence, unlike the borrowed categories of Aristoteli- anism incorporated in contemporary Christianity. He asks: Where do Marxists deal adequately with questions on "the existence of God, the definition of man, the meaning of mankind, the mystery of death, etc."?[46] Clarification of these concerns is not a peripheral issue but central to the traditional project of Christian theology. Their relega- tion by positivist Marxism to the unfalsifiable realm of metaphysical dependency demonstrates the fundamental incompatibility between the two great philosophical systems. So, while Ratzinger sees the ad- mission of atheism and the demise of theology as a consequence of Marxist social analysis, López Trujillo sees these positions as neces- sary preconditions for the development and application of any aspect of Marxist philosophy.

Another Latin American cleric, Father Juan Gutiérrez, has also fo- cused on the a priori claims of Marxist philosophy in his critique of Gustavo Gutiérrez's use of Marxism. In *The New Libertarian Gospel* Juan Gutiérrez expands the argument begun by López Trujillo con- cerning the implications of Marxism's positivist atheism for theol- ogy.[47] He begins by noting that Gustavo Gutiérrez claims merely an interest in Marxism for the selection of a technique for social analy- sis. Presumably, then, with a better understanding of social condi- tions, clergy and theologians can make the application of their theology more relevant to the needs of their charge and concerned readers.

Juan Gutiérrez argues, however, as with the other critics, that an inseparable fusion exists between social analysis and philosophy in Marxism operating with a materialist base fundamental to its intel- lectual pursuit. Furthermore, the enterprise of social analysis itself is dependent upon the larger philosophical framework for guidance in its application. And, of course, this framework maintains the a priori assumption of atheism that prevents it from taking seriously any theological arguments concerning the existence of God and re- vealed Truth.[48] Consequently, if theologians consult Marxism on how better to relate theology to society as does Gustavo Gutiérrez, Marx- ist advice is to apply a particular secular, social theory to understand the nature of religious behavior. In this way, Marxists claim, both practices and beliefs of theology and religion in general and Christianity in particular can be understood as to their real nature. According to Juan Gutiérrez, then, this approach to understanding the relevance of theological reflection for society incorporates a one-sided emphasis with fatal results for theology. The Marxist attitude essentially denies the transcendental content of religion by explaining it in terms of sociological phenomena; and this in turn denies and destroys any basis for the faith of the believer and ultimately the rationale for the theological enterprise itself. In effect, Gustavo Gutiérrez's attempt at dialogue between Christian theology and Marxism will eventually move toward the intellectual subordination of Christianity to Marxism and finally to the annihilation of Christianity altogether; "instead of 'understanding' Marxism, theology will be 'understood' by it."[49]

Relatedly, to substantiate his claim that philosophical dialogue between theology and Marxism results in Marxist co-optation of theology, Juan Gutiérrez argues that Gustavo Gutiérrez's purportedly theological use of *praxis* is in fact strictly political and Marxist and not theologically based. He points out that this central concept from Marxist philosophy is never satisfactorily defined by Gustavo Gutiérrez but only used in the same way as the Marxists. That is to say, praxis is used with regard to politics only, dealing with the social relationships of the particular material conditions of society.[50] According to the value judgments of the ideological assumptions in Marxist philosophy, the application of social analysis reveals that the development of the material conditions of society are only based on the dynamics and politics of class struggle. Furthermore, Juan Gutiérrez maintains that such an analysis reveals the dependent, political dimension of religious teachings and practices. And again, as later echoed by Ratzinger, the political efficacy of these teachings and practices to the ultimate goal of human liberation can only be determined by the praxis of class struggle "which itself becomes the criterion of truth."[51]

Now we are closer to understanding the problem conservatives perceive in any attempt at an amalgamation of Marxism and Christianity. While the moral and social consequences of such an enterprise are not to be discounted argues Ratzinger, the philosophical and theological possibility of such an enterprise itself is doubtful according to López Trujillo and Juan Gutiérrez. Ratzinger claims that religion will be destroyed as a result of any union between Marxism and Christianity; López Trujillo and Juan Gutiérrez claim that in terms of theoretical integrity and compatibility, a philosophical union is impossible from the start. Clearly, all three rule out the possibility of maintaining a productive tension between Marxism and Christianity.

Marxisms and Marx

Historically, the result of using Marxist analytical frameworks has indicated for radical social critics the moral bankruptcy of religious foundations and the deceptive use of religious institutions and beliefs by oppressive states. In turn, conservatives have generally criticized Marxists for their apparent atheism; they accuse Marxists of holding the view that religion has no authentic contribution to make to alleviate human suffering in the world. In fact, radicals have generally accepted the conservatives' accounts as accurate, only disagreeing with their denunciation of Marxism for having revealed the awful truth about a superstitious portion of social reality. The use of Marxist assumptions by liberation theology, then, would indeed seem to undermine the very legitimacy of liberation theology itself—whether perceived from the right or the left.

First, however, it should be noted that despite the claims made by these critics, no consensus exists among Marxists on the indivisibility of Marxist philosophy with regard to social analysis and ideology. According to many contemporary theorists, these standard interpretations of Marxism and religion lack accuracy and sophistication. One philosopher has pointed out that adherence to atheism is not an essential element of Marxist social analysis, nor is the imposition on society of deterministic mechanics originating with the economic base a necessarily appropriate reading of results from class analysis.[52] In fact, much of the debate on interpretation of Marx's thought and development of Marxist theory has focused on the question of determinism. Is Marxism indeed a mechanical theory of social relations where all social activity is caused by and only by prior economic activity with no room for autonomous, even irrational, behavior? Among several schools of radical political thought, the growing influence of the Frankfurt School of *critical theory* and the resurgence in popularity of the writings of Antonio Gramsci and Georg Lukács would seem to dispel any idea of consensus on economic determinism.[53] Their writings present arguments demonstrating the importance of a long-neglected, humanistic aspect of Marx and his observations for critical, social theory.

In fact, it is the conservative treatment of Marxism as embodying a unified set of doctrine within an impregnable philosophy as just discussed, that has itself drawn recent criticism from liberation theologians and others. For example, in *Theology and the Church: A Response to Cardinal Ratzinger and a Warning to the Whole Church,* Juan Luis Segundo has responded directly to Ratzinger's first document on liberation theology and its assessment of Marxism.[54] He discusses Ratzinger's refusal to recognize the possible acceptability of carefully selected and delineated aspects of Marxism by Christian theologians. As we have seen, although he recognizes the diversity of Marxist schools, Ratzinger claims that all Marxisms are flawed. The use of any aspect of Marxist philosophy necessitates the adoption of all aspects and assumptions of Marxist philosophy, so that this enterprise will eventually culminate in the ultimate ruin of religion as well as theology itself. Yet Segundo points out that this claim does not accord with actual practice. Frequently writers from one school of thought borrow and incorporate an element from another school with no apparent harm. Even the pope on occasion has used elements of Marxist analysis—for example, *alienation*—with no apparent adverse consequences to his theology or the Church. The problem with Ratzinger's claim, then, is his failure to clarify the "distinct epistemological status" of Marxism that prevents the borrowing of elements prevalent from other systems.[55]

Furthermore, although Ratzinger fears that any adoption of Marxist social analysis leads to atheism, Segundo reminds him that there is no consensus on the centrality, if any, of atheism in Marxism and its importance for analytical theory development and application among social theorists.[56] The ambiguity of Marx himself has fueled unending debate among contemporary heirs of his tradition; many treat the problem in a variety of ways, from viewing it as a core problem of metaphysics to a periphery problem of science. Segundo concludes that Ratzinger's publication, with its lack of specificity with regard to any serious philosophical discussion of Marxism, can only be understood as an impassioned if serious polemic against Marxism.[57] Consequently, while Ratzinger's claim to deal with the issue of Marxism's epistemological status is indeed crucial to his concern, he never fulfills his objective.

In another response to the Church's concern over the use of Marxism by liberation theology, the theologian Joseph Kroger has also focused on Ratzinger's dogmatic conflation of Marxist analysis with Marxist ideology.[58] He demonstrates that far from settled is the issue of the relationship between theory and practice among Marxists. In particular, he presents a general discussion of the project of contemporary critical theorists, such as Jürgen Habermas, who have attempted to deal with the problem of reconciling general social theoretical assessments with individual autonomous behavior. Furthermore, referring explicitly to Gustavo Gutiérrez and Segundo, Kroger argues that the style of social criticism in liberation theology is quite similar to that found in critical theory. Both attempt to bring general assessments of the structural dynamics, rationality, and politics of industrialized and industrializing societies to bear while clarifying the role of autonomy.[59]

The potentiality in Marxist social theory, then, for recognition of autonomous behavior on the part of individuals and institutions other than economic classes, invites speculation on the possibility of utilizing Marxist social analysis apart from other aspects of Marxist philosophy. If the issue of autonomous behavior can be resolved with its possibility defended, one effect of a successful separation would be to permit an analysis of socioeconomic conditions without necessarily denying the moral traditions nor the political efficacy of revolutionary change originating from a variety of sources, including from religious institutions.

At this point, an unsettling situation exists. Conservative critics of liberation theology argue against any union of Marxism and Christianity given their assessment of these two traditions. Each appears to them as monolithic, having been founded upon comprehensive, mutually exclusive, and incompatible philosophical frameworks. Yet among theologians generally there is no consensus on the uniformity of Marxism, nor apparently on that of Christianity. Conversely, that there is a close intellectual relationship between Marxism and Christianity has been suggested by many philosophers. For example, Alasdair MacIntyre contends that Marxism via Hegelian thought utilizes philosophical categories derived from earlier Christian thought, primarily those of *alienation, objectification,* and *becoming.* He demonstrates the influence of Pauline eschatology on G. W. F. Hegel's thought, on that of the Left Hegelians and Ludwig Feuerbach, and, finally, on that of the writings of Karl Marx and Friedrich Engels. Thus, Marxism "shares in good measure both the content and the functions of Christianity as an interpretation of human existence, and it does so because it is the historical successor to Christianity."[60] Indeed, even some critics of liberation theology, such as the theologian Dennis P. McCann, have conceded that, while it would not be easy, a reinterpretation of the Christian tradition itself could be effected to allow for the incorporation of certain aspects of Marxist philosophy.[61] The conservatives' criticism of the supposed compatibility of the two systems still deserves consideration, however, with regard to the issue of the sociology of religion. For even if atheism and strict determinism need not be adhered to in the application of Marxist social analysis, the origins and practices of religion still will not necessarily be explained as anything other than socially created behavior with society's machinations as their reference point. Ironically, Marx's own assessment of religion appears to give credence to the conservatives' concern.

Marx's Critique of Religion

Although radical theology often uses Marxist social analysis and categories, one aspect of Marxism is indeed its usual criticism of religion. To the extent that Marxism may be presented as a complete philosophical system, how can the use of one part of the philosophy not accompany other parts that apparently are integrally connected? It would seem that radical theologians must take Marx's criticism of Christianity seriously and ultimately face questions concerning the compatibility between the two.

In his essay "On the Jewish Question," Marx provides insights into his understanding of the nature and role of religion in individual and social life.[62] With regard to fellow social critic Bruno Bauer's attempt to deal with the problem of anti-Semitism in an officially Christian society, Marx maintains that Bauer does not go far enough in his analysis. "It was by no means sufficient to ask: who should emancipate? who should be emancipated? The critic should ask a third question: *what kind of emancipation* is involved?"[63] What must be examined is *"the relation between political emancipation and human emancipation."*[64]

These two differing types of emancipation, political and human, are crucial to a proper understanding of the role of religion in Marx's thought. Political emancipation refers to the emancipation of the state from various constraints. For example, Marx maintains that the state has been emancipated in some places—such as, North America—by preventing private property from acting as a constraint on politics. Such abolition occurs when property qualifications for electors and officeholders are no longer mandatory. Marx remarks: "Is not private property ideally abolished when the non-owner comes to legislate for the owner of property?"; and he concludes, "The *property qualification* is the last *political* form in which private property is recognized."[65]

Although removed as a formal restriction in electoral politics, private property yet continues to reside in civil society. Only the state and those citizens involved in lawmaking have been emancipated from this formal constraint. Yet other aspects of civil society continue to be affected by the existence of private property. Similarly, political states may emancipate themselves from the direct relationship with, and control by, religion and its detrimental consequences—for example, the Christian state with its attendant persecution of Jews. As with private property, the state must refuse to recognize any religion as having exclusive authority over other sects to influence official public policy. Traditionally this has been the stance of those who have advocated "separation of Church and state." Yet, according to Marx, this political emancipation does not emancipate individuals from religion. "Man [has only emancipated] himself *politically* from religion by expelling it from the sphere of public law to that of private law."[66]

The problem of complete human emancipation has yet to be resolved, according to Marx. Even though the liberal state may have become emancipated from private property and religion, it still presupposes their social existence and thus continuing ability to restrict individual freedom. Political emancipation has now merely institutionalized a dichotomy between public and private activity, social and personal beliefs. According to Marx,

> one should have no illusions about the scope of political emancipation. The division of man into the *public person* and the *private person,* the *displacement* of religion from the state to civil society—all this is not a stage in political emancipation but its consummation. Thus political emancipation does not abolish, and does not even strive to abolish, man's *real* religiosity.[67]

This formally institutionalized opposition between public person and private person, between man as a social being and man as egoistic, by the liberal state, has yet to be overcome. Human emancipation ultimately can only be realized with the abolition of those elements found in civil society that differentiate individual interests. Yet the liberal state is limited by its ability to overcome all oppression; for the politically emancipated state to totally abolish the very foundations of its existence for its existence clearly involves a contradiction, and, according to Marx, the remedy for this contradiction can only be achieved through "permanent revolution."[68] Hence, to maintain its own survival, the liberal state (public sphere) accepts as legitimate for civil society (private sphere) all of the very elements from which it has struggled to free itself. In this way, Marx claims to reveal the limitation of political emancipation under classical liberalism with regard to individual liberation.

The problem with classical liberalism and its imposed distinction between civil society and the state involves, according to Marx, a misguided reflection upon moral values. The political revolutions of the eighteenth century emphasized "the rights of man" as the legitimate foundation for moral authority. Yet these rights became "simply the rights of a *member of civil society,* that is, of egoistic man, of man separated from other men and from the community."[69] Instead of being liberated from religion, property, and "the egoism of business," man received religious liberty, the liberty to own property, and "the liberty to engage in business."[70] Consequently, Marx argues, the supposedly authentic man of civil society is alienated from political man or man as citizen. The maintenance of this artificial and repressive alienation is the final barrier to the achievement of human emancipation. The development of man's true identity as a social being will occur when the abstraction of political man has been overcome and merged with the reality of individual man.[71]

With regard to religion, then, a morally liberated society will have no need for religious beliefs to explain certain phenomena nor the attendant religious institutions that preserve those beliefs. Marx believes religion merely reflects the inadequacies of civil society where human emancipation has yet to be achieved. He demonstrates this notion with regard to "the Jewish question." "Let us not seek the secret of the Jew in religion, but let us seek the secret of the religion in the real Jew."[72] This secret manifests itself in Judaism's aggressive characteristics of "self-interest," "money," and "huckstering." But to be emancipated, these characteristics must be understood in terms of their social origins. And their social origins will be discovered in a society guided by egoistic principles. Hence,

> An organization of society which would abolish the pre-conditions and thus the very possibilities of huckstering, would make the Jew impossible.[73]

And,

The tenacity of the Jew is to be explained, not by his religion, but rather by the human basis of his religion—practical need and egoism.[74]

Thus, as soon as the "empirical essence" of Judaism is abolished, "the Jew becomes impossible";[75] and as with Judaism, so, too, with religion in general.[76] The existence of religion, then, is merely a symptom of deeper social inadequacies.

This critical assessment of religion did not originate with Marx. For many critics, it was simply a continuation of the critical studies of religious beliefs initiated in the modern era with the shift from scholasticism to Cartesian philosophy and Newtonian science.[77] Modern science founded on a positivistic epistemology, it was claimed, could now fulfill those needs originally satisfied by religion in ways subject to final verification; thus knowledge would replace belief, and reason faith.[78] Marx, too, felt that religious explanations for natural phenomena could no longer stand up to the objective scrutiny of modern science and would eventually be shown to be mere explanations based on superstitions that have historically fulfilled certain psychological needs.

This particular assessment of religion by Marx becomes clearer in another essay, "Introduction to the Contribution to the Critique of Hegel's Philosophy of Right." According to Marx, "The struggle against religion is, therefore, indirectly a struggle against *that world* whose spiritual *aroma* is religion."[79] Given what he took to be the intellectually insupportable claims of religious beliefs, Marx recognized their presence as a genuine reflection of other more important and very real concerns.

> *Religious* suffering is at the same time an *expression* of real suffering and a *protest* against real suffering. Religion is the sigh of the oppressed creature, the sentiment of a heartless world, and the soul of soulless conditions. It is the *opium* of the people.[80]

Under current social conditions, religion serves as a sedative to ease the pain of the harsh requirements for mere survival. Nevertheless, Marx felt that religion must be critically evaluated to reveal its earthly foundation. And in turn, it is this foundation, the socioeconomic conditions, that must be understood and modified to construct a proper reality for man without the medicinal needs of false illusions and hopes.

Thus the criticism of heaven is transformed into the criticism of earth, the *criticism of religion* into the *criticism of law,* and the *criticism of theology* into the *criticism of politics.*[81]

To effect comprehensive human liberation, then, Marx argued that a critical theory must be developed and applied to all aspects of society. But in the intervening decades, from the published writings of Marx and Engels to mid-twentieth century theories of orthodox Marxists, the topic of religion has typically been treated in a cursory fashion of secondary importance when compared to questions dealing with the establishment of just socioeconomic arrangements. The importance of religion has often been dismissed altogether. Thus, as Fierro notes, the development of the orthodox Marxist theory of historical materialism accounted for the phenomenon of religion in a way that "reduces it to a mere ideological superstructure engendered by relationships based on economic domination."[82]

Perhaps the conservative critics of liberation theology are justified in their criticism of the use of Marxism by religious thinkers. The ultimate legitimacy of religion may not be sustained in the face of Marxist social analysis. Nevertheless, Fierro notes that many Christians who utilize Marxist social analysis make a critical distinction between "religion" and "faith." They can accept the traditional Marxist criticism of religion when directed at the Church's role in society, including its teachings as a particular ideological aspect of the superstructure, while accepting faith as a set of beliefs not included in that critique given faith's own transcendence.[83] Yet other Christians doubt the validity of this bifurcation. They argue that religious forms, symbols, and rituals are indeed revealed as well. Should this be the case, then it would appear that the distinction between religion and faith would collapse and hence not avoid the devastation of Marxist criticisms. On the other hand, should the distinction collapse and religion prove to be a potential agent of social change, the Marxist criticism of religion may itself be invalidated as a general "law."[84]

Notwithstanding the conservative critics' assessment of Marxism and Marx's own assessment of religion, liberation theology is flourishing. Many of its most noted proponents utilize in some way Marxist social analysis, including Hugo Assmann, Leonardo Boff, Gutiérrez, José Míguez Bonino, Miranda, and Segundo.[85] They reject the existence of the dilemma described by their conservative critics and claim to maintain a viable and productive tension. But if tension is indeed maintained between the two great philosophical traditions, what conditions are necessary? The answer seems to lie in the area of concern raised earlier by López Trujillo and Juan Gutiérrez: the problem of theory compatibility. According to liberation theology, however, the conservative critics avoid any debate over the proper methodology for doing theology itself as their primary area of disagreement. Yet as discussed earlier, it is indeed the *methodology* of liberation theology that provides the justification for the use of Marxism.

Furthermore, given Marx's concerns, a study of the Scriptures reveals no analytical scheme for explaining contemporary intricacies of political, economic, and social institutions and conditions. And of crucial importance for a Christian adoption of a Marxist interpretation of historical totalities is the role religion plays as part of the superstructure. That is, how independent, if at all, is the religious dimension of the superstructure? For if religious institutions exhibit a certain autonomy from the socioeconomic base, then potentially they could act as agents of social change. And such an insight, if substantiated and convincing, should be of significance as a legitimate response to the conservatives' concerns as well as for the development of a Marxist-Christian tension as the basis for political ethics for the religious individual.

Furthermore, how do theologians of liberation respond to Marx's own criticisms of religion? Is there no revolutionary role for religion? Our assessment must now focus on how liberation theology perceives Marxism, both as to its limits and possibilities. Specifically, where does Marxism permit, if at all, the possibility for religious autonomy?

Liberation Theology's Critique of Marx

Many liberation theologians accept Marx's criticisms of the role religion often plays as an aspect of the oppressive institutional and ideological superstructure of the state, but they do not see it necessarily as a mere epiphenomenon. They claim that religion has a certain amount of autonomy that allows it to assist in the transformation of the socioeconomic base. To defend this claim while applying Marxist class analysis, liberation theologians point out Marx's own neglect in analyzing religion for its revolutionary potential. Using the general outline of his hermeneutic circle to analyze Marx's treatment of religion, Segundo attempts to demonstrate that, given the dynamics of the hermeneutic circle, Marx fails to fulfill its and his own intellectual requirements, a failure rectified by liberation theology itself.[86]

According to Segundo, Marx's assessment of the social consequences of the Industrial Revolution provoked from him a sense of moral outrage. He blamed the bourgeois owners of capital, with the protection of the state, for using their property in a way that benefited the wealthy few to the psychological, social, and economic detriment of the working class or proletariat. It was through his writings and political activities, that Marx attempted to bring justice to an unjust world. With this personal commitment to changing the world through, and on behalf of, the proletariat, Marx can be understood as embarking upon the first step of the hermeneutic circle, "an act of will."

During the latter half of the nineteenth century the industrial societies did indeed appear to be increasingly divided between two classes, the bourgeoisie and the proletariat. And the proletariat also appeared to be gaining more strength with victory imminent. But the final revolution failed to materialize. Suspicion as to why this should be so, says Segundo, led Marx to develop a peculiar theoretical explanation. Corresponding to the second step in the hermeneutic circle, "ideological suspicion," Marx developed the general theory of "historical materialism" to explain why the proletariat, despite its superior strength, nevertheless failed to revolt. According to his theory, the ruling classes typically impose particular arguments or ideologies on the rest of society to justify the skewed socioeconomic arrangement and to protect their political and economic interests. These ideological justifications that provide popular legitimacy for the status quo consist of selected philosophical, religious, and political claims for their support. Hence, before a social revolution may proceed, it would appear that the proletariat must be liberated from false ideological assumptions.

Segundo finds, however, that Marx's writings are unclear as to whether the economic mode of production must first be changed to destroy false ideologies or the nature of false ideologies should first be exposed. Segundo maintains that in this situation it will be necessary for the emergence of a revolutionary faction to enlighten the proletariat concerning their true situation before they can revolt. A vanguard organization will be necessary to accomplish such tasks and will require a scientific approach to understanding the nature of various institutions in the superstructure, especially the relationship of religious thought to other beliefs and the economy. This presupposes that religious thought has a place in the ideological superstructure, that the prevailing religious thought derives from the dominant classes' own experience, and that "the process of discovering this connection abets the revolutionary forces of the proletariat."[87] In other words, the religious dimension of the superstructure must be taken seriously and investigated as to its potential for revolution.

It is in this second step of "ideological suspicion" of the hermeneutic circle, where Segundo maintains that a serious analysis of contemporary religion would have revealed it to be both the actual means through which the ruling classes use a particular interpretation of Scripture to support their dominant social position as well as the potential means through which the proletariat can use a more accurate interpretation of Scripture and thus "convert religion into their own weapon in the class struggle."[88] With this realization, the third step of the circle, "exegetical suspicion," should have taken on extreme importance for Marx given his own assessment of the relationship of religion to ideology and society, as just discussed. Yet, Segundo argues, he failed to follow through with his own methodology of scientific analysis that would have examined "the specific concrete and historical possibilities of religion and theology."[89] Instead, Marx was satisfied to accept the traditional claims of religion as strictly an ahistorical spiritual matter opposed to the insights of historical materialism and thus worthy only of abolition. With this reductionist and nearly deterministic attitude toward religion, according to Segundo, Marx failed to complete the intent of the hermeneutic circle by scientifically analyzing the dynamics of religious faith and thus failed to appreciate the autonomy of religion and to recognize the revolutionary potential of religious beliefs, symbols, and institutions.[90]

Despite Segundo's critique, it is not clear to what extent Marx was in fact bound to materialist explanations of history and social change and to what extent he ruled out the possibility of elements in the superstructure acting in revolutionary ways on the socioeconomic base. According to Engels, their position never was intended to be understood as one of strict determinism as suggested by Segundo. In a letter to the political newspaper editor Joseph Bloch, Engels attempted to refute those who applied the deterministic materialist label to his and Marx's writings. He wrote that many aspects of the superstructure are indeed capable of acting on the socioeconomic base to effect change, including "religious views and their further development into systems of dogma, [that] also exercise their influence upon the course of the historical struggles and in many cases preponderate in determining their *form.*"[91]

We may imagine, though, what effect Segundo's claim might have had were Marx to have taken it seriously. Had Marx admitted the revolutionary potential of religion, he would have had to have given social theoretical legitimacy to religion, a legitimacy he himself was unwilling to accept; for religion had no normatively acceptable place in his personal life nor in his moral prescriptions. Furthermore, the revolutionary potential of religious institutions and beliefs and thus their social legitimacy would have undermined the materialist if not deterministic basis of modern, positivist theory, thus raising the specter of inconsistency that would haunt his work. The paucity of Marx's writings on religion and the lack of systematic and coherent treatment of religion in the writings that do exist suggest that Marx was not convinced of the need to study religion to effect social change. According to the philosopher Delos B. McKown in his treatment of Marx on this subject,

The point here is not to give a catalogue of opposing views on the origin of religion but to show that Marx's opinion on the essence and origin of natural religion suffers acutely from lack of information.[92]

Marx's critique of religion, then, indicates that the socioeconomic base need not be nor may well not be as completely mechanistic and one-sided as orthodox Marxists and conservatives have maintained. According to Fierro, the correct assumption should be that, depending on the concrete circumstances, aspects of this superstructure may effectively interact with the base to produce novel outcomes.[93] Many neo-Marxists, however, have also seen the potential for religion as an effective force for liberation from oppressive social structures.[94] Yet still lacking, says Fierro, is any well-thought out historical-materialist theory of Christianity that would clearly explicate "the relationships between the socioeconomic base and theological ideas of a period and a society."[95]

Even so, regardless of the inadequacy of Marx's treatment of religion, it is precisely the argument for the revolutionary potential of religion that provides the counterbalance to the weight of the typical Marxist critique of religion with its sociology of knowledge and that liberation theology claims as its unique contribution to social criticism.

Maintaining the Tension

Marxism, then, appears to many liberation theologians to be normatively and methodologically compatible with their religious values and theological frameworks. Yet if such is the case, why do these thinkers require Christian values at all, given the moral values and interpretive enterprise of Marxism? In his review of recent attempts in political theology to bring about a convergence of Christianity and Marxism, the theologian and political scientist Douglas Sturm points to the failure of radical theologians to provide "public validation" for their religious convictions.[96] Unlike other ethical arguments advanced by such social theorists as John Rawls and Habermas, Sturm claims that liberation theology provides no theoretical justifications for its Christian ethical roots; it simply accepts them as given. But we should be reminded, as just discussed, that liberation theology claims only to offer a methodology for doing theology for believers; it does not propose a systematic, theological defense of Christian social ethics before nonbelievers. Still, if moral commitments and social activism is all Christianity has to offer, Marxism can match it. And if Christianity has nothing more to offer, where is the tension that permits the use of Marxist social analysis as required by liberation theologians but prevents the annihilation of Christianity by the same analysis as feared by conservatives?

In fact, explains Assmann, it is precisely at the level of the superstructure where liberation theology can contribute most to revolutionary theory. The traditional bourgeois values found in the superstructure, including values derived from traditional Christian beliefs, contribute to the defense of the status quo in economics and politics. Because of the pervasiveness of Christianity in Latin America and the faith of the citizenry, Assmann argues, liberation theology can provide a morally superior critique of authoritarian ideologies to that of Marxism. Given their Christian roots and theological methodology, radical theologians participating in liberation movements are in a unique position to undermine the legitimacy of the state that is supported by religious traditionalists by offering a credible critique of "pseudo-Christian traditions and values."[97]

This moral critique also transcends the Marxist perception of man by accepting him as more than simply a human being with the potential to exercise his creativity. Assmann accepts Marxism's emphasis on creativity but extends the argument; "Man is born of the gift of the Lord; he is created, as man, from outside."[98] That is, man is more than a mere product of social processes; he also possesses a real need to emulate his creator. The scriptural accounts of God's dealings with man indicate a moral standard of behavior of how one human being should be treated by another, and God acts out of a commitment based on love for his creation. Thus, liberation theology presents a humanizing component in political action because of the presence of Christian thought. This is a new revolutionary ethic that should be at the heart of the liberation process, Assmann maintains, similar to the revolutionary ethic that guided Latin American revolutionary and Marxist Ernesto Ché Guevara. But this revolutionary ethic will have a far greater humanizing influence because of the presence of Christian thought that has more to say than an atheist position regarding the ultimate meaning of the human condition.[99]

Now the divinely inspired, sensitivity of man to the plight of his neighbor, plus the commitment to liberation of the oppressed; the necessity and use of social science; and the engagement in political action to change society, result in the transformation of history itself. This transformation then provokes in the sensitive individual reflection upon the meaning of history. And it is at this crucial moment of mortality, says Assmann, that Christianity avoids existential dread in a way unattainable through Marxism. The superiority of Christianity to Marxism is found in its affirmation of victory over death—"the final alienation to which Marxism can find no answer."[100] Alongside God's example of ethical concern with human affairs, belief in the immortality of the soul and the potential for eternal peace provide a richer purpose for life than the simple humanism of Marxism and its focus on the satisfaction of material wants. Consequently, political action also takes on a greater sense of importance as both God and man unitedly seek justice. In this way, Christianity provides an opposing, counterbalance to orthodox Marxism's materialist sociology of religion and thus maintains the tension in liberation theology.

Yet the claim that Christianity is superior to Marxism because it includes treatment of death in its explanation of the meaning of existence can only be upheld if Marxism is asking the question of the meaning of death and fails to answer it on its own terms. One theory cannot claim superiority over another to the satisfaction of the other in terms of a particular issue if both are not asking and answering the same question. What Assmann sees as an inferior response by Marxism to questions of death, may only be indifference on the part of Marxist theorists, not a fault. From a Marxist perspective, Christians may simply be embellishing their philosophy of life with eccentric explanations concerning the baffling meaning of death. So far, liberation theologians have not penetrated beyond this superficial criticism with regard to Marxism and death. What they must show is the need on the part of Marxist theorists to provide an explanation to a vexing problem originating in Marxist theory, and then to demonstrate how liberation theology can assist in providing a unique and adequate response to a Marxist problem.

Conclusion

We have now come full circle to the concern raised initially by the conservative critics of liberation theology: The utilization of Marxist social analysis will negate the essence of Christianity with its unique understanding of the transcendental nature of the relationship between God and man. Liberation theologians claim to preserve this essence, and to do so with the partial assistance of Marxism's contribution to theological development. As Boff succinctly states, "There is, then, a Christian appropriation of Marxism."[101] Obviously, an alternative methodology to that of the conservative critics is necessary for the liberation theologians to engage in appropriate theological reflection. The methodology of academic theology utilized by the conservative critics is inappropriate for several reasons, as discussed earlier. The essence of the conflict between the two sides, then, should entail arguments over the acceptance or rejection of a particular theological methodology, not for or against Marxism per se. In fact, both sides agree on many of the limitations of Marxism for Christianity. But this is not the direction the debate has taken. If this is indeed the real problem—that is, a dispute over esoteric issues of theological methodology—then why the debate over Marxism? Perhaps the debate should be seen less as a theological dispute over political methodology and more as a political dispute over theological methodology.

The conservative critics want religion to preserve a *meaning* structure of reality that, among other things, ultimately subordinates the importance of life in this world to that of the next. Liberation theologians want religion to deal with social *values* in this world and to de-emphasize the importance of a particular static description of reality. The latter claim that an important dimension of theological development must include social science, and many select Marxist social analysis as most effective in this regard; the former, of course, find this unacceptable. But if the maintenance of a Marxist-Christian tension is indeed a theoretical possibility, conservative critics may well fear more the demise of their own social status than the annihilation of religion.

The methodology of liberation theology induces changes in perceptions of reality that tend to affect all aspects of religious as well as social life. The conflict over perceptions is crucial at several levels. All perceptions perform the function of infusing coherency, order, and meaning into an otherwise chaotic world. Politically, they provide the legitimacy for the institutionalization of power and its authoritative uses in society. Any modifications in perceptions of social reality may threaten the legitimacy of those exercising authority. Moreover, a theological transformation of religious perceptions may also redefine the teachings, practices, and goals of the institutionalized Church. The practical activities of the Church are tied to a particular interpretation of the religious values of those who guide it as well as those who participate in its activities. For those conservative critics who occupy ecclesiastical offices and uphold current positions and practices of the Church, a threat to their interpretation of values may well call into question the legitimacy of their leadership, goals, and policies. And currently, with increasing public doubts concerning some activities of the Church fueled by critical evaluations and alternative proposals from liberation theologians, a political problem exists.

Because popular fear of Marxism persists, particularly in much of Latin America, the conservative critics' counterattack on liberation theology calls attention to the role of Marxism in radical Christian thinking. In fact, this may be a successful tactic to deal with a political problem. The emotional appeal of fighting Marxism certainly holds greater public attention than focusing strictly on contemporary problems of theological epistemology. Yet it is their refusal to deal with the implications of their own as well as alternative epistemologies—particularly, the problem of ascertaining the most appropriate methodology for theological reflection upon questions of social injustice—that may well portend the greatest threat to the legitimacy of the ecclesiastical positions, policies, and theologies of the conservative critics. For regardless of its merits, it should be understood that liberation theology contains an internal, critical dynamic of its own—with or without Marxism. And for those critics who ignore the methodological issue in favor of the political dimension, the cost of neglect may present a political problem indeed.

The Ethos of Liberation

Marx, of course, did not wish to engage solely in philosophical speculation. Indeed, he stated in his now ubiquitous phrase that "the point of philosophy is not merely to understand the world but to change it."[102] A sense of moral indignation at the impoverished conditions of industrial workers motivated his search not only for the cause of poverty, but for the key to liberation from poverty. Ironically, Marx saw the key in the very exploitative system itself. He thought that internal contradictions in the very goals and arrangements of capitalist economics—between forces of production and relations of production—would contribute to the system's eventual demise while providing the basis for a new social order premised on more acceptable values. His claim of having found the source for a more just society had been, and no doubt will continue to be, debated; but of greater influence on liberation theologians as well as others was his emphasis on political action to achieve the just society. This was coupled with a theoretical understanding of reality that would itself undergo change as society changed, thus the emphasis on *praxis*.

As we have seen, then, Marxism holds an appeal for liberation theology from at least two angles: as moral denunciation of social injustice and as a method of social analysis. While Marxist methods of social analysis find compatibility in Latin America, many normative aspects of Marxist epistemology find comparable analogues in much Christian theology. This sense of identity contributes to the justification for the incorporation of Marxist social analysis by many radical Christian thinkers. But a number of philosophical difficulties must still be overcome when attempting to incorporate Marxist sociology into any complete Christian theological framework. The mixed results of recent Marxist-Christian dialogues attest to such difficulties. For example, questions concerning the professed atheism and ostensible materialism of many Marxist theorists have typically been seen as major obstacles to effective compatibility. Again, can part of a theory be appropriated and the rest discarded without destroying the efficacy of any single part?[103]

But for liberation theology, perhaps the most important common theme running through both Marxism and Christianity is the idea of *hope*. MacIntyre addresses this theme in his early work. "Both

Marxism and Christianity rescue individual lives from the insignificance of finitude (to use an Hegelian expression) by showing the individual that he has or can have some role in a world-historical drama."[104] Marxism offers the only modern perspective that provides man once again with hope to understand social conditions and to liberate himself from an oppressive present to a constructive future. Such hope had earlier found its expression only in religious terms, terms inherited by Marxism through Hegel. And it is this emphasis on hope, says MacIntyre, which has been abandoned by liberals. "For liberals the future has become the present enlarged . . . the Marxist project remains the only one we have for re-establishing hope as a social virtue."[105]

For liberation theologians, the use of Marxist social analysis assists them not only in liberating the poor and oppressed, but in liberating theology itself, thereby liberating the Church to become an agent of social change, and fulfilling the hope of Christianity. They have generally appropriated Marxist social analysis with no serious reservations with regard to atheism and materialism or any other potential theoretical obstacle. They claim that Marxist class analysis reveals the sources of social injustice in Latin America. Such revelation then permits liberation theologians to render judgments on social issues and to work with Marxists toward the elimination of injustice. So while it may not be obviously apparent whether the limitation of Marxism strictly to class analysis is theoretically possible,[106] in practice there has been little problem.[107] (Indeed, originally it was out of a sense of survival under repressive regimes and hope for the future that they worked alongside Marxists.)

Yet from the foregoing sketch, it also appears that Marxist theorists should take seriously in their sociology of religion the political possibilities of an autonomous Church. Individuals engaged in practical politics have often recognized the revolutionary potential of the Church in Latin America; according to Ché Guevara,

When Christians are bold enough to bear integral revolutionary witness, the Latin American revolution will be invincible; for up to now Christians have allowed their doctrine to be used as a tool by the reactionaries.[108]

And, of course, theologians of liberation view the Latin American church as not only a potential, but a proper agent of social change in their confrontation with repressive social orders.

97

The Political Theory of Liberation Theology

So how do liberation theologians understand current social orders? What is their assessment of Latin American political economies? As discussed earlier, social institutions and structures play key roles in determining the morality of economic conditions and public policies. And this determination in turn influences the political ethics of liberation theology. Now that the importance of social scientific analysis for this alternative methodology to doing theology has been established, an evaluation of particular social analyses will reveal more of the logic and dynamics of liberation theology's political theory. Furthermore, a clearer understanding of how social conditions are evaluated will assist our attempt to clarify the moral arguments for various forms of political activism, especially with regard to the use of violence.

\

Chapter 4

Assessing Latin American
Political Economies

Introduction

The methodology of liberation theology takes politics seriously, but not merely as an additional aspect of religious life; it places it squarely in the center of theological development itself.[1] Given the centrality of politics in theological development and religious practice, then, liberation theologians are interested in assessing the dynamics of Latin American society in their search for the causes of social injustice. They claim that an intelligent layout of the political landscape and economic terrain will permit them to explore solutions to social problems in a more sophisticated manner; otherwise they will continue wandering blindly in society and stumbling into overwhelming barriers of power if they follow inappropriate, irrelevant, and detached theological certitudes.

Lacking any original critical social science in either biblical or theological work per se, liberation theologians have been impressed with a variety of modern social analyses that shed some light on contemporary politics. Furthermore, as we have seen, they utilize those studies that assist their initial moral commitment to liberating the poor and oppressed; particularly useful in this regard is Marxist class analysis.[2] In other words, studies of social conditions in Latin America are of particular value when they identify those social phenomena, including their dynamics and directions, that are inimical to human dignity and freedom. Hence, studies that provide critical assessments of the status quo—that is, military juntas, ruling oligarchies, U.S.-dominated international trading policies, and capitalism itself—find greater audience among liberation theologians than studies that claim to be "objective" and "value-free." Nevertheless, liberation theologians are aware that the latter studies enjoy wide circulation. But they point out that those claiming such objectivity are themselves generally supportive of the status quo in politics and economics, a status quo that is responsible for the misery and suffering of the vast majority of Latin Americans. Then how do liberation theologians themselves, given their capacity for, and adoption of, critical social theory as required by step two of the hermeneutic circle, generally perceive the dynamics of Latin American political economies, a perception that currently makes for a revolutionary situation?

There is general agreement among liberation theologians that the existence of mass poverty alongside political oppression is not a mere coincidence, but that the two are inextricably linked. Hence, they use studies that demonstrate and critique this conscious relationship between political power and the wide disparity in the distribution of wealth. Even so, not all social scientific assessments of this relationship find agreement on the causes nor their dynamics; likewise liberation theologians disagree on where to place the ultimate responsibility for social injustice. However, two differing approaches to social analyses are most widely used by liberation theologians: one emphasizing the structural dynamics of the world economy with a particular relationship among nation-states, the other emphasizing the preeminence of the nation-state and its role in international politics.

In the writings of liberation theology, social analyses based on the dynamics of the world economy are more common. This can be attributed to Gustavo Gutiérrez's initial acceptance and use of such social analyses that have had enormous influence throughout the development of liberation theology.[3] Generally, this approach finds its own origins in critiques of capitalism and imperialism, hence the use of various Marxist insights and explanations as required by the hermeneutic circle.[4] Other liberation theologians, such as José Comblin, assess the origins of destructive social dynamics as found in peculiar characteristics of the nation-state itself. The following discussion will reveal the basic thrust of these two approaches.

The World Economy

From Gutiérrez's reading of history, contemporary capitalism was born out of the transition from the medieval to the modern era.

The eighteenth century marks the beginning of revolution in different fields of human activity. In this period, humanity acquired a clear awareness of its capacity to know and transform nature and society; that is to say, to transform history by taking it into hand. This exercise of human reason appeared to be radically free in the measure that persons recognized themselves as able to change the conditions of their lives and to situate themselves differently within social relations. It is in this context that bourgeois society sprang up.[5]

Gutiérrez argues that "the modern spirit" of the bourgeoisie found its initial impetus in the confluence of rapid social changes brought about by widespread discoveries in the natural sciences, ever-growing demands for popular government, and the irreversible impact of the Protestant Reformation with its emphasis on personal salvation. Furthermore, the Enlightenment and the French and Industrial revolutions all provided fertile soil for expressions of "individualism" as the basis itself for the growth of a new public philosophy or ideology to challenge the social ethics and public morality of the classical and medieval eras.[6]

With an increasing emphasis on, and acceptance of, the importance of rationalism in private decision making and the concern for individualism in public policy making, the bourgeois class gained strength as feudalism declined. But this fluid time had disturbing social consequences, according to Gutiérrez. "The former serfs were emancipated, but, at the same time, they lost their direct access to the means of production."[7] Nevertheless, with the shift away from mercantilism toward reliance on market forces to determine production methods and decisions as well as distributive patterns for commodities, merchant capitalism gained strength. Eventually, economic and political power fell into the same hands of those who also owned and controlled the means of production. The reorganization of the state along lines emphasizing individual rationality and freedom with regard to personal ethics and social activities, concludes Gutiérrez, was well on its way by the end of the nineteenth century in most Western nations.

The Political Theory of Liberation Theology

Gutiérrez's brief critique of the early history of Western industrialization is certainly not unique. But its theme has been developed further by many contemporary social analysts. The usual thematic focus of these critiques has been the subservient relationship of the political and economic concerns of most Latin American countries to those of the industrialized West, especially the United States. Gutiérrez also continues with this same focus.

Developmentalism

After the Second World War, Latin American countries attempted to shift their economies away from dependence exclusively on foreign trade—that is, according to Gutiérrez, "exportation of primary products"[8]—through the development of domestic economies with an industrial base and extended markets. Various studies had indicated to policy makers that modern development was economically possible and with populist movements demanding greater prosperity it appeared politically feasible as well.

The United Nations, the Organization of American States, the International Monetary Fund, the Inter-American Development Bank, the Agency for International Development, and the Alliance for Progress, comprised the international organizations and programs that supported increased economic development in Latin America. But this support, claims Gutiérrez, resulted in the institution of a particular model of development "oriented towards a model abstracted from the more developed societies in the contemporary world."[9] In order to be mirror images of the industrialized West, Latin American societies were expected to remove or neutralize the political power of any traditional social organizations and forces that were perceived as obstacles to modernization. Considered as backward countries, then, the less developed nations were expected "to repeat more or less faithfully the historical experience of the developed countries in their journey towards modern society."

Furthermore, says Gutiérrez, advocates of this model explained "economic development" as merely the ultimate stage on a historical continuum along which developing nations must travel. They expected transition from traditional society to modern society to be fueled by the emergence of groups opposed to the traditional way of life. Although only accomplishing partial changes at first, the hope of "developmentalism" (*desarrollismo*) rested on the belief that the accumulated effect of groups agitating for change eventually would transform completely "Latin American societies from traditionalism to modernism, from underdevelopment to development."[10] The basic thesis of developmentalism as a solution to problems of poverty in the Third World has, however, not yet proved itself, Gutiérrez maintains. Latin American societies were not transformed along the lines of the example set by the history of the more industrialized countries of the West. By the 1960s the optimism over developmentalist policies had largely given way to the realism of ever-increasing poverty, not only between the rich and poor in each country, but between the rich and poor countries of the world. Regardless of the cause, "the developmentalist approach has proven to be unsound and incapable of interpreting the economic, social, and political evolution of the Latin American continent." Thus Gutiérrez finds, "Today it is evident that the developmentalist model suffered from grave problems of perspective. It did not sufficiently take into account political factors, and worse, stayed on an abstract and ahistorical level."[11]

The essential flaw in the developmentalist model, argues Gutiérrez, was its view of development as historically linear and independently situated. That is, not only did various stages of development exist through which all societies must pass to achieve greater standards of living, according to this model, but any nation could do so with proper assistance to reach a point economically approximate to that presently of the United States.[12] As Gutiérrez notes, "The developmentalist and modernizing approach made it impossible to appreciate both the complexity of the problem and the inevitable conflictual aspects of the process taken as a whole."[13]

Dependencia

The developmentalist model's perception of economic conditions of the world in terms of two sets of sovereign countries, either developed or undeveloped, may indeed overlook a crucial relationship between the two. Gutiérrez maintains that the condition of undevelopment is itself the end result of a more pernicious process, and is better understood as a condition of *under*development. And it is the comprehensive nature of this particular process that must be grasped. An historical perspective will demonstrate that underdevelopment can only be understood in terms of its "relationship to the development and expansion of the great capitalist countries." That is, the inferior political and economic condition of Latin American and other Third World countries has historically resulted from the development activities of other, more powerful countries. Gutiér-rez maintains that

> the dynamics of the capitalist economy lead to the establishment of a center and a periphery, simultaneously generating progress and growing wealth for the few and social imbalances, political tensions, and poverty for the many.[14]

Appreciation for the relation between "center" and "periphery" is crucial to understanding the dynamics and effects of capitalism found in liberation theology's assessment of Latin American political econo-mies. The general theoretical framework from another liberation the-ologian, Enrique Dussel, will assist in clarifying the general perception of this relation.

Dussel, using Hegelian imagery, maintains that there is a carefully defended intention on the part of the industrialized West to prevent "face-to-face"—that is, democratic and equal—encounters between First and Third World countries. Yet these encounters are a neces-sary condition for the retention of freedom and dignity, themselves necessary for full human expression. Nevertheless, the United States and other Western countries that dominate the economics, politics, and other social aspects of the Third World, have refused to partici-pate in any democratic and equal encounter.[15] Dussel characterizes this domination as a relationship between "oppressor" and "op-pressed." By defending its political and economic exploitation of the oppressed in the Third World, the oppressor refuses to recognize and thus denies the humanity of the oppressed. The international market aids this exploitation by allowing the wealthier capitalist countries to operate with virtual abandonment. According to Dussel's assessment,

> the present world order (economic, cultural, sexual and aesthetic) is the prevailing rule of sin, inasmuch as it oppresses the poor. The "rulers" have their group projection which they objectify as the projection of the whole system and which expands as an imperialist projection by means of conquest in Latin America, Africa and Asia.[16]

And to justify these otherwise morally indefensible relationships, the dominating nations utilize various ideological arguments. That is, says Dussel, the "I-Thou" relationship between oppressor and oppres-sed is presented as not only economically *necessary*, but socially *nat-ural* by those who wish to defend and maintain status quo political and economic relationships. But it is precisely this ideological attempt—that is, presenting specious arguments that current social conditions are necessary and natural—at justifying oppression that must be revealed to show its basis in sin.

Dussel begins the elucidation process with an extensive analysis of Western development practices. The center of the modern world, he argues, has shifted location during the past few centuries from Western Europe to the United States, always with less-developed countries at its periphery. The wealthier and more powerful countries have encouraged both public and private enterprises to engage in economic and political penetration of the periphery to exploit other peoples and cultures for their own benefit. Historically, the shift in the location of the center has made no difference with regard to Latin America, which remained on the periphery. Using fifteenth- and sixteenth-century historical accounts of Spanish conquests in the New World as the pattern as well as a metaphor for modern political and economic activity, Dussel says,

> Latin America is the *child* of the European conqueror and its Indian mother, Amerindia. For almost five centuries it has been prevented from explicating its own "distinctiveness," its own way of participating analogically in the catholicity of Christ's one and only church.[17]

Furthermore, the child, Latin America, is in a situation of oppression as his father, the European conqueror, has forced his mother, Indian women, into a condition of prostitution; hence both child and mother are in a position of subservience to patriarchal authority and paternal domination.[18] Thus, the oppressive social relations of the economic arrangement induce a ripple effect throughout society.

In political terms, Dussel maintains that this arrangement has had the effect of turning the political economies of Latin America and other Third World countries into "neocolonies," primarily of the United States.[19] He refers to dependency theorists' assessments, demonstrating "that 80 percent of the benefits that the center realizes in its commercial interchanges come from the periphery." But it must be understood that this unequal distribution results from a particular process. And it is in explicating this process that the use of Marxist social analysis becomes timely. Applying it on a global basis, Dussel looks at the creation and unequal distribution of surplus value.[20] In effect, current international economic arrangements cause "capital-labor surplus value to leave the country in the form of center-periphery surplus value."[21] That is, the unequal power relationship between worker and owner that forces the former to alienate the productivity of his creative activity to the latter, as found in the firm, is the same relationship that exists between the Third and First worlds. And, of course, this relationship is one of unjust domination.

Dussel maintains that this "praxis of domination," whereby one set of countries says no to or denies and thus refuses to accept the humanity of another set of countries through asymmetrical political and economic relationships, is sinful. Sin occurs when those dominating countries "usurp the position of God and exalt themselves."[22] What is necessary is a "negation of the negation" in order for the oppressed, as well as the oppressors, to say yes to the humanity of the other and thus to cease support for the current system of exploitation foisted on Third World countries. Dussel's analytical framework is sufficiently comprehensive to normatively assess the role of all potential actors with regard to the unacceptable social conditions of Latin America. Nevertheless, liberation theologians must not only pierce the ideological facades that offer justifications for the prevailing relationships of domination, but they must also understand the relationships in themselves so as to effect social change. To this end, they attempt to explicate the dependency relationship found in Latin America itself.

The history of Latin American societies since the colonization by Spain and Portugal, according to Gutiérrez, reveals a "history of successive modifications of their conditions of dependence." Although these conditions have differed in degree of underdevelopment, few societies have been able in modern times even to attempt to break out of their dependent status short of nationalist, populist, and generally leftist revolution—for example, in the cases of Cuba and Nicaragua.[23] Of course, each country brings significant differences in terms of internal social structures and cultural background to its particular situation. Nevertheless, Gutiérrez accepts Dussel's argument that the key and virtually common element throughout Latin America is the economic and political dependence of weak nations on the stronger and domineering nations of the industrialized West.

Regardless of each country's peculiar manifestations, this element of dependence continues to affect adversely internal political and economic development in Latin America. For example, Gutiérrez notes that old forms of imperialism do still exist, such as the existence of foreign-owned and foreign-run plantations and mining centers. Furthermore, newer and more subtle forms of domination have emerged. Foreign financial arrangements continue to co-opt nascent local industry and to maintain the dependent relationship of Latin American economies on Western industrialized countries. Thus, even the modern sector of local economies continues to be bound to the demands of international capitalism.

More importantly, says Gutiérrez, this new form of dependence does not support the status quo of traditional political and economic arrangements. It fosters widespread social change throughout Latin American societies by encouraging greater inequality of wealth and less assistance to the poor. "Modernization and the introduction of greater rationality into the economies is required by the vested interests of new economic groups."[24] And the emergence of these new indigenous, elite groups have become less nationalistic and hence less identifiable with the heritage of their respective countries; today they are more internationally oriented and hence more identifiable with the interests of multinational corporations. Gutiérrez concludes that "the imbalance between developed and underdeveloped countries—caused by the relationships of dependence—becomes more acute if the cultural point of view is taken into consideration."[25] Thus, to explain the nature of poverty and oppression in Latin America, a dependency theory of development must take into account the indigenous effects of multinational corporations and trade policies.

The theologian Michael Novak, perhaps the most prominent critic of liberation theology on issues of political economy, criticizes Gutiérrez and other liberation theologians for adopting a dependency theory explanation of social conditions in Latin America. He maintains that dependency theory fails to account for recent "economic miracles" in other Third World nations.[26] In the Far East, for example, Hong Kong, Singapore, Taiwan, Japan, and South Korea have surged ahead of more established capitalist countries such as the United States and Canada in key sectors of economic production.[27] Since the end of the Second World War, these countries were as economically devastated as those in Latin America; yet they "experienced an almost miraculous uplifting of the poor" by 1970, their Third World status notwithstanding. The reason for the continual existence of massive poverty in Latin America, says Novak, has less to do with the exogenously imposed dependence on more powerful capitalist nations of North America and elsewhere, and more to do with the indigenous culture, law, and politics of Latin American society itself.

The problem for Latin America, argues Novak, is not the presence of capitalism, but its absence. Liberation theologians mistakenly identify and critique their economies as capitalist when in fact "most of Latin American countries exhibit economies that are pre-capitalist."[28] Furthermore, the institutions of Latin America are not only pre-capitalist, but mercantilist and patrimonial as well. And this is the case precisely because they retain the cultural ethos of "Iberian Christianity," not having grasped "the metaphysics of liberalism nor the social role of markets."[29] That is, the corporatist bias of traditional Christianity continues to pervade Latin American social thinking, including that of policy makers, long after the emergence, implementation, and success of capitalism in other parts of the West. The real source of the problem, then, for impoverished Latin American countries is the current attempt by misguided governmental policy makers to impose economic development policies from the "top down" with attendant incentive-destroying behavior, instead of allowing the economy to build from the "bottom up" freely, efficiently, and productively.[30]

Novak maintains, in fact, that "Latin Americans have *chosen* to depend on the more developed capitalist countries."[31] Business elites in Latin American society lack the courage necessary to invest and take risks; instead they prefer relying on others, especially other countries, for new market discoveries, business innovations, and technological developments. This cultural ethos of safety permeates Latin American society as it has done since the earliest days of Iberian colonization. Yet instead of advocating educational programs aimed at correcting this cultural "defect," Novak insists that the only way Latin America can renounce its self-imposed dependency and bring about economic development is to change the laws and governmental policies that inhibit and discourage the spirit of private entrepreneurship.[32] After removing the stultifying and disfiguring presence of the state in the economy, market forces will surge forth, bringing economic development and prosperity in their wake.

The problem of economic development, however, is not one strictly of selecting the most efficiently appropriate means. Liberation theologians are concerned with the same moral questions Christianity has asked at least since the advent of the Industrial Revolution. What are the moral values associated with the drive toward materialist production in a market economy? And, given those values, what are the spiritual consequences for the soul and the social consequences for the community of the new individualist ethic?[33] Even assuming the moral appropriateness of liberal individualism found in Novak's assessment, what would it take to encourage economic and political elites in Latin American society to back away from extensive use of governmental authority and law, and to move toward a deregulated state and more reliance on market forces for economic growth? Furthermore, could it be that these elites have other interests, perhaps class interests, that would inhibit any move toward deregulation?

Liberation theologians argue that current Western political economic arrangements encourage not only a widening of the gap between rich and poor nations within a dependent relationship, but between rich and poor classes in the poorer nations themselves. And it is the logical relationship between these widening gaps, internationally and nationally, where one should focus attention. An indispensable tool in this regard, says Gutiérrez, is class analysis. Understanding international politics as simply a contest between nation-states based on self-motivation and endurance with unlimited resources, as Novak suggests, misses the point. Something more is at work. Gutiérrez suggests that "the theory of dependence [itself] will take the wrong path and lead to deception if the analysis is not put within the framework of the worldwide class struggle."[34] Already apparent to Gutiérrez and other liberation theologians are the many political as well as economic factors indicating that "autonomous Latin American development is not viable within the framework of the international capitalist system."[35]

Yet even though dependency theory may be useful for liberation theologians to explain the skewed economic relationship between First and Third World countries, it may not be comprehensively adequate to explain all impoverished conditions inside the Third World. It would seem that enough political "sovereignty" exists to allow each country to pursue domestic policies within a relatively broad range of choices. Dependency theory may adequately explain how the limits of the range of choices were determined, but it would seem insufficient to explain the direction of policies within the range of possible options. Brazil, for one, need not be impoverished to the extent that it is, logically speaking; it could, for example, spend less on military armaments and more on social welfare programs. With regard to political oppression, Colombia has been far less repressive of dissidents than has Argentina, yet both are dependent economically on Western industrialized countries and international financial institutions. The use of dependency theory seems incomplete with regard to explanations of the causes of human rights violations. In fact, an alternative theory might find more empirical evidence for support were it to focus on internal socioeconomic factors. For example, a study of the relationship between levels of domestic military spending and military decision making and levels of human rights violations might prove enlightening. Given current debates over the nature of the state and political power, then, reliance by liberation theologians on some version of dependency theory may not allow for sufficient recognition of the autonomy of the state with regard to domestic policies.[36]

But in addition to the emphasis on analyzing the structure of the world economy found in liberation theology, is the emphasis on analyzing policies at the nation-state level. Also of particular concern to liberation theologians are the adverse social consequences of the domestic policies of the "national security states" in Latin America. An assessment of the national security state finds its clearest exposition in Comblin's book, *The Church and the National Security State.*

The National Security State

Comblin argues that the emergence during the late 1960s and early 1970s of the national security state in Latin America can be attributed to the creation of a "national security system" in the United States after the Second World War.[37] In 1947, the National Security Act created two new political institutions: the National Security Council (NSC) and the Central Intelligence Agency (CIA). These institutions were created to further the imperialist role of the United States in world affairs. But the negative impact of this legislation would be felt both domestically (in the United States) and internationally. Through the NSC, says Comblin, more political power shifted away from Congress to the president as the executive branch arrogated to itself more of the responsibility for initiating, directing, and supervising defense and foreign policy.[38] The CIA became more secretive as it assumed "the right to supervise the lives of citizens and officials and the right of intervention in foreign countries according to the secret interests of the United States—or more precisely, those of the National Security Council."[39]

Nevertheless, the creation of the national security system in the United States has had far more socially devastating consequences for Latin America. Comblin describes how many of the countries that currently exhibit or recently passed through the "national security state" phase, established their own national security council and secret service patterned specifically after those of the United States.

For example, in 1964 the Brazilian National Security Council assumed complete political power with regard to Brazil's constitution, congress, and other policy-making apparatus. Comblin states that

the same thing happened in Argentina in 1966, and not long after in Uruguay, Bolivia, Chile, and other nations. And as these councils, which are basically military dictatorships, came to power, they organized duplicates of the CIA—the SNI (National Information Service) in Brazil, the DINA (National Intelligence Division) in Chile, and so on.[40]

Unfortunately, points out Comblin, "neither the national security councils nor the secret services in Latin America have to cope with the limits of constitutions or the reaction of a congress. There is no longer either a constitution or a functioning congress in most Latin American countries." In their place a new type of regime was constructed wherein the traditional legislative, executive, and judicial functions are simply administrative services and auxiliaries to the new institutions of the national security state.

The Latin American national security state also has an ideology that "covers virtually all individual and social activities of the nation and gives a new meaning to all human existence, it is universal and totalitarian enough to exclude any interference by another philosophy."[41] According to Comblin, this ideology finds its point of origin, like the national security institutions, at military officer educational and training facilities or war colleges in the United States.[42] In fact, many Latin American countries have also created their own war colleges patterned after those found in the United States to teach the ideology of national security to their own officers. But the Latin American theorists who devised the national security state ideology incorporated tendentious social scientific elements in their explanations of politics, so as to present their ideological claims as "objectively true." Comblin presents a critique of the ideology of the national security state and its "social sciences" of "geopolitics" and "strategy."

Geopolitics

While many Latin American proponents of geopolitics as a science differ on the basic question of how the concept of geopolitics itself should be defined, Comblin finds that they do tend to agree that the primary focus of any theory of geopolitics is the state.[43] Theorists of geopolitics propose comprehending the state as a center of power

111

that is geographically situated and conditioned, and in rival competition with other states for the expansion of power; "Thus it may be said that geopolitics means the most thorough pursuit for maximum power for the state at any given time."[44] Furthermore, they describe the state as a viable "organism" that lives and dies like any other organism. Most theorists of geopolitics agree with "the basic notion of Rudolf Kjellen, the Swedish founder of this science, who wrote that the state is a person with its own life, its own features, its own behavior, its own world of feelings and wishes, always competing and fighting with other states."[45] After endowing the state with anthropomorphic characteristics, these theorists then attempt to identify the citizenry with the nation, the nation with the state, and ultimately the state with power.

According to the science of geopolitics, the state is made up of three essential elements: "territory, populations, and sovereignty." Territory and population, necessary material conditions for the existence of any state, are static elements that serve the dynamic element of sovereignty. And sovereignty is defined as absolute power that the state has over its territory and population. Hence, to maintain its sovereignty, the theorists conclude, the state must be the final repository of all power. As Comblin explains the relationship of the state to power,

> Power is the ability of the state to make its own will reality. Domestically, it is the ability to rule the population in such a fashion as to make the people the executors or agents of the will of the state. In foreign relations, power is the ability of the state to submit other states to its will in order to achieve its national purposes.[46]

The living state, then, exists with an imperative to conquer all the geographical territory it feels is necessary for its security, development, and survival. Consequently, according to the ideology of the national security state, the history of political systems operating on the basis of geopolitics should be understood as a history of the domestic glorification of power coupled with an aggressive and militaristic foreign policy.[47]

But in fact, is the primary objective of the proponents of geopolitics in Latin America merely to increase the territorial boundaries of the state at the expense of its neighbors? Or could there be other uses for the science of geopolitics? While this science claims to justify the foundation for centralized and extensively applied state power, Comblin maintains that in fact, the absolute power of the national security states in Latin America "is not intended to face other states, but rather, the people, the citizens who are to submit to and be involved in governmental programs."[48] This claim becomes clearer in his discussion of the dynamics of the second science, "strategy," promulgated and adopted by theorists of the national security state.

Strategy

The proper understanding and application of strategy is the next science that is dealt with in the ideology of the national security state. Historically, Comblin observes, strategy has typically been thought of as "the art of war, of preparing and conducting military operations."[49] But he points out how this concept has been redefined in more comprehensive terms in modern times as a result of technological advances in, and attitudinal changes about, warfare. According to the proponents of the national security state, the concept of strategy, once understood as a straightforward battlefield problem of military science, has now irrevocably evolved into a comprehensive methodology for the state's conduct of war. They link this evolution of the concept to the complex evolution of political problems themselves. And by accepting a contemporary, extended concept of strategy, theorists of geopolitics defend the transformation of society into military dictatorships.

As Comblin explains, the theorists of geopolitics point out that strategy with regard to war has become increasingly more comprehensive since the French Revolution. That upheaval inaugurated the concept of an "armed people" to redirect and thus redefine the application of military strategies. Later, as a result of the widespread destruction of the First World War, the concept of "total war" emerged as a further refinement of military strategy. Since all aspects of each nation's social and economic resources were impressed into the war effort, all sectors of society were appropriately redefined as potential military targets. This redefinition had the effect of abolishing the heretofore generally accepted, qualitative distinction between "military" and "civil" activities, and between combatant and noncombatant. The global reach of the Second World War further extended the concept of total war, as few nations were able to escape any impact of modern warfare. And finally the exacerbation of East-West tensions, particularly during the cold war era, has abolished any lingering idea of neutrality. Technological advances in armament research has expanded the use of nuclear weapons, such that their impact will be felt by all nations of the earth.[50]

The national security state theorists further argue that war itself is a continuing and perpetual state of existence. Consequently, the definition of peace as itself a viable state of existence is thereby abolished, since the traditional distinction between peace and war no longer applies. Augmenting this expansion of the concept of war, these theorists have further redefined and more widely applied the concept of strategy. The importance of this extension of the concept of strategy takes on stark relevance in contemporary Latin American politics. For, as Comblin points out, according to the military governments founded on the national security system and ideology, all politics has become a politics of war.[51] Consequently, total military planning not only encompasses military strategy, but national economic strategy and political strategy as well. Thus, according to the Latin American theorists of geopolitics, "All times are times of war.... All peoples are permanently in a state of war."[52]

Now, in order for theorists of geopolitics to give coherency and direction to a national security strategy, they must devise a "national plan," explains Comblin. The national plan is a synthesis of policy-making strategies that aggregate and coordinate all interests in society to work for the survival of the nation as the permanent and absolute end of the state. That is, the enactment of a master plan will incorporate every aspect of society in the survival of the state and its "national interests." However, Comblin points out that when these theorists attempt to explain and define the national interests to be protected, they provide only a nebulous description that "is concentrated around the ability to survive against negative forces—in other words, to obtain national security."[53] The beginning and the end of politics, then, is national security, and it is negatively defined in terms of what the leaders find objectionable.

Since the goal is national security, the means to achieve it is through "national power." Obviously, then, the proper end of politics is to build up national power to achieve national security. According to Comblin, "national power is the whole expression of all the means (political, psycho-social, economic, and military) available to the nation at any time to guarantee its national objectives."[54] Consequently, all of the social and political institutions and offices of the state, both public and private, must be subordinated to the national security institutions—that is, the national security council or the CIA-like secret service—since these institutions were created specifically to serve national security interests, the most important objectives of the state.

As mentioned earlier, economic development is also subordinated to the demands of national security. But as Comblin explains, "Ultimately, in the national security ideology, economic development becomes the process by which the state may acquire more and better weapons to defend itself."[55] The priority of developing the warfare state to the exclusion of the welfare state or any other form of the state, is justified by reference to the hostile and technologically developing world where a more powerful state by virtue of its nature poses a serious threat to its less powerful neighbor. Furthermore, national security theorists describe the process of economic development as also characterized by fierce competition among states in their attempt to secure optimum results from technological progress and industrial growth; in other words, "development is the economic side of the war."[56]

Moreover, not only must the state be secure from threats by other states, but the state must be secure from internal threats as well. It must even be free, through its secret service, to act unrestrained against the behavior of its citizens when it perceives a threat to national security. As Comblin explains,

> According to national security ideology, enemies are powerful and the consciousness of the masses is always receptive to infiltration. Therefore, all citizens are suspected of subversion, and it is appropriate to study them closely; this is the task of the secret service.[57]

Even so, the secret service does not want to thwart all citizen activities, since widespread satisfaction is ultimately necessary for the support of national policies. However, it does want to be certain that most of those aspirations citizens want to satisfy will also be in accordance with national security aims.[58]

Yet theorists of the national security state are aware of the potential for negative social costs associated with any program to increase dramatically national defense spending and production. They recognize that at some point development policies should also support a structure for social harmony necessary for internal stability. Consequently, says Comblin, the theorists will argue for a certain amount of economic progress in nonmilitary areas as necessary, otherwise popular support for the system will collapse. Hence, a minimal amount of social welfare policies is tolerated, even though these

unavoidably cut into the priorities of defense spending. For the max-
imization of national power, though, reasonable sacrifices by citizens
are necessary and expected.[59] The ideology of the national security
state, then, maintains a certain tension between social welfare needs
and national security demands.

The same holds true, explains Comblin, with regard to individual
liberties. The national leadership perceives its situation as the classic
dilemma between security and liberty; "Generally the national security ideology answers it by requiring the sacrifice of individual liberties."[60] As with the desire to minimize social welfare spending and
maximize defense spending, but not at the cost of social stability, the
national security state must find the point at which any further abolition of liberties will destroy itself, and then maintain policies slightly
above that point. And the determination of this point must be left to
those most capable of leading the nation.

Elites

Yet given the sciences of geopolitics and strategy, how does the
ideology of the national security state justify the military expropriation of political power? If ruling elites are necessary, why must they
come from the military? According to Comblin, national security
theorists posit two reasons: "the betrayal by citizens" and "the necessity of war."[61] With regard to the first, the theorists perceive fatal
flaws in the general political behavior of the citizenry in a democracy.
Citizens are too susceptible to demagoguery; they are easily persuaded by those who would do the state harm, such as Marxists.
Civilians are also administratively inefficient and thus basically incapable of proper national leadership. In a world of competitive and
powerful states in a fierce struggle for survival, the often inconclusive
and erratic behavior of pluralist politics and the pervasive corruption
of politicians place the nation in grave danger.

Furthermore, prolonged political crises have resulted from inept
democratic politics, crises that are incapable of being dealt with satisfactorily by pluralist compromises. The internal structure of state
and society must be strong and stable with a unified public will. The
moral task of the military, then, is to re-create the nation on solid
foundations. According to the national security theorists, "a true re-
birth will take place by military salvation."[62] As Comblin notes, military leaders "place themselves on the same level as the founding
fathers; they are the second founders of nation and state." And from
where does their ability to guide the nation properly originate? Only

in force and power; since the essence of the state, according to the national security ideology, is indeed force and power. The military, in their professional capacity as the only legitimate possessors of real power to use force and violence, must be the legitimate and proper heirs to rule the nation. As Comblin explains, within such a system the significance of military force is comprehended at a more transcendental level:

> [the] level of a metaphysical attribute: life is power, military power; the essence of being is violence. It is the old argument of Pan-Germanism, linked with some Hegelian concepts, some intuitions proceeding from Nietszche, and, at bottom, Hobbes's political philosophy with its sublimation of violence.[63]

The other reason why the military should assume political control refers to the state's environment of total war, as discussed earlier. This condition of total war is identified with and explained as the standard conflict between East and West, between the "communist world" and the "free world." For example, the national security theorists argue in favor of the subordination of Latin American security interests to North American foreign policy objectives. They do not perceive this subordination as a threat to their own national sovereignty, but as a protection and guarantee of their national sovereignty. Comblin notes that all nations that have employed the national security ideology have taken up the Brazilian doctrine that "the war against communism is the fundamental opposition in the present condition of the world."[64] In the vociferous denunciation of communism as well as Marxism and other theoretically and sociologically related movements and activities, the national security states consider this fight to be "an all-out war within the present definition of total war." With the United States leading the fight against the Soviet Union and communism, the Latin American countries must employ all their resources and mobilize effectively to join the United States in the face of a mutual challenge. Of course, only the military is properly trained and equipped to meet this challenge; and thus military governments are necessary for national survival.

Conversely, civilian governments, they argue, have historically been open to, if not tolerant of, Marxist infiltration and extremist subversion. This claim plays a central role when analyzing the political conditions of oppression today in many Latin American countries: for, according to the national security theorists, the enemy is not only

117

outside the borders, but within as well. As Comblin explains, from the perspective of the elites of the national security state, "the enemy is inside the country; every citizen is potentially a Marxist, and thus an enemy."[65] Consequently, in their claim to save Western civilization, the primary domestic concern of the military is to suppress communism at home; and to do this effectively, the military must seize control of all power in the state.

But, asks Comblin: What is this "West" that the imposition of military dictatorships is supposed to protect? According to the national security ideology, the national security states in Latin America were instituted to protect "science, democracy, and Christianity." But, observes Comblin, "to protect democracy and achieve a Christian society, the most far-reaching dictatorship is established. . . . A basic postulate of the ideology is that war and dictatorship are the means with which to establish democracy and Christianity."[66] But in practice, war and dictatorship never seem to end, because the military cannot give up power for fear of undermining the stability of the state; continuation of its war upon the citizenry in the name of anticommunism is the only way it can justify its position. Consequently, the national security ideology is unable to justify an end to war or to provide provisions for transition to a peaceful government. Although the theorists of the national security state refer to their ideology as simply nationalist, Comblin cites various texts to demonstrate that it transcends simple nationalism to the point of subordinating all values, even religious values, to those that best serve the state. Ultimately, concludes Comblin, in national security ideology "the nation takes the place of God. . . . [Where the] Christian God is only a cultural symbol [for the military]."[67]

Limitations of Liberation Theology's Assessments

Are the two approaches utilized by theologians of liberation to assess the social conditions in Latin America—that is, from the perspectives of the world economy and the national security state—incompatible? Gutiérrez and Dussel are certainly aware of the dynamics of the national security state and its ideological justification;[68] similarly Comblin is aware of poverty and the distorted economic relationships between countries.[69] And, of course, larger social theoretical debates continue in academia and elsewhere as to the proper approach to political analysis and to the study of international relations with regard to whether particular structural relationships transcend and control national sovereignty or whether nation-states are relatively autonomous.[70]

But reliance on some version of dependency theory by liberation theologians is under additional pressure. For Gutiérrez and others, moral imperatives require immediate political action to address social problems in Latin America. Hence, dependency theories must be especially attentive to details of their theoretical assumptions and sociological analyses, so as to allow those who utilize the "new-found" approach to make as few mistakes as possible in their efforts to effect social change. This concern should give pause to liberation theologians to reflect further upon the theoretical enterprise itself. Reliance on a particular worldview places great pressure on the accuracy of theory development and perhaps even greater responsibility on the religious individual who acts on perceived theoretical insights within the confines of liberation theology's peculiar methodology. The methodology itself maintains that on the one hand the individual must be convinced of the efficacy of his theory, while on the other hand the individual must retain his skepticism concerning any theory that claims universal insights as absolute certitudes. In tension, then, is the activist compulsion to act in the world however noble the cause, and the conservative hesitation to leave things as they are out of fear of unexpected and intolerable costs as a result of mistaken claims as well as ever-changing insights.

The Need for a "Historical Project"

While the question may not be definitively nor generally resolved in favor of one social theoretical approach over another, liberation theologians are in general agreement that the results of their analyses reveal that the majority of political economies in Latin America are not functioning in accordance with traditional precepts of respect for human dignity and rights; certainly these societies evince no collective interest in liberating their impoverished and oppressed masses. Whether or not more emphasis should be placed on one social factor over another, virtually all liberation theologians agree that a revolutionary situation exists in various societies throughout Latin America. For many, the problem is now one of political strategy.

Several liberation theologians advocate drastic social change in Latin America to bring about a just society. Some have even begun to theorize about the nature of the process necessary to achieve their desired ends. José Míguez Bonino refers to the object of this process as a "historical project."[71] To grasp better what the project might look like after completing one of the two political economic analyses just discussed, he sets forth seven essential characteristics.

The first characteristic of the historical project is the establishment of its own moral position as a normative guide for proper political and economic development. It begins by defining itself in contradistinction to the current models of development that place Latin American societies in a condition of dependency on the international capitalist system. Instead, it will argue for the necessity of an independent economy, though not isolated from other countries.

The second characteristic extends the concerns of the first with regard to the project proponents' desire to move society away from a condition of political and economic dependency. Here they argue for the necessity of social revolution. According to Míguez Bonino, the goal of a revolution driven by popular movements is to displace the oligarchic elites who are dependent on foreign interests and who in turn dominate the indigenous social institutions. He recognizes, however, that theoretical differences exist among project proponents as to the proper balance of political weight to be given to the roles of the peasants, the industrial proletariat, the military, the revolutionary elite, and the nondependent groups of the bourgeoisie.

Related closely to the issues of personnel composition and political direction of the social revolution is the third characteristic of the project: the appropriate structure of the new state. Given the democratic ethos of the project's movement, the successful revolutionary government will continue to encounter resistance from economic and political elites. At a minimum, then, "a strong, centralized state is a necessary step in the process" to assure the survivability and success of the revolution. But Míguez Bonino warns that proponents must be cautious of the authoritarian dangers inherent in each step.

The fourth characteristic displays an awareness of the need for changes to be wrought in social relations throughout society, and not just in foreign and domestic economic considerations, after the revolution. To this end, the project must attempt to "awaken" the dispossessed as to their true condition of oppression. Míguez Bonino argues that this will have the effect of fostering within them a genuine desire for change which will assist further in the transformation of society. Closely related to this process of political awakening is the fifth characteristic: recognition that the project's primary route of change will come through the political sphere. That is, all other changes—technical, cultural, social, and economic—are subordinate to the "primacy of the political in the present Latin American struggle."[72]

The sixth characteristic reveals careful consideration for the creation of an authentic Latin American socialism. Here exists a strong awareness of the problems and errors of contemporary political economies founded on dogmatic interpretations of Marx. And closely following this, the seventh and final characteristic of the project insists that proper social development in Latin America must not focus strictly on formal political and economic change, but must incorporate all dimensions of society. Fulfillment of this final characteristic will complete the total liberation of Latin America by transforming all aspects of political economic development, including ethical aspects. Thus, according to Míguez Bonino, "liberation is the process through which a 'new man' must emerge, a man shaped by solidarity and creativity over against the individualistic, distorted humanity of the present system."

Míguez Bonino recognizes, however, the presence of realistic limitations on the project. For example, he notes that the various armed uprisings of guerrilla bands in recent years have generally proven inadequate. What may be needed instead is mass mobilization of the citizenry. However, this can only be achieved by working with the oppressed and helping them to understand the nature of their oppression completely and thus be in a position to assist efforts aimed at social change. Yet he also recognizes that even the mass educational and organizational efforts among the poor have often been met with the force and intransigence of the state, frequently ending in violence. In this case, he argues, it may be necessary to accept a temporary and transitional stage wherein "a restricted change in coalition with military or national capitalist groups opposed to imperialism may offer an opening for a socialist society."[73] Nevertheless, in those extreme situations where revolutionary violence is the only alternative, Míguez Bonino exclaims that Christians should continue supporting and participating in the effort to bring about the creation of a "new man."

Revolutionaries greet it also with surprise and joy, welcoming their [the Christians'] participation, without being able to understand this phenomenon which runs counter to all their theories about the role of religions and religious people![74]

Beyond the general outlines and characteristics of the historical project, Míguez Bonino's strategic thinking is vague. How are we to define more clearly and operationalize his concepts? What practical problems should be anticipated? What tactics will be necessary? Specifically, what kinds of problems of economic development vis-à-vis concern for social justice will be encountered, and how should they be resolved? And what about ethical conduct and political violence? First, economic development.

Economic Development and Social Justice

Market economic theory generally argues that efficient use of resources can be achieved under ideal circumstances.[75] Individual producers, sellers, and consumers must have equal participation rights. Furthermore, not only is wealth distributed in such a way that all members of society can participate in the market, but full information is available with all logically possible options necessary for each individual to make a rational choice. In addition, there must be no cost to the enforcement of contracts and property rights; there must be no "externalities" at all to otherwise voluntary transactions. So with a well-functioning market economy, material production will increase dramatically.

Ideal social conditions, of course, are never fully realized.[76] With unequal starting points some citizens and firms have advantage over others. This unequal beginning can distort market efficiency as prices are set according to the influence an individual or firm exercises over some portion of the economy, rather than according to the equal but competing forces of supply and demand. And this situation holds for both national and international economies. Furthermore, complete information is rarely available. And methodological debates continue regarding economic theories that assume individual rationality. Nevertheless, the political and economic advantages of a market economy include its recognition of individual rights and its efficient allocation of resources; the moral disadvantages of a market economy include its lack of a concept or standard of justice, wherein goods are allocated according to ethical criteria other than that of rights of appropriation justifying the unequal distribution of wealth.

The problem, then, would seem to be one of balancing the necessity for greater economic productivity with the moral imperatives of a just society. Liberation theologians, of course, want both. Greater productivity is desired to meet basic, material needs of an otherwise impoverished citizenry. But they also recognize that public policy oriented toward greater productivity with unequal centers of economic power has often been the source of abuse of human dignity and rights. However, despite their general critiques of the failure of developmentalist economic policies to promote peace and justice in Latin America, liberation theologians noticeably lack rigorous analyses of the theoretical justifications for current economic arrangements.

Yet of crucial importance for any moral critique of capitalism should be an analysis of market economic behavior itself; and for liberation theology, this should be done in terms of exploring the possibility of a viable relationship between productive efficiency and ethical concerns of social justice. After all, theoretical arguments of market efficiency, as just discussed, and empirical claims of increasing productivity from private capital accumulation provide powerful support for current Latin American economic arrangements. Nevertheless, liberation theology falls short of offering a general critique of the role of the market with regard to the interrelationship between individual and community, rights and obligations, and productivity and justice.

This failure may result in part from an uneasy discourse between the language of economics and the language of moral philosophy. While productivity is relatively easy to measure, the concept of justice encounters more formidable obstacles, both in terms of definition and in comparative evaluation with demands for greater productivity.[77] It may also result from the contingency nature of public policy making itself. When the two normative concerns for economic development and social justice confront each other after a social revolution, policy debates generally focus on the issue of economic redistribution. And, ultimately, it becomes a problem of resolving the theoretical conflict between property rights and social welfare.[78] Consequently, any satisfactory resolution of the problem must involve complex factors that moral denunciations and platitudes—for example, those of Gutiérrez and Míguez Bonino—easily neglect. An example of the policy difficulties encountered once moral proclamations have been exhausted can be seen in Nicaragua. Guided by a political theory similar in many respects to that of liberation theology, the Sandinistas continue to search for a synthetic solution to the problem of maintaining economic development and of simultaneously achieving social justice.

The Political Theory of Liberation Theology

Sandinismo and the Case of Nicaragua

Since the revolution of 1979, Nicaraguan society has undergone a thorough reexamination of its political values for which Sandinismo as well as religious discourse, including liberation theology, are playing important roles of clarification. Today, it appears that a coherent political theory of the ruling Sandinista "party," the Sandinista National Liberation Front (*Frente Sandinista de Liberación Nacional,* FSLN), is emerging that is far more sophisticated than that initially set forth in 1961.[79] The political theory of Sandinismo criticizes dependent capitalism, while supporting a commitment to some kind of market socialism or mixed economy. It also argues for a commitment to freedom of expression, especially political pluralism, and to racial and sexual equality, which provides the theoretical foundation necessary for the Sandinista attempt to democratize political processes at virtually all levels of society. As with liberation theology, the political theory of Sandinismo also emphasizes the necessity of analyzing the political, economic, and cultural conditions of Nicaraguan society for descriptive and prescriptive purposes. Before the regime of the Somoza family could be successfully overthrown, the revolutionaries developed their own sophisticated understanding of the social dynamics of Nicaraguan society. From Augusto C. Sandino in the 1930s to his contemporary intellectual heirs, Sandinistas have engaged in wide-ranging analyses of Nicaraguan social conditions in their attempt to discover the root causes of political disorder and thus to assist better in suggesting long-term remedies.[80]

Sandinismo borrows heavily from neo-Marxist and other political economy assessments of international relations and their effects on local conditions. Similar to the description of the Third World by liberation theologians, Sandinistas describe the Nicaraguan situation as one of an impoverished Third World country caught in a peripheral-dependent economic and political relationship with countries of the First World, primarily with the United States. Until 1979, this dependent relationship required the establishment of a political dictatorship in Nicaragua, militarily armed and economically supported by the United States. The primary objective of this relationship was North American hegemonic domination of Latin American economic and political activities. Furthermore, this objective continues to threaten the sovereignty of Nicaragua.[81]

The external conditions of political and economic domination has also had a mirror effect on internal social relationships in Nicaragua.

The Sandinistas argue that the exercise of authoritarianism in both the state and the economy, in terms of unjust social behavior and public policies, is primarily structural or institutional in origin. Consequently, programmatic attempts to counter authoritarianism must include more democracy. They have called for the restructuring of all Nicaraguan social institutions along democratic lines.[82] To this end, the political theory of Sandinismo encourages all citizens to become involved in the decision-making process in virtually every organization that involves collective citizen participation, from economic enterprises to neighborhood associations.

From the beginning, the Sandinistas seem to have grasped the importance of the criticism made earlier by the political theorist Hannah Arendt concerning the essential problem that modern revolutionaries have failed to solve: how to assure that political power in a revolutionary society will be used in morally appropriate yet competently effective ways.[83] They recognized that political power is a primary attribute of nearly all social relationships. They further understood that mere attainment of the political power of the state would be insufficient to deal with the pervasiveness of unjust social relationships inherited from the previous regime. Indeed, while new social relationships in the state may themselves be structured more appropriately according to procedural principles of democracy, they also realized that inappropriate social relationships in civil society would continue to maintain their authoritarian structure and exploitative practices—practices that could ultimately undermine the newly formed democratic state. Consequently, with their commitment to human liberation and individual freedom in all aspects of social life, the Sandinistas have argued for the restructuring of social relationships along a more equalitatarian basis throughout society.[84]

The Sandinistas argue, too, that the presence of unjust social relationships was itself a function of, as well as a contribution to, the inequitable distribution of political and economic resources. They perceive the existence of social inequality as a threat to individual liberty. Since Aristotle, of course, the problem of the appropriate relationship between liberty and equality has been analyzed. Social philosophers have generally recognized that a political regime that emphasized one element to the neglect of the other would surely be doomed. That is, a regime that professed the presence of both elements but leaned more strongly toward equality would find itself ultimately with the threat of liberty being extinguished in the name of majority rule. And a similar regime leaning more heavily in the

direction of liberty would ultimately find the right of property dominating in a way that democratic politics would be subverted.[85] Consequently, modern political theorists began to argue for a political
system that would emphasize the importance of both equality and
liberty. But as heirs of modern political thought, how could the Sandinistas, as with the liberation theologians, call for full democracy
while maintaining an economy with an extensive disequilibrium in the
distribution of wealth?

Their revolutionary commitment to a democratic society out of
necessity has required that the Sandinistas think not strictly in *procedural* terms, but in *substantive* terms as well. With regard to the "programmatic suggestions" growing out of their theoretical commitment
to democratic decision making, the political theory of Sandinismo appears to be essentially "Rousseauist." That is, a revolutionary attempt
is under way to build a unique society where the individual is both
citizen and lawmaker, both democratically accountable and individually autonomous.[86] For example, the entire process of writing and
shaping the new constitution in Nicaragua consisted of an extremely
energetic attempt to involve all economic, political, and social interests in Nicaraguan society. Furthermore, the constitution itself attempts to maintain an effective arrangement of separation of powers
(procedural considerations) with popular controls (substantive considerations).[87] Nevertheless, the formal mixture of procedural and
substantive elements poses serious theoretical problems. In theory,
procedural democracy argues for the establishment of rules of fair-
ness in the public sphere of state politics while usually ignoring the
nature of politics in other social organizations of the private sphere,
such as in economic enterprises. Substantive democracy, on the
other hand, argues for an equitable distribution of resources necessary for the game of democratic politics to be played fairly, and thus
its concerns extend beyond the public sphere.[88]

In Nicaraguan society, an uneasy tension between liberty and
equality has arisen as the revolutionary process unleashes theoretical
and practical contradictory concerns, while the Sandinistas attempt
to merge the requirements for procedural democracy with the demands of substantive democracy.[89] Current domestic policy has resulted in the complex organization of a mixed economy as well as a
pluralist political system.[90] With their concerns for both economic development and social justice, the Sandinistas have encouraged engagement in a variety of economic activities and wide-ranging
political organizations. The development of "generic" or mass

organizations along with special-interest groups has undercut and thus diminished the depth of social cleavages; and this, in turn, apparently has had the positive effect of diminishing potentially divisive social conflict.[91] However, the simultaneous development of complex and overlapping social organizations appears also to have diminished the overall efficiency of national policy making. Furthermore, the continual evolution of the mixed economy has encouraged conflicting economic policies and goals as the government encourages the simultaneous development of private, cooperative, and state-owned enterprises—all with different and conflicting interests—while attempting to promote a sense of national identity with corresponding citizen commitments.

For the Sandinistas, then, the attempt to deal with the conflicting goals of economic development and social justice has demanded considerable detailed and sophisticated refinements in political theoretical development as well as in policy design and application. Liberation theologians, though, have yet to experiment in this logical sequel to their own political theoretical foundation. While their general assessments of the dynamics of political economies in Latin America provide a key point of departure for further theological development, the departure itself still requires specific attention to the political theoretical explication of the assessments.

Conclusion

Liberation theologians have yet to work out a resolution to the problem of reconciling economic development with social justice, if they wish to develop fully their political theory. In addition, a related concern remains with regard to the most appropriate path to achieve and maintain their goal of human liberation. This concern for liberation theologians is essentially one of selecting the social analysis which best suits the question being asked; and *the* question they ask has to do with the most efficacious and ethical path of political action to effect social change. Does the path to social change lead through the political sphere and reform politics? Or must change come as a result of economic transformation, probably necessitating a social revolution?

Many radical critics of Latin American politics still perceive the Church as held "captive" by the current political economic state. If this perception is accurate, crucial questions arise concerning not only the human liberation of the poor and oppressed members of society, but the institutional liberation of the Church from domination by either the national security state or corporate economic interests or both.[92] Theology and politics, as formal disciplines and separate endeavors, may well be completely incompatible, thus ruling out the possibility of developing a genuine political theology. And if the development of a political theology is not theoretically possible, then debate over religious political ethics may be irrelevant as well. Consequently, any theologically oriented assessments of the political economies of Latin America must stop short of advocating either comprehensive reform or social revolution.

Liberation theologians disagree. As discussed earlier, Juan Luis Segundo's analysis of Karl Marx's theoretical shortcomings demonstrates a basic misunderstanding by radical critics of the role religion plays with regard to social change. Having established the critical dimension of religious beliefs and the autonomy of religious institutions, Segundo suggests that much greater support for morally justifiable political action may exist, from passive disobedience to violent revolution. In fact, liberation theologians maintain that ethical dualisms of the modern era are ideologically suspect. For example, Hugo Assmann argues that there is no sphere of abstract truth separate from the sphere of social reality: thus, political ethics cannot be separated from theology.[93]

Furthermore, Gutiérrez notes, liberation theology as one form of political theology is indeed a "theology of the world."[94] This means that regardless of the efficacy of the various critiques of capitalist political economies in general, and Latin American political economies in particular, liberation theologians must attempt to use the logic and rationale of contemporary economic and political arrangements as a source of moral criticism. The amalgamation of traditional values with modern analytical techniques from the social sciences provides a critical function that can restore to modern rationality the two-dimensionality of normative critique and prudential practice. By accepting modern rationality as a critical tool but not as the end of being, liberation theology provides a radical critique of modern social conditions that includes yet transcends existentialist positions. According to Gutiérrez,

Perhaps this initial theological effort comes from another perspective and not only from another perspective, but also from a contradiction of the dominating elements of the process. . . .[95]

The selection of an analysis of social conditions is a crucial move, then, whether from a world economy or national security state point of view. For, in fact, the crucial assessment relates directly to the advocacy of particular political solutions. Perhaps reform is preferable to revolution; but to justify the former, the "relative autonomy" of the political sphere must be argued. One must argue that the oppressive social conditions are not influenced exclusively by the dependent status of Latin American economies on a world economy controlled by powerful, corporate capitalist interests. Comblin's social analysis of the national security state claims to reveal that the state is more flexible than dependency theorists suggest. If this is the case then social change may be possible without entailing the additional costs of a revolutionary approach. Yet in many cases lack of rule of law persists and threatens any possibility for reform-minded politics. Such conditions usually invite another look at the possibility, both ethically and politically, of social revolution. And even if the political sphere is relatively stable and legally coherent, the economies of Latin America remain heavily tied to international corporate interests—thus providing another formidable barrier to reformist politics.

From either point of view, liberation theology offers a powerful if limited critique of social conditions that contributes to the development of a revolutionary situation. Liberation theology as critical theory has dual emphases. As a critical theory *of* Christian faith, it offers a critique of religious beliefs, rituals, institutions, and practices. And as a critical theory *from* Christian faith, it becomes itself the methodology for a radical critique of society. Hence, liberation theology claims to provide the framework for more than an assessment of the political economies of Latin America; it also claims to provide a moral grounding for engaging in political action. Their moral justifications for both reformism and revolution now demand careful consideration.

129

Chapter 5

The Ethics of Reform and Revolution

Introduction

Imagine a confrontation between two gunmen, one of whom has unjustifiably threatened the life of the other. If the threatened gunman is quicker at the draw than his unjust adversary, his violent and lethal action might well be considered justifiable as a legitimate act of self-defense. Suppose, however, before the confrontation the innocent gunman has conclusive evidence that his unjust adversary is in fact quicker at the draw. Prior to the appointed time may the threatened gunman, knowing he will lose in a direct confrontation, continue to claim self-defense as justification were he to ambush his opponent? Furthermore, suppose that an ambush is also not feasible. As a last desperate act to avoid certain death, what if the threatened gunman were to kill one of his own friends so that he could falsely accuse his opponent with responsibility for the innocent death in order to discredit him publicly and thereby avoid the initial confrontation? Could this last approach be morally justified as legitimate self-defense?

Juan Luis Segundo presents this scenario in an early article on the problem of violence for a Christian.[1] He prompts two basic questions: Is the use of violence, even for self-defense, ever justified? And, if violence can be justified, do limits exist as to how violence may be used? The first question is certainly not unimportant in moral philosophy. Pacifism, however, is not a central theme of liberation theology's concern about political ethics, although some activist clergy and theologians have adopted nonviolent moral commitments.[2] Segundo uses this scenario to deal with the second question: that of when violence may be used legitimately. His response will be assessed a little later.

Citing recent papal encyclicals and other Church documents and describing the existence of violence pervasive in Latin American society, most liberation theologians conclude that present social conditions demand a response from Christians that at times may legitimately include the use of counterviolence.[3] The question of when and how to use violence, then, is fundamentally more difficult to answer other than with the absolutist position of pacifism. It entails the search for limits on the use of violence, limits that are themselves shaped by the exigencies of a socially unstable and volatile world. Moreover, the limits to violence are simultaneously limits to nonviolent reform. For to define what is morally legitimate or illegitimate in terms of violence presupposes moral categories of nonviolence. And therein lies the possibility for a variety of expressions of ethical political action.

In chapter 2 we saw how the methodology of liberation theology focuses on the two essential elements of its political theory: *praxis* and *hermeneutics*. We also saw in chapters 3 and 4 how this foundation led to the inclusion of modern social science—especially some version of Marxist social analysis—as a necessary aspect in the development of a political theory for a contemporary assessment of political economic conditions. Furthermore, recall from chapters 1 and 2 that the impetus for the development of a "liberation theology" is the moral commitment to human liberation, a commitment involving not only social analysis, but political action as well. Now given their assessment of contemporary social conditions, how do liberation theologians go about assessing the moral legitimacy of certain behavior in the realm of political ethics? Specifically, where is the place for violent as well as nonviolent political action? Dealing with this question brings us to the third essential element of the methodology of liberation theology: *evangelizaton,* proclaiming the message of salvation to oppressor and oppressed alike. Once again, we begin with Raúl Vidales and Segundo to set the stage for the development of an ethics to deal with violent and nonviolent politics.

131

The Political Theory of Liberation Theology

Evangelization

According to Vidales, the problem of evangelization is posed by the question: "How are we to proclaim Jesus Christ here and now?"[4] The traditional goal of the religious individual is essentially to change the morally errant attitudes and behavior of others by proclaiming the Christian message of salvation. This message, Vidales notes, reveals that God finds meaningful and universal expression in the Incarnation—that is, God's intervention in human history—and requires a moral response from human beings by bringing attention to it. The moral content of this religious message includes an affirmation of human dignity and an exhortation to take responsibility for the welfare of one's neighbor. The committed Christian can bring attention to this message only through participation in the liberation of fellow citizens from unjust situations. But a qualification exists. "The gospel message cannot be held equally by the exploiter and the exploited. That is why it is so dangerous to reduce the gospel's range of action to the purely spiritual realm, to concentrate exclusively on the salvation of the human soul."[5]

As discussed earlier, to avoid a situation of quietism in the face of social injustice, liberation theologians have abandoned the traditional religious acceptance of "ontological dualism," a dualism that places inordinate limits on ethical behavior. In other words, by imposing the dualism of "natural" and "supernatural" realms and then relegating religious concerns solely to the supernatural realm, they feel that most mainstream theology is incapable of sufficiently resolving ethical problems in the natural or this-worldly social life. For example, governmental officials who abuse and violate the rights of others typically compartmentalize their ethical commitments by claiming to be Christian (other-worldly) with regard to religious beliefs and practices while areligious (this-worldly) with regard to political and economic attitudes and behavior.[6] For liberation theologians, the appeal of the dualism found in traditional Christianity must be resisted to allow theological development and religious teachings to speak once again to social problems and thus to develop an evangelization of liberation. Vidales is quick to point out, however, that reflection upon problems of social injustice are not the only normative concerns for developing a theology for salvation; nonetheless, they are crucial concerns that have been neglected in the past and must now be recovered.

Evangelization of liberation, says Vidales, includes attempts at revising the traditional Christian understanding of prophetic warnings from Scripture. He points out that the ancient prophets were not engaged in discourse on abstract principles of the divine, but instead actively denounced concrete situations of sinful behavior from the standpoint of the divine. What this means for contemporary radical thinkers in modern times is that the problem has now become one of deciding how to exercise the prophetic tradition of denunciation when the very nature of sin "has hardened into structures, institutions, and systems," and how to annunciate grace with regard to transforming effectively an unjust society. Vidales states,

> The Christian message is not simply a word whispered to individuals in their isolated lives as lone persons. It is also a public proclamation to society, uttered in the face of its concrete structures and the prevailing system.[7]

This element of evangelization in conjunction with the other two elements of praxis and hermeneutics raises several questions for the development of a political theory. Notice that problems of properly evaluating contemporary social conditions become paramount in attempts to implement this radical interpretation of the prophetic tradition. Consequently, the emphasis on evangelization when combined with a commitment to liberation will encounter serious ethical questions in its attempt to justify various forms of political action.

Grounding

As discussed in chapter 2, liberation theologians rule out reliance on universal propositions and theological certitudes to guide ethical action. We will recall that theological development itself is in response to an individual's moral commitment. Religious individuals commit themselves to the liberation of their fellow citizens from poverty and political oppression by developing a theology to explain their commitments and justify their behavior. Consequently, the development of political ethics cannot be grounded sufficiently upon a set of abstract, moral criteria, as has been done in academic and orthodox theologies of both the present and the past. For example, José Comblin points out that the traditional criteria for a "just war" is inappropriate as a model for developing criteria for a "just revolution" or especially a "theology of revolution."[8] He maintains that

133

the subject matter of a theology of revolution is sometimes misunderstood. Its problem does not consist in determining the legitimacy or illegitimacy of a revolution itself. Neither does it consist of a search for abstract conditions of a right revolution; it is not an attempt to develop a theory of "just revolution," like the "just war" theory.[9]

The avoidance of a methodology based on moral absolutes, nevertheless, demands that liberation theologions find another aspect of their methodology to provide a coherent, consistent, and stable approach toward the development of an ethics for political action. Segundo clearly recognizes this situation.

Our theory, in other words, assumes that there is an empty space between the concept of God that we receive from our faith and the problems that come to us from an ever-changing history. So we must build a bridge.[10]

Notice that Segundo recognizes the necessity of reconciling two contrary if not contradictory concepts: a being of transcendence (infinite) and the existence of history (finite). Implicit in his statement is a dualism of his own: transcendental vs. existential dimensions of reality. It would seem that this acceptance of these two dimensions undermines Vidales's criticism and rejection of the ontological dualism found in traditional Christianity. There is, however, a subtle but distinct and hence crucial difference. Vidales's criticism aims more at the ideological definition and use of a particular understanding of ontological dualism that has historically resulted in the religious justification of, and support for, the status quo in worldly affairs. This common ideological approach maintains that God spoke to certain religious concerns and not to others. This common delimitation of the character of God's pronouncements has been criticized by liberation theologians for encouraging the compartmentalization of moral attitudes and behavior in a way that often leads to social injustice. The shattering of this traditional approach to religious dualism and its replacement with one that allows the active participation of God in both dimensions of reality is the goal of liberation theologians. Thus, there is a need to construct, theoretically, a bridge between the infinite and the finite, the objective and the subjective, to explain the proper relationship between the divine and the social.

Segundo presents the clearest example of how such bridge-building might occur. First, he calls attention to the crucial aspect of each individual's socialization process that facilitates the selection and instillation of a particular set of values. The initial formation of this set of values emerges generally through trust in other human beings. The child, for example, begins by "identifying himself with the values of his parents"; later this human trust tends to develop into a broader religious faith.[11] Moreover, this maturing set of values then becomes the focal point for faith itself. Now, with changing historical situations, analytical assessments of social conditions as well as interpretations of scriptural meanings and their attendant values also change, as suggested by the hermeneutic circle. Consequently, the solutions ethically appropriate to problems of social injustice will differ as well.

Yet what provides the grounding necessary for reasonably stable political ethics? For without a stable, transcendental basis for ethical judgments found in any radical theological framework, it would seem that particular values would conflict, being devoid of any capacity for evaluation and lacking ability for application in a consistent manner. Thus, the very resolution of questions concerning the appropriate selection of ethical values would not be possible without an arbitrary selection process that would harm all standards of political ethics. Consequently, the selection of any set of political values would be difficult to implement legitimately, if not comprehend completely. Liberation theologians, then, must establish a central core or thread of consistency as an ethical standard to judge the merits of political behavior.

In liberation theology, the religious faith itself is the key: Faith continues unchanged. It is the unchanging and constant faith of the religious individual that provides for ethical stability. Yet the nature of this constant faith must be such that it avoids both absolute and general identification with particular ideologies and with the epistemological problems associated with existentialist ethics. Consequently, the nature of absolute faith in liberation theology is not the same as that found in traditional Christianity. Traditionally, the acceptance of a static body of truth itself as absolute has provided a clear delineation between the values of good and evil, with an individual's faith placed in the truth of these immutable givens. As José Míguez Bonino explains the traditional notion,

Truth belongs, for this view, to a world of truth, a universe complete in itself, which is copied or reproduced in "correct" propositions, in a theory . . . which corresponds to this truth. Then, in a second moment, as a later step, comes application in a particular historical situation.[12]

For example, "freedom" has traditionally been defined in terms of rigid constraints imposed by the demands of propositional truth. But according to Segundo, a better understanding would define freedom as "precisely the capacity to absolutize what nature and history always present to us as something relative."[13] That is, the proper conception of freedom should not be defined in terms of the constraints of propositional certitudes, but in terms of the constraints of historical context; and these latter constraints are constantly in flux. Consequently, proper social ethics must be understood as relative to the particular historical situation from which they arise at any given time. That is, through a commitment, an individual can absolutize a value—for example, liberation—by merging it with objective reality— for example, the oppressed—and then declaring the merger unconditional—for example, a moral commitment to liberating the oppressed. For faith to be in operation, the individual must entrust his commitment to human liberation with complete hope, regardless of the probability of success. For Segundo, then, such subjective absolutization comprises the essence of faith; thus,

the process of faith begins by absolutizing persons rather than disembodied or abstract values. However, it does not absolutize a static person. Instead, it attributes value to the person as a companion in existence, as a guide through the wilderness of the unknown and the unexperienced [sic].[14]

Other liberation theologians have also arrived at similar positions concerning the connection between faith and politics, and the relationship between truth and action, theory and praxis. Míguez Bonino concludes that only through proper activities can "correct knowledge" be known.[15] And Hugo Assmann further emphasizes that faith has a political dimension of its own such that one cannot "live a life of faith in isolation from daily life."[16]

Furthermore, Segundo points out that the theological shift in absolutization, from abstract certitudes to individuals with particular social needs, has the effect of attributing "absolute value to a person as educator."[17] That is, the evangelizing individual must evaluate his own social circumstances with his moral commitments in mind, exercise his prophetic function by denouncing social injustice, and actively assist in the liberation of others by "teaching" them what he has learned. It is the process of learning itself that alone transcends historical situations and thus can alone claim ontological status as abstraction, although it manifests its quality conditionally. According to Segundo,

Thus, in and through faith, we absolutize one concrete pedagogical process in history, placing it above and before any other such process.[18]

Therefore, absolutization is a subjective and free act of the individual's will, although it is an objective process in history, says Segundo, "directed by God himself . . . an absolute educator."

Segundo maintains that this objective process for liberation also reveals that religious faith can be "converted into freedom for history, which means freedom for *ideologies*."[19] A logical relationship now exists between the commitment of faith and the argument for political action, since both have the same object or end in mind. Segundo refers to this relationship of interconnected values as *ideology*, where means-ends arguments are advanced.[20] The "foundation stone" of ideology, then, is faith. And it is the complementary relationship between the two that provides the bridge between a "conception of God" and "the real life problems of history." So in liberation theology, faith exists as an absolute educational process subjectively applied to problems of social injustice, while ideology represents possible explanations of, and relative solutions to, problems in the historical situation. As Assmann succinctly notes,

Once the ideological function, in the pejorative sense of idealizing everything, has gone, then it becomes possible to use ideology as an instrument for the transformation of the world.[21]

Reformist Politics

Now that they have grounded their ethics in a peculiar concept of faith, have revitalized the ancient concept of the prophetic function to provide their moral impetus, and have defined the important but limited function of ideology, liberation theologians must devise strategies that are ethically appropriate yet efficaciously applied to achieve their social objectives. In political ethics, efforts at social change generally fall into two categories of strategic approaches: reform and revolution.

With regard to reform, a number of variables must be taken into account, including the primary variable having to do with the nature of *rule of law* in society.[22] Does an independent judiciary exist? Is access to lawmaking processes possible? Another important variable is an assessment of the degree of economic and political power possessed by reformist groups and their antagonists. An appropriate amount of power is a necessary ingredient for reformists to bargain successfully with the institutionalized powers historically intransigent with regard to reform efforts. Specifically, do reform-minded groups have the sufficient wherewithal to force the status quo to negotiate if lawmaking is nonexistent, arbitrary, or intractably skewed?

Many activist clergy, influenced by liberation theology, in fact, engage in nonviolent politics as an active expression of their ethical commitment to human liberation. Their reform efforts include organizing peasant and labor unions, farm cooperatives, and health clinics. But the most dynamic and politically challenging organizations to arise in the last two decades in Latin America have been the "Christian base communities." An analysis of these "communities" provides a case study of the possibilities and limitations of reformist ethics in liberation theology.

Christian Base Communities

A little over five decades ago, the reaction of the Catholic church in Europe to the adverse social consequences of industrial society as well as the growing appeal of socialism resulted in the establishment of the program, Catholic Action. This program attempted to involve lay members who, under the guidance of professional clergy, sought solutions to social problems. Later in Latin America, a variant of this program was instituted in Brazil to deal with its own pressing social problems.[23] It was also used to help deter the appeal of socialist solutions that were perceived by political and ecclesiastical elites alike as a threat both to society and the Church. However, the experience of working with the poor radicalized many of the younger members of Catholic Action as well as some of the clergy, who then pressed for more structurally far-reaching social changes. But the conservative character of the Church's ecclesiastical structure purged Catholic Action of its radical membership. Yet the overall impact of the radicals far outlasted the short-term gains of the conservatives. An increasing number of individuals, both lay members and clergy, including higher ecclesiastical authorities, had become increasingly sensitized to the plight of the poor. However, a shortage of traditional clergy left the

Church in the awkward position of outwardly speaking on behalf of the poor while institutionally unable to do very much for them.

In response to the demands of activist clergy, the Catholic church again instituted a number of programs to reach the poor in a way that also included many lay workers. With a lack of more moderate clergy, the Church had to employ many of the radicalized former participants of Catholic Action. These radicals then implemented innovative techniques developed by the educator Paulo Freire, to overcome illiteracy among the poor. Freire's method of "conscientization" (*conscientização*)[24] extended beyond simply helping the poor overcome debilitating problems of illiteracy; it included an ideological critique of prevailing socioeconomic conditions to help them become literate about and overcome the oppressive state as well. His method utilized an approach to language instruction that focused on a vocabulary and set of concepts drawn not only from problems in agriculture or fishing, but from problems of social dependence by the poor on wealthy landowners, unjust city functionaries, and ultimately on the authoritarian state itself. In these Church programs peasants were educated in such a way that they became aware of the "true nature" of their socially dependent and unjust situation. From their new religious perspective, they saw the state as supporting and thus giving legitimacy to that which was illegitimate in the eyes of God. Nevertheless, the gains toward social change made by the literacy programs of the Church were muted in 1964 when the conservative military junta forced the efforts of the Church educational programs away from social criticism.

Yet here too the radical legacy begun with Catholic Action and passed on to later educational programs continued to find expression in small "communities" of worshippers. Initially instituted as part of the educational program of the Church, many neighbors would gather periodically in groups to discuss the relevance of Scripture in everyday life. In fact, "Christian base communities" (*as comunidades eclesiais de base,* CEBs) often developed spontaneously with no official connection to the Church. Today these CEBs are generally motivated by intellectual and social dynamics of a democratic and participatory nature. Community members discuss and reinterpret the relevance of scriptural teachings in light of their contemporary social problems (fourth step of the hermeneutic circle). According to Leonardo Boff,

Christian life in the basic communities is characterized by the absence of alienating structures, by direct relationships, by reciprocity, by a deep

139

communion, by mutual assistance, by communality of gospel ideals, by equality among members.[25]

Furthermore,

> The specific characteristics of [current societies] are absent here: rigid rules; hierarchies; prescribed relationships in a framework of a distinction of functions, qualities, and titles.

With over one hundred thousand CEBs currently operating throughout Brazil and thousands more throughout Latin America,[26] many ecclesiastical officials have expressed concern over their growing influence in religious affairs. However, Boff sees the real contribution of CEBs in religious life as a bridge over the gap that currently exists between the needs of the individual believer and the broader, variegated concerns of the institutionalized, global Church.[27] Consequently, he argues that CEBs should not be perceived as an alternative religious institution attempting to replace the established Church, but instead understood as a source of dynamic resurgence of faith within the Church; the CEBs "can only be [the Church's] ferment for renewal." In a similar vein, Gustavo Gutiérrez maintains that the interaction between CEBs and liberation theology itself during the past two decades has yielded positive social effects for Latin America. Primarily, the established Church has become more active in dealing with problems of the poor as result of this union.[28] The growth of CEBs, then, has had a noticeable impact in at least two areas: They have become influential in the development of liberation theology, and they have become a significant factor in politics.

As we saw in chapter 2, liberation theologians find much fault with any approach to theology that assumes the a priori existence of propositional truths upon which to build a theological system and from which to derive a set of guidelines for social action. Instead, liberation theologians emphasize *orthopraxis* over *orthodoxy*, beginning with concrete conditions, not abstract doctrine for theological reflection. The same dynamics are present in both CEBs and liberation theology. In fact, out of the growth and activities of CEBs has emerged a *Latin American Bible,* a translation of the sacred writ of Christianity with a commentary from liberation theology perspectives and CEB experiences. So with their religious "conscientization" as to the nature of the social injustices they are experiencing, CEB participants often organize themselves politically to improve local social conditions.

But with regard to current socioeconomic conditions in Latin America, a crucial question challenges the political effectiveness of CEBs as well as the normative foundation of reformist ethics in liberation theology: What long-term effects will CEBs and reformist politics have in terms of affecting the destiny of certain Latin American nations, particularly the national security states? For example, what are the implications for the future of politics in Brazil as a result of the activities of CEBs? Two very real possibilities exist, one optimistic, the other pessimistic. With regard to the optimistic possibility, CEBs do appear to provide a training ground for democratic politics, not unlike the effects of local government in federal political arrangements, in otherwise authoritarian political systems. The emphasis on open discussion, compromise, and consensus may indeed prepare individuals for the future pressures of citizenship, with the return of democratic politics. In fact, CEBs appear to have played a significant role in the recent transition from military rule to democratic politics in Brazil.[29]

Already in thousands of base communities, local residents are learning how to take responsibility for their destiny and to cooperate to overcome various local problems. For example, villagers often pool resources to clear a field, buy a community tractor, dig wells, or deal with recalcitrant landlords. Slum dwellers have organized in a way that is politically effective; they have exerted pressure on local magistrates to provide material assistance for the improvement of local health care and other living conditions, while those living in the affected area donate their labor, thus working together to improve their community.

Yet in the long-term, how much impact can CEBs have on transforming society from within? And what about their revolutionary potential? From a more pessimistic point of view, it appears that their contribution to the transformation of society through reform efforts may only be marginal at best. Of course, the success of CEBs is not marginal to those whose lives are directly improved, and such marginal activity may be ethically worth pursuing for its own sake. But with regard to long-term prospects for democratic politics, CEB leaders and theorists do not appear to fully address fundamental questions dealing with the nature of political and economic power—that is, the particular relationship between the economic arrangements and political institutions, and how those institutions themselves are defended and justified.

Certain basic assumptions concerning the nature of private property and political rights guide policy makers. And the disproportionate emphasis on the confluence of property and political power along with the emergence of the national security state pose the most serious problems for the overall long-term effectiveness of CEBs. For the key to the effectiveness of CEBs—that is, the CEBs' reform orientation in a system based on rule of law—may well be the source of their ineffectiveness. Reformism in any nonviolent sense requires a certain amount of legal respect for the reformers from those elites who are the targets of reform. This respect is generally only forthcoming as a result of the elites' maintenance of, if not greater respect for, the rule of law. But the recent history of the national security states, such as those of Brazil, Chile, Paraguay, and Argentina, would indicate that the elites' respect for rule of law itself has limits. No consensus exists as to whether the proper interpretation of the political economies in Latin America indicates that the state acts at the behest of powerful economic interests or in fact subordinates all social questions—even those of the private economic sector—to certain military priorities. But that the national security state will not always abide by the rule of law—even its own—becomes all too obvious in the face of overwhelming evidence of state condoned and instigated terrorism and violence.[30] For the rule of law implies the existence of certain limits on the prerogatives of governmental authorities. And it is precisely the claim by the national security state to unlimited authority and the right to rule unhindered that poses the greatest threat to the concept of rule of law as a restriction on violence and to CEBs dependent on the rule of law for their reformist politics as well as for their very survival.

Consequently, to the extent that CEBs have had political successes, they have generally been marginal, not major and decisive with regard to the basic structure of institutional relationships throughout society. These institutional relationships preserve a particular and crucial arrangement in the distribution and retention of political power such that when the distributional scheme is threatened, the entire system unites to resist its subversion. Presumably, then, the reformist activities of the CEBs will be tolerated by the national security state only to the point at which CEBs threaten those elites who hold political power.

Of course, it should not be surprising that ultimately the real question of attaining a just society has to do with preserving individual liberty and designing a particular distribution of power such that liberty can have its fullest expression while meeting basic needs. This has been a recurrent theme throughout Western political philosophy. For example, Jean-Jacques Rousseau grappled with the problem of liberty and how best to preserve it;[31] James Madison also grappled with the same problem and actually constructed a system of countervailing power to protect individual liberty.[32] Yet neither theorist, for example, could foresee the extent to which industrial capitalism would develop by the late twentieth century. And it is the nature of this contemporary form of social organization in Latin America and elsewhere not accounted for in classical liberalism that liberation theologians perceive as not only threatening individual liberty, but in fact failing to meet even the most basic of human needs. It is, then, this particular form of organization that must be analyzed to understand its relationship to political power and the rule of law, especially in the Third World. And depending on the nature of this relationship, the reformist attempts of CEBs to alleviate mass poverty and political oppression may only yield marginal benefits at best.

The problem, then, found by those who have organized CEBs in particularly violent societies, such as in El Salvador and Nicaragua (pre-1979), is the lack of rule of law that inhibits their overall, long-term efficacy.[33] Again, the emergence of CEBs to effect fundamental social change through reform efforts assumes that peaceful reform is possible and that these local associations can make a positive contribution to easing the plight of the poor and oppressed. But if reform is not possible, what is to be done? Social revolution? Under these circumstances what is the role of the CEBs? And what about the amount of violence that a successful revolution might entail? Perhaps the ultimate rational discussion on the viability of a theory of political ethics is the treatment by that theory of the ultimate irrationality: violence.

Revolution and Violence

Just War and Just Social Revolution

Liberation theologians generally find arguments in favor of a just war too confining to serve as a role model for developing a theory of a just revolution.[34] Such arguments fall short of meeting their needs

143

on two accounts: "absolute certitudes" and "restricted domain." With regard to the first, liberation theologians reject theoretical frameworks that rely on absolute certitudes. By contrast, theories of a just war depend on recognizable and changeless moral propositions. Such a framework might be useful were religious individuals to be searching only for moral justifications of self-defense against repressive regimes. In light of abstract principles, then, the individual could resist the state, even violently if necessary. Yet liberation theology's methodology affords the opportunity to construct a comprehensive theory of both religious and political thought and behavior.[35] And to do so, its methodology consists of an approach that rules out a priori the existence of certitudes. So, while a modification of a just war theory may have limited strategic usefulness, it is philosophically incompatible with the methodology of liberation theology.

With regard to restricted domain, just war theories tend to define the moral categories of "innocent parties" and "guilty parties" in such a way that the innocent party's acts are only justified when restricted to reactions directly aimed at the aggressor. That is, the innocent party may only defend itself when attacked by particular agents of repression. What tends to be ruled out as morally justifiable are subversive activities directed at faceless economic and political institutions. In other words, just war theories generally avoid dealing with the causes of social injustice; they limit the domain of morally justifiable use of violence to reactions against the effects of social injustice. Furthermore, they tend to rule out nongovernmental leadership possibilities as lacking political legitimacy. If only officially recognized heads of state may lead the citizenry in war, then armed insurgencies would find no legitimate standing in a theory of the just war.

For liberation theologians, then, theories of the just war tend to be ineffective in providing moral justification for widespread social change. However, what liberation theology lacks is a theory of the just social revolution. At a minimum, such a theory must consist of arguments based on general guidelines, not certitudes, compatible with liberation theology's methodology. The theory itself must continually be subject to reinterpretation as values are redefined, social conditions are reassessed, and objectives are modified. Furthermore, criteria for such a theory must remain focused on the causes, not just the effects, of social injustice. In this way, the success of a morally justifiable revolution might be able to continue building new social institutions to complete the revolutionaries' goal of complete liberation.[36]

The use of a theory of the just social revolution for the development of a theology of social revolution provides opportunities for liberation theology to find its own moral justifications for radical social change. Comblin points out that liberation theology originally emerged out of considerations given to European theologians of revolution as applied to Latin America.[37] Yet as liberation theologians developed their own distinct methodology for reflection on the moral dimension of Latin American political economies, the scope of liberation language expanded and eventually extended beyond the concerns covered by the original language of revolution.[38] Consequently, the development of theologies of liberation came to express and strive for greater social goals than the objectives of European theologies of revolution. Nevertheless, the European criteria for a just social revolution continue to challenge liberation theologians, especially with regard to the issue of revolutionary violence.[39] Indeed, questions concerning the proper role of violence pose the most vexing moral problem in the political ethics of liberation theology. While the details of a theory of the just social revolution have yet to be worked out, liberation theologians have had much to say about the problem of violence.

Violence

The moral difficulty posed in Segundo's scenario at the beginning of this chapter is embedded in the search for the balance between the efficacy of violence with regard to certain normative objectives, and the costs, both physical and spiritual, incurred in the use of violence to achieve those objectives.[40] Furthermore, the use of violence raises an additional problem: Toward whom or what should violence be directed? Three basic issues must be dealt with by liberation theologians with regard to the justification for political violence by Christians: an adequate explanation of the nature of existential social conditions and objectives in which violence would be used, the nature of transcendental moral concerns with regard to violence, and the relationship between the two. In liberation theology's approach to the problem of ontological dualism, the relationship between the existential and the transcendental dimensions provides the crucial framework that guides the search for comprehensive and appropriate political ethics.

Furthermore, a certain irony exists as to the nature of violence for many liberation theologians. For example, Míguez Bonino sees the presence of violence as a naturally inherent aspect of all human action. The individual as human being is "a project of liberation that constantly emerges in the fight against the objectifications given in nature, in history, in society, in religion."[41] Furthermore, in this fight with the social environment, the individual is creator as well as defender; and as creator, he acts out of a sense of love. Yet inasmuch as violence is also a part of creation, a need exists to discover a beneficial mix between love and violence. Consequently, as creators, human beings employ some measure of violence with their love. And since violence delimits love, love itself, then, may become an increasingly effective weapon of liberation. Nevertheless, does Míguez Bonino's approach contravene the standard Christian teaching that all of humanity is equally deserving of each individual's love? If not, have the concepts of violence and love undergone a transformation in their meaning and usage? Segundo deals more directly with these questions.

Violence and the Economy of Energy

Although the presence of violence is pervasive in Latin America, the role of violence may be such that no social arrangement can dispense with it entirely. For Segundo, the moral problem is less one of choosing between violence and nonviolence, and more one of recognizing the degree of violence inexorably present, and then determining how much emphasis to place on violence and to what or to whom it is to be directed. Yet Christians have traditionally argued against the morality of violence by arguing in favor of love of enemies as well as of friends. But Segundo maintains that it is through a precise understanding of the meaning of love that the religious individual can determine the meaning and value of violence.

Now with regard to love, Segundo claims that an "economy of energy" exists.[42] Each individual has a finite amount of available energy to expend out of concern for others such that only a certain number of persons can be truly loved in a meaningful and effective way. Consequently, the more persons an individual includes, the greater the dissipation of the finite amount of energy one possesses for loving; and if the focus were greatly expanded to include all of humanity, the expenditure of an individual's love would become "vague and ineffectual." Furthermore, Segundo argues that the economy of energy in the process of love implies that there is some mechanism whereby we can keep a whole host of people at arm's length so that we can effectively love a certain group of people. . . . This mechanism is not precisely hatred, it is *violence*—at least some initial degree of violence.[43]

In this sense, the use of violence is a natural method whereby the caring individual limits the range of recipients who may receive care, thereby making his love more effective.

The argument thus far maintains that the ability of an individual to love others effectively is limited. Furthermore, the existence of limitations suggests that where love is not found, violence, not hatred, is encountered. Consequently, violence is an inherent and an inescapable aspect of an individual's attitudes and decision-making processes. Given that limits do indeed exist as to how many people can be effectively helped, the religious individual is forced to direct his love toward some and away from others in an effort to increase the quality of assistance. Yet this raises the practical problem of how to keep at a distance those who cannot, and presumably should not, benefit from one's concern so as not to usurp another's love. The solution to this problem, says Segundo, is found in the organization of society.

To segregate those who are loved more from those who are loved less or not at all, requires a mechanism that has the effect of reducing the caring individual's perception of the latter group to mere objects or social functions. Accordingly, says Segundo,

our inclination is to treat them in terms of the role or function they represent and perform. . . . Furthermore, even though this violence begins as an internal thing, the need to make this segregation and economy effective means that the underlying violence soon surfaces directly.[44]

The social mechanism that reifies the existence of others as roles or functions is *law*; "Law constitutes the most generic expression of these functional, impersonal relationships with other human individuals."[45] And the existence of credible laws requires society to possess and threaten the use of "physical violence" to exact citizen compliance with established public policy. Since all societies employ structural violence to maintain the efficacy of law, the problem now becomes one of ascertaining the degree to which love "guides" the use of violence.

At this point, Segundo has only made the argument, albeit an important and crucial argument, that love and violence are complementary, not contrary, for both the individual and society. Yet if everything can be characterized as having a violent component, why talk of violence at all? How can we distinguish between the guilty and the innocent in terms of violence? How can the use of violence itself be restricted? Can some individuals and societies be preferred morally to others without consideration of how prevalent violence is in a society? How, then, does liberation theology provide the religious individual with the ability to discern moral, social distinctions?

Segundo points out that the real antithesis to *love* as "love-of-others" is "self-love" or *egotism*, which involves inappropriate prejudices and other morally unacceptable attitudes. As with love, egotism is also subject to the economy of energy. It, too, has limits, such that where egotism is not found violence exists. And, as with love, egotism can influence the use of violence.[46] He argues that this understanding now leaves the religious individual in a better position to assess the moral dimension of politics. For example, a society that enforces its laws through love is to be preferred to one that does so through egotism, although both societies use violence. And for liberation theologians a critical analysis of Latin American political economies quickly confirms the degree to which the violence of egotism dominates social policies, policies that contribute to the maintenance of poverty and political oppression.

Part of the moral problem of justifying the use of violence involves ascertaining who should be the proper recipients of the violent act. Presuming that there is a just cause for the use of violence, as in the case of the gunman scenario; that an economy of energy is at work with regard to love and violence; and that egotism is the source of unjust societies, toward whom should violence be directed? Presumably, any just return of violence should be aimed at the unjust perpetrator of violence in the first place. Not so obvious in Latin America, however, is the source of violent injustice. In fact, it is not even clear that the intent of the question—to identify the perpetrator—is more properly focused on "who" rather than "what" is responsible for poverty and oppression. In other words, should individuals be blamed more than institutions or ideas for the origins and maintenance of social injustice? The answer to this problem of moral responsibility has enormous implications, for depending on how much emphasis is placed on one "cause" over another, political ethics will be directly related. Again, for liberation theologians, notice that the hermeneutic circle is in full operation. As discussed in chapter 1, the official documents of the CELAM meeting held in Medellín encouraged Latin American religious observers and others, to focus attention on the violence endemic in particular social institutions and economic arrangements. The bishops argued that the maintenance of "peace and order" in society by authoritarian regimes without the prerequisite correspondence of justice, remains violent.[47] The emergence of "institutionalized violence" and the rejection by the ruling elites of social reform proposals occurs, they realized, when

> the privileged many times join together, and with all the means at their disposal pressure those who govern, thus obstructing necessary changes. In some instances, this pressure takes on drastic proportions which result in the destruction of life and property.[48]

And as can be seen from the last two chapters, furthermore, the use of Marxist social analysis in its application to the social structures of institutionalized violence reveals for many liberation theologians the dynamics of social forces that limit and constrain the will of the individual. The use of various theoretical frameworks, such as that of dependency theory, also reveals to them the essence of violence inherent in the relationships among and within contemporary social institutions. The nature of these relationships—generally a domestic continuation of the oppressive relationships between industrialized countries and Third World countries—is the key to understanding the source of human suffering and thus to devising various strategies for its elimination. Consequently, this understanding requires concerned individuals to focus on the structural arrangements of economic and political institutions to find the source of misery and suffering. The perception of violence as originating with institutional arrangements, then, takes on primary importance in liberation theology. In fact, discussions on conditions of economic poverty and political oppression by radical thinkers often revolve around the problem of institutionalized violence, a violence that has become institutionalized because of its relationship to the logic of capitalist rationality and egotism, both of which guide the institutional arrangements of Western economic and political behavior. But this realization of the sources of injustice complicates attempts to induce social change.

149

Generally, it seems, successful behavior modification consists of two elements that must be taken into account and balanced in a way to effect social change: individual personalities and social structures. Current economic arrangements and practices of production and distribution heavily influence members of society to behave in ways that individual good intentions to end poverty are insufficient. That is, in order to survive economically, most members must behave in a rationally maximizing fashion, competing with each other for scarce goods and services. Consequently, there is little if any incentive for members to behave altruistically. Recognizing the importance of both of these elements—personality and structure—liberation theologians, unlike traditional Christians, criticize religious activities and teachings that are limited solely to the moral conversion of personalities. While they recognize that appeals to personal conscience are a necessary aspect of Christian evangelization, they find them insufficient. Míguez Bonino refers to this one-sided approach as "idealistic-Christian-bourgeois social ethics."[49] While they profess a genuine expression of concern for justice and the proper treatment of the weak in society, even "a call to a stern morality," mainstream Christians generally stop short of dealing with the origins of broader socioeconomic questions; they lack any additional critical evaluation of existing social structures and thus avoid active attempts to change those structures to improve social relationships.

Liberation theologians, then, describe social injustice as a problem of morally unacceptable social relationships, not merely attitudes. Furthermore, they maintain that these social relationships result not only from egotistic personalities, but primarily from behavior that members of society rationally adopt to survive and, perhaps, prosper economically in accordance with prevailing societal expectations. These prevailing expectations, of course, are defined by the established methods and arrangements of economic production and distribution, the formal institutions of politics, the interaction between economics and politics, the institutional support from other sectors of society, and the ideological arguments generally accepted and propagated throughout society by the status quo elites.[50] The overall nature of Latin American society, then, is perceived by liberation theologians as possessing a fatal flaw: the exercise of violence that has an egotistic, systemic, and rational basis for its existence.

The nature of violence endemic in Latin American social relationships and the lack of rule of law in many social settings have meant that unjust social conditions have often been impervious to reformist challenges. The bishops at Medellín argued that an integral relationship exists between the institutionalized violence of the oppressors, and a response of violence from the oppressed that most certainly will be forthcoming barring any structural changes. And this latter violence, of course, carries with it its own set of moral problems.[51] Often, attempts to challenge institutionalized violence through peaceful and legal reform have had an augmentative effect on the social dynamics of violence itself. Frequently referred to as "the spiral of violence,"[52] this phenomenon has been a standard occurrence in many Latin American countries, such as Brazil (1968–71), Chile (1973), Argentina (1976–77), and Nicaragua (especially 1978–79).

Influenced by this understanding of the spiraling dynamics of violence, the late Archbishop and the current Archbishop of San Salvador, Oscar Arnulfo Romero and Arturo Rivera y Damas, respectively, explained their assessment of the situation in El Salvador, a country plagued with poverty, political oppression, and lack of rule of law.[53] They argued that the social pathology of violence comprises several stages in its spiraling effect. The deprivation of the basic necessities of life to a majority of the population occurs as a result of the egotistic monopoly of economic power held by a small privileged class. This condition of institutionalized violence encourages various social movements and institutions, religious and otherwise, to attempt to organize the poor and to protect their human rights. This activity is perceived by the elites of society, however, as a threat to their own economic and political power; and it is this perceived threat that triggers an even more vicious form of violence. According to Romero and Rivera y Damas,

> Alongside institutionalized violence there frequently arises repressive violence, that is to say the use of violence by the state's security forces to the extent that the state tries to contain the aspirations of the majority, violently crushing any signs of protest against the injustices we have mentioned.[54]

Furthermore, there exist no limits to the use of "repressive violence" against reformers—including religious individuals and groups—attempting to ameliorate the effects of the institutionalized violence. The number of victims, including Romero and other clergy, has been well documented in the continuing condition of repressive violence in El Salvador, as well as in other Latin American countries.[55] According to the Latin American specialist Brian H. Smith,

A major reason for their being attacked, claim the bishops, is their demand that society meet the basic needs of their people in a more just fashion—employment, housing, education, and health care.[56]

Typically, the government justifies its use of violence by invoking national security concerns. Guided by the ideology of the national security state, it perceives the presence of foreign-influenced internal subversions as a greater threat to social stability and national existence than the random violation of human rights by government security forces.

Continuing with the spiraling effect, the escalation from institutionalized violence to repressive violence creates an atmosphere wherein self-defensive "spontaneous violence" erupts. Romero and Rivera y Damas defined the nature of this violence.

We call violence spontaneous when it is an immediate, not a calculated or organized, reaction by groups or individuals when they are violently attacked in the exercise of their own legitimate rights in protests, demonstrations, just strikes and so on. . . . [Spontaneous violence occurs when] a group or an individual repels by force the unjust aggressions to which they have been subjected.[57]

But as increasingly ferocious counterviolence to spontaneous violence emerges from the government, social stability deteriorates even further, often yielding to "revolutionary violence" and even terrorism. In this way, according to Romero and Rivera y Damas, the spiral of violence accelerates as each side attempts to use greater force to overcome the force of its opponent.

The Limits of Violence

As a result of critical theoretical analyses of social injustice, liberation theologians recognize the reality of oppressive structural violence, the violence that serves egotism, and the potential for the spiral of violence to be set in motion. Where does this leave the religious individual who is morally committed to the liberation of his fellow citizens? Traditionally, Christianity has exhorted all individuals to love their enemies as well as their neighbors. However, according to liberation theologians, this exhortation has had the effect of precluding any discriminatory discernment of political actors and institutions as to who or what is responsible for social injustice and thus who or what would be deserving of further corrective attention.

Gutiérrez warns that any notion of love remains "an abstraction unless it becomes concrete history, process, conflict."[58] Love becomes concretized in liberation theology by opting for the oppressed—the commitment to human liberation—and by seeking as well, to liberate the oppressors from their own mistaken path; that is, "by combatting the oppressive class." According to Gutiérrez,

> In the context of class struggle today, to love one's enemies presupposes recognizing and accepting that one has class enemies and that it is necessary to combat them.

To love one's enemies, then, is to combat them, to liberate them from their own oppressive behavior that not only affects adversely the physical lives of others, but their own spiritual salvation as well.

In moral philosophy the problem of violence is typically a problem of justification in the first place, and then a problem of its limits once justification is established. In liberation theology the two problems may be synonymous. For following the logic of Segundo's analysis wherein violence is a necessary aspect of love and Gutiérrez's exhortation to demonstrate love for one's enemies by combatting against them, the problem of violence now becomes a problem of historical circumstances; that is, according to Segundo, "the problem of violence, within a given civilization, consists precisely in the introduction of it."[59] Furthermore, the very nature of liberation theology's methodology has "ruled out any possibility of a gospel-inspired ethics or morality deciding in advance whether some line of action is consistent with divine revelation or not."[60] The hermeneutic circle reveals that the Scriptures contain no absolute injunction against violence; on the contrary, it may be justified depending on the historical context. For example, the Scriptures exhibit the violent aspect of love in Jesus' use of a whip to drive the merchants from the temple (John 2:13–15) and in the parable of the wealthy Samaritan who presumably denied his loving care to a number of needy individuals before finally choosing one to assist (Luke:29–37).[61]

Other liberation theologians have come to similar conclusions in their exegeses of biblical Scripture. For example, Míguez Bonino finds that violence does not appear in the Scriptures "as a general form of human conduct which has to be accepted or rejected as such.... Thus, the law forbids certain forms of violence to persons and things and authorizes and even commands others."[62] And Ignacio Ellacuría has also discovered that "[God's violence] possesses not only the element of moral denunciation but also the elements of chastisement, punishment, and the rehabilitation of an order that has been out of kilter by the abuses of the unjust people in power."[63]

In traditional moral philosophy, violence itself is never considered a moral good; only an unjust situation may require violence as a necessity to remedy the situation in the name of a greater justice. For liberation theologians, the conditions of social injustice in Latin America often require violent remedies. Míguez Bonino has even concluded that class struggle is inevitable. In fact, under conditions of poverty and oppression, he maintains that God requires man to create a new society. Hence, through class struggle, the oppressed must gain the power to reshape economic and social institutions along different and morally appropriate lines. Unfortunately, history has shown that those with positions of power rarely yield their positions voluntarily; generally, then, the use of violence will be necessary to attain "a new and more just situation."[64] Segundo cautions, however, that the amount of violence must be limited to achieving the just goal of the revolution. He stipulates that

> [one should] use the least amount of violence compatible with truly effective love. The proper proportion, then, must be figured out in the context of each different historical situation.[65]

Liberation theologians have easily merged the necessity for class struggle with their assessments of Latin American political economies as a result of their use of Marxist social analysis. Overall, it is this encounter with Marxism, Comblin argues, that has led theologians to redefine Christianity in light of the call to revolution.[66] With the incorporation of Marxist social science into their theologies, oppressive social structures have been identified, critically analyzed, and morally assessed as "sinful." And given this recognition of the source of sin in the modern world, exhorts Ellacuría, "Christian love must be framed as a struggle to eliminate sin from the world."[67]

For Assmann, the economic institutions in Latin America can only be changed through revolution. To be effective, Christians must be open in stating their revolutionary objectives and they must be engaged in developing revolutionary theory. But more importantly, they must involve themselves with other revolutionary groups so as to influence the direction of the revolution given their position as "the true theorists of the aims and methods of the process of liberation."[68] Assmann maintains that "Christians will more easily become authentic revolutionaries the more they identify their way of life with that of the exploited."[69]

But with regard to the creation, formation, and coordination of revolutionary movements, liberation theologians lack consensus on the leadership role for radical Christians. Segundo recognizes that differences in intellectual capabilities and spiritual perceptiveness exist. As a result of different experiences with social injustice and incomplete assessments of socioeconomic conditions, a certain few individuals will be in a stronger position than the rest to offer critical insights for decision-making purposes; consequently, there will always be the dichotomy between "the minorities and the masses—the former to lead the latter."[70] Both Segundo and Assmann agree that Christians should form the vanguard of the revolution. However, in a less elitist approach toward revolutionary leadership, Míguez Bonino argues that, in the struggle for social justice in Latin America, "there is no divine war, there is no specifically *Christian* struggle."[71] In their identification with the oppressed, he says, radical Christians will participate in class struggles; however, they have nothing unique to contribute to the revolution.

Conclusion

Of course, not all Latin American clergy and exegetes accept the liberation theologians' typical assessments of the use of violence as depicted in Scripture.[72] Many point out the normative biblical injunction against violence toward the state: "For all who take the sword will perish by the sword" (Matthew 26:52). Should this passage be understood as a universal prescription or moral certitude with regard to political ethics? Throughout the history of Christian theology, interpretative claims regarding the moral implications of such passages have long been debated, at least since Augustine.[73] Yet can disputes over the normative dimension of biblical passages be definitively settled by exegesis alone? In this passage, for example, Jesus indeed rebukes Peter with the warning about the life of the sword for having cut off the ear of the High Priest's servant. But this particular admonition is found only in the Gospel account of Matthew; the other three Gospel writers are silent. Furthermore, in Luke (22:35–38) Jesus himself actually orders that swords be purchased shortly before the violent confrontation at Gethsemane. And in all four Gospel accounts, the apostles are brandishing swords until the end of Jesus' life (Matthew 26:47–56; Mark 14:43–47; Luke 22:47–51; John 18:10–11). Furthermore, John the Baptist, an ally of Jesus, permitted his disciples to serve in the military (Luke 3:14). Thus, one could make the argument—and indeed the violent phases of the history of Christianity bear this out—that the decision to carry and use weapons is at least a personal matter, not subject to conformity with an idealized, transcendent, and universal principle, but based on the concrete exigencies of the historical context.

In liberation theology, then, the lack of propositional truth rules out the possibility of transcendentally originating limits on the use of violence; the historical context sets the limits. That is, the legitimacy of violence seems to set its own limit in any circumstance depending on the objective sought. But even so, liberation theologians may well only be participating in the great spiral of violence with no possibility of escape; they may actually be intensifying the ferocity of violence and not contributing to its demise. The assumption implicit in liberation theology is that violence employed for a just cause will incur fewer costs than acquiescence in the face of social injustice, and, furthermore, that the religious individual's violent participation in the struggle to overcome social injustice will make a difference—a difference for the better. Yet can there be any certainty in this assumption? The bishops of Medellín recognized that "revolutionary insurrection can be legitimate" under certain circumstances while simultaneously warning that " 'armed revolution' generally 'generates new injustices, introduces new imbalances and causes new disasters.' "[74]

Sensitive to this dilemma where liberation theologians have committed themselves to human liberation and peace while recognizing the presence and necessity of violence, Míguez Bonino suggests a utilitarian meta-consideration. He advises the politically motivated, religious individual to calculate the probability of the amount of human costs involved should revolutionary action be taken, and next to compare this to the probability of the amount of human costs involved should revolutionary action not be taken. The individual, of course, should then pursue the option that contributes to the lesser amount of violence.[75] Yet Míguez Bonino's approach would engage the calculator in an infinite regress of calculations and thus preclude the radical Christian from ever engaging in revolutionary action. Perhaps only the existential plunge itself into the irrationality of violence remains alone, as the religious individual simply commits himself to Segundo's stability of faith and forges ahead.

But regardless of the limited if unsatisfactory response to these issues, revolutions have occurred in Latin America with the participation of radical Christians. And particularly instructive in this regard, again, is the case of Nicaragua. In the revolution of 1979, liberation theology played a highly significant role. Radical clergy had earlier organized a version of CEBs, known as "Delegates of the Word," around clandestine activities, that would later assist the revolutionary effort.[76] In fact, many of the leaders of the Sandinista National Liberation Front (*Frente Sandinista de Liberación Nacional*, FSLN) and subsequently of the Governing Junta of National Reconstruction (*Junta de Gobierno de Reconstrucción Nacional*, JGRN), including members of the FSLN Joint National Directorate (*Directorio Nacional Conjunto*, DN), had their beginnings in the CEBs, having been "conscientized" morally with regard to problems of social injustice during the previous regime of Anastasio Somoza.[77]

Many Christian clergy, in turn, identified their moral commitment to liberation with the armed struggle led by the FSLN.[78] The biography of Ernesto Cardenal, a Nicaraguan Catholic priest, exemplifies the intellectual journey of an individual driven by a desire to see spiritual values respected in a world of social conflict. At some point in his life, Cardenal faced the inescapable realization that a political dimension exists of all spiritual values as well as in all social conflict, and that he must incorporate a sophisticated political awareness to achieve his goal of spiritual, social harmony.[79] To this end, he felt compelled to embrace social theorizing and to develop his own theology of liberation. Cardenal not only identified his theological methodology and moral commitment with that of liberation theology, but he finally came to identify his political theory and struggle with that of the Sandinistas. After the revolution, he described how the Sandinistas were praised by religious believers as liberators sent to bring peace to a violence-torn nation. Today, Cardenal argues that the struggle for freedom from despotism, was born out of love; "Revolution . . . is a synonym for love."[80] Futhermore,

In Nicaragua, in the rebellious states and cities, we experienced how an entire people can put the Gospel into practice, sacrificing their lives for the lives of others. . . . For us Christians, participation in this revolution has meant faith in Jesus Christ.[81]

157

Many Christian clergymen and CEBs continue to support revolutionary change in Nicaragua. And some ordained priests even serve in prominent positions in the Sandinista govenment.[82]

Yet while the revolution was indeed popularly supported and successfully prosecuted, the cost included 50,000 lives out of a population of approximately 2.5 million inhabitants. Had the cost of achieving victory been known ahead of time, would the attempt to overthrow the government have been popularly supported? During the revolution one Sandinista in a moment of doubt reflected upon recent revolutionary failures in other Latin American countries and the thousands of deaths that would be necessary to defeat the Somoza regime. He regained courage to pursue the struggle only after looking to his comrades-in-arms for support. As he recalled, "You are saved by the fact that the FSLN inculcated in us a historical will, an infinite, boundless stubbornness."[83] And to die fighting the regime was to die with absolute honor, "Because, as the Christians say, we denied our very selves."[84] The act of self-denial may well be the only rational response to the problem of violence.

Thus far, the elements necessary for liberaton theology to develop its political theory have been analyzed, including its peculiar methodology for theorizing as well as its relationship with Marxism, its assessments of Latin American political economies, and its political ethics of reform and revolution. Now, in an essay on values and social theory, the philosophical significance of the political theory of liberation theology will be evaluated as to the success of its attempt at a reconvergence of social values and social science.

Chapter 6

Ethics and Social Theory

Introduction

The Problem of Modernity

As discussed in chapter 1, the modern era has awkwardly maintained a peculiar tension in an attempt to avoid problems of social instability. Historically, the rise of individualism and the limited state in the advanced industrial societies and their progeny, such as in Latin America, has resulted in a significant shift away from the paternalistic, social ethics of the classical and medieval eras. This earlier communal bond was based on a specific and commonly held religious worldview that defined civic virtue and individual moral virtue as one. But as a result of a complex series of events, including the impact of the Scientific Revolution and the Protestant Reformation, the intricate cosmology of the classical and medieval eras was dissolved and eventually replaced with an alternative understanding of the mechanics and dynamics of nature and human associations.[1]

This new understanding was also compatible with the emergence of the individualistic ethics and secular social order of classical liberalism. Consequently, the early liberal state attempted to remove itself from the debate on social morality and virtue and to relegate itself to the role of improving the conditions for the development of market society. Social stability itself was to be precariously maintained with the enforcement of a "social contract" premised upon recognition of individual rights and obligations.

The moral inhibitions placed on natural and social scientific investigation characteristic of the earlier eras were also removed as Western civilization moved into the Enlightenment. This removal of constraints stimulated wide-ranging investigations of nature, often regardless of moral concerns. And with the application of new scientific insights to solve technological and economic problems, the Industrial Revolution surged forth to test and promote the new social agreement and relationships of the modern era.

But along with material growth, rapid industrialization also brought a host of new "social evils." And with these evils, from dangerous working conditions to poor living conditions for the growing working class, socially concerned, interest groups increasingly put pressure on government to modify its attitude of simply maintaining order among society's disparate parts, by including a positive role in regulating the relationship among those disparate parts. During the past century, then, as the limits to growth have approached, the liberal state has been forced to reconsider its restricted moral role, especially in terms of redistributive policies. It has now been transformed into varying hues of the paternalistic, welfare state with a mandate to remove selected, social obstacles that impede individual freedom of choice while protecting the economic base of capitalism. It has encouraged members of society to develop a civic virtue while simultaneously pursuing their self-interests. But with increased frequency modernity's emphasis on individualism has been sidetracked by the ascension to political power of influential interests or factions that use the state to their own benefit. A crisis then appears over the struggle for power and the meaning of legitimate claims to the use of that power. And with increasing socioeconomic problems, modernity has been challenged by a broad array of social criticisms.

Modernity (both Enlightenment and post-Enlightenment eras), then, has arrived at a confusing, if not crisis, state with regard to theories of political, social, and individual ethics.[2] Consequently, the defense of the relationships of the new order has encouraged a variety of thinkers, from Immanuel Kant to John Rawls, to find political theoretical justifications for a more secure foundation. In the contemporary attempt to resolve disputes over meanings of legitimacy, several disparate theories have been set forth dealing with the proper ends of the state, the ethics of public policies, and the morality of various forms of political action.[3] Today this current state of mass

Ethics and Social Theory

proliferation of ideas is often perceived as itself a state of conflict with regard to social theory and a state of anarchy with regard to moral philosophy.

Although the impact of industrialization in the Third World has often been significantly different and in many regions the religious culture has remained far more homogeneous and pervasive than in the First World, the primary political and moral effects of the dynamics of Western industrialization have also been felt. In particular in Latin America, the influence of the *fact-value dichotomy* of the modern era is ever present, as are the conflicts it has generated in moral and political philosophy. Liberation theology, as one radical or "neo–orthodox" approach to doing political theology, attempts to grapple with the concrete manifestations of conflicts over the proliferation of social theories and the anarchy of moral values. To this end, liberation theologians have produced their own political theory that may provide alternative assessments of, and novel solutions to, ethical and social problems of Latin America as well as those of contemporary Western society. Liberation theologians claim that they have successfully merged together traditional, religious values with analytical, social science. They argue that this merger restores a critical dimension to contemporary social issues with regard to economic and political policy making. And, as a result, they maintain that they are in a much better position to bring about the social liberation of their fellow citizens.

In order to comply with their moral commitment to liberate their fellow citizens from poverty and oppression, liberation theologians require a peculiar methodology for critical thinking and action. This methodology, as represented by the *hermeneutic circle,* allows them to subject continually their analytical descriptions and moral assessments of prevailing religious and political activities and arguments to critical evaluation. This avoidance of preestablished absolute assumptions concerning moral dictates on belief and behavior allows them to enlist the assistance of "secular" social analyses and to engage in radical politics. Liberation theologians, then, have generally found it expedient to adopt Marxist social analysis as the most appropriate framework for understanding the origins and dynamics of social injustice in Latin America. And, as we have seen, many have found moral justification for their participation in various reformist and radical political activities, including revolutionary violence.

But it is in specific reference to questions concerning its methodology and the incorporation of Marxism that liberation theology may

161

or may not sustain itself as an important contribution to political theory. For it is precisely at the point of tangency between methodology and Marxism that liberation theology claims to reconverge social values and social science. Of what significance are the claims of liberation theology? Has it adequately achieved its goal? If so, what novel insights does it offer? If not, what else is necessary? A look at the *liberation* project of liberation theology will now set the context for discussion of the merits of the *political theoretical* aspect of liberation theology's purported contribution to political ethics and social theory.

Avoiding the Monolith of the Rational State

Historically, projects of social liberation have often attempted to accomplish certain radical or revolutionary goals. But what makes a project revolutionary? It may be revolutionary in the two respects that political theorist Hannah Arendt, for one, has pointed out are inherent in any revolution.[4] First, the project attempts to restore what has been lost or taken away; this is the first stage of revolution: to look to the past. In this case liberation theologians have much in common with traditional conservatives: both want to restore the tension between the individual and the community of an earlier era and both want to restore ethical primacy to the community to promote the proper end of human existence, whether it is virtue and happiness, or human creativity and freedom. However, they part company with the conservatives inasmuch as they also want to restore individual liberty as conceived by classical liberals but denied under capitalist economics; conservatives sense a certain hubris in such talk of liberty.

Secondly, says Arendt, the project of revolution focuses on formal structures. In this stage of revolution, new—looking to the future, not to the past—social, political, and economic structures must be built around the ethical values of respect for social equality and human dignity, the demand for democratic participation in decision making at all levels where appropriate and feasible, and the maintenance of individual liberty, including provision for basic material needs. Liberation theologians argue that these are crucial aspects of any liberation project.

In this sense, then, the project of liberation attempts to restore the sense of community of classical and medieval eras while maintaining the scientific, technological, and economic advances achieved in the modern era. In this regard, liberation theologians propose no less than the construction of a new, and third, form of the state based on a new tension to hold the disparate parts of society together; a tension similar to, yet significantly different from, the tensions of both feudal societies and liberal states.[5]

Yet one wonders if the project itself—however noble and sincere— is too late in its recommendation of a solution to the problem of human alienation, social oppression, and environmental degradation. Of late, concern has been expressed over the current developmental tendencies of technology and its impact on society. Many social theorists argue that the human condition is not simply one of lack of freedom for the many as a result of the aggrandizement of power by the few, but lack of freedom for all as a result of a "new master" that has taken control over all aspects of social, political, and economic processes and institutions: technological rationality.[6]

As alluded to earlier, the liberation of mathematics from the moral domination of theological criticism and its subsequent unification with science in the liberal state, unleashed a particular logic of efficiency that has attempted to coordinate human activities along increasingly complex, rational lines.[7] The growth and development of scientific theories became more difficult to falsify. As scientific hypotheses became more acceptable, significant impact was felt in two key areas: the metaphysical structure of cosmologies and the material foundations of existence. With regard to the first, the relationship of religious values and ethics eventually became severed from the scientific enterprise; and with regard to the second, initial solutions to problems of economic necessity were in reach as scientific theories were applied to technological innovations.[8] Thus, developments in mathematics and science and their role in education, society, and economics, became a wedge whereby the critical dimension—that is, the importance of normative questions—of science was severed from the purely hypothetical, or at least material, aspect of science.[9] This separation has had far-reaching consequences for Western societies.

A dialectic has developed between abstract science and liberalism as the two challenged the conservative state of traditionalism. With its near-monopoly on ethical values, the conservative state had historically set the context for scientific investigations as well as for maintaining the social tension between individual and community.[10] But the success of this dialectic provided for the emergence of nascent capitalism and bourgeois revolutions. These in turn restructured the political community by founding it upon a new tension between individuals. This new foundation permitted the unlimited use of

163

scientific investigations and ultimately the use of scientific rationality as tools of powerful interests in society. Yet the tools themselves, in defining what was possible, metamorphosed into guides to what was rationally expedient given their own internal logical consistency; and in the absence of normative critiques, they became masterless guides of their own definition and construction of the future. Consequently, what are the possibilities for normative philosophy today to challenge the seemingly inevitable monolith of the rational state? Some social theorists, such as Herbert Marcuse, have argued that resistance to this one-dimensionality may be preventable, and that the Third World may be the key.[11]

In several cultures, such as in Latin America, Asia, and Africa, the remnants of religious traditions have survived despite several centuries of liberal colonialism and capitalist imperialism. The limited but culturally important role of religious institutions has encouraged the development of religious teachings, practices, and rituals that have retained legitimacy throughout society. In particular, theological development has remained a socially acceptable activity despite the importation of liberal cultural values. Furthermore, it is the promise of recent theological developments that often utilize modern social theoretical insights alongside traditional religious values that has raised renewed hope for confrontation with, and transformation of, modern industrialization and technology. In particular, the development of "theologies of liberation" as critical theories of resistance and revolt has instilled in many concerned individuals the real possibility for social change, especially if religious institutions can occupy the position of revolutionary vanguard in reinvigorating the radical project of liberation. And the ultimate fulfillment of the promise will be the reversal of the dialectic of exploitation of Third World countries by unraveling the logic of technological rationality and capitalist dynamics, thereby eventually forcing the industrialized nations to restructure themselves along humanistic and democratic lines.

The discussions in this book have explicated and evaluated the attempt made by liberation theology to reconcile *faith* and *politics* in a way that will achieve revolutionary ends. As we have seen, thinkers in this movement provide an intellectual framework that they claim allows as well as demands the merging of the traditional Christian commitment to values of human dignity and rights (faith) with contemporary social scientific analysis (politics); and with this synthesis, theologians of liberation justify a broad range of political activities. What are we to conclude, then, on the legitimate possibilities of this new, philosophical movement with regard to its claim of possessing a viable social theory of politics and political ethics? Does it in fact present an adequate and sustainable critical alternative to the unbridled, egoism or egotistic rationality that guides modern scientific, technological, and economic development?[13]

Two problems suggest themselves. The first problem involves the possibility of a reconciliation between two traditionally separate theoretical approaches to explaining the human condition. That is, what can be done, if anything, to unite legitimately the use of Marxist social analysis with Christian theological considerations? And, how will such unification satisfy the quest for the reconvergence of social values and social science? The second problem involves the actual practice associated with overcoming the "oppressive present" and the hope for an "improved future." That is, given human nature, what can be realistically expected of reformist and revolutionary attempts at social change? How are we to understand the relationship between human nature and politics? The latter problem will be dealt with first to provide closer scrutiny of the ultimate problem of theory accommodation, social values, and social science.

Human Nature and Politics

A close relationship exists between theories of human nature and theories of political regimes. In the modern era, political theorists have attempted to answer the essential question of what kind of political regime is legitimate by beginning with an analysis of human nature. Whether man is basically competitive, egotistic, and depraved, or cooperative, altruistic, and innocent, the justification for a particular regime would be adjusted or argued accordingly.[12] In fact, debates over theories of human depravity and human innocence have raged perennially among students of theology as well as politics. Hence, many philosophical criticisms have been directed at liberation theology based on arguments concerning human nature.

The theologian J. Andrew Kirk, for example, is skeptical of revolutionary movements, including liberation theology, and their messianic claims concerning the establishment of the perfect, just society on earth. He suggests that "revolutions have failed because they have accepted the theory of human innocence."[13] Of course, this a priori

165

acceptance of the depravity of human nature precludes him from accepting, without reservation, the attempts of revolutionary elites to construct the just society. But more importantly, Kirk's position is exemplary of larger questions concerning the nature of politics itself. For as long as theories of human nature set the conditions for determining which form of political regime is superior, studies of politics will have only secondary relevance. That is, acceptance of Kirk's or any other position advocating theological ascendancy over politics proscribes from the start any serious consideration of the merits of liberation theology.

Conversely, whether an observer accepts the depravity or innocence of man may matter little in explaining the attempts and results of a variety of political movements and policies. That is, the failure of revolutions may have nothing to do with the revolutionary theoretician's acceptance of the theory of human innocence. And if this is the case, arguments and criticisms based on human nature would have no bearing on predicting the success or failure of revolutionary politics supported by liberation theology. Such an understanding, then, of the significance of either the theory of human innocence or the theory of human depravity suggests that attention should be paid less to assessments of human nature and more to the nature of politics itself.

Furthermore, the study of politics reveals that individuals act and behave in a way responsive to the actions and behavior of others. Institutional arrangements and policies have an impact on individuals in a way that forces or entices them to behave in ways other than they had planned. Generally, three methods are available for governments to achieve their objectives: Citizens can be *forced* through superior authority to do something; they can be offered goods and services in *exchange* for a particular behavior; and they can be *persuaded* to change their behavior voluntarily.[14] Any one or a combination of these approaches may result in beneficial or devastating social consequences, regardless of their implementation by bourgeois or revolutionary officials.

In fact, whether the intentions of public officials are basically "good" or "evil" is of less significance than the fact that not all citizens agree with every policy decision. Furthermore, that human nature is one of innocence or depravity is of less importance than the lack of universal agreement of what innocence and depravity consist. Indeed, it may be the case that human nature is one of depravity; nevertheless, a lack of consensus continues to elude any aggregation of individual assessments, thereby providing the condition for politics. And the same holds for human nature as one of innocence. This lack of consensus and agreement is itself, then, the essence of politics. Consequently, it is an understanding of the *dynamics* of politics—not human nature—on which judgments concerning the viability of a particular political theory ought to be based. Thus, any assessment of human nature ought not to play a crucial role in judging revolutionary claims and evaluating messianic movements. The lack of consensus on moral imperatives is itself the breeding ground of politics and it is politics itself that finds constancy in history and the world. And it is politics that one must take seriously immediately; theories of human nature will follow.

With the demotion of the importance of developing a theory of human nature as a standard to judge the worthiness of political claims, politics can now be extolled as amoral, if not good in itself for itself.[15] From this perspective, then, the competition over ideas and the struggle for power are simply factors of human existence. Revolutionary claims and status quo policies must be evaluated on their own merits, without reference to theories of human nature; for to do otherwise is to misunderstand the nature of politics altogether.

It is for this reason that the traditional primacy of scriptural exegesis has been downgraded to the level of secondary concern in liberation theology. Of course, many biblical exegetes continue to dispute the understanding (*aktuelles Verstehen*) that liberation theologians apply to their account of scriptural stories;[16] similarly many theologians disagree on the meaning and significance of the liberation theologians' interpretations (*erklärendes Verstehen*) of the scriptural accounts of the prophets.[17] But the crucial significance for normative political philosophy, and by implication for social scientific methodology, is the extent to which liberation theologians are able to adapt contemporary social theoretical perspectives—particularly Marxist perspectives—on economics, politics, and culture, including religion, while retaining the viability of theology's claim to transcend temporal concerns, thus maintaining the legitimacy of religion in itself and for itself.

Given the centrality of politics, then, what is the viability of liberation theology as political theory? While discussions in the foregoing chapters have evaluated aspects of liberation theology's political theory, conclusions concerning the ultimate problem of liberation theology have yet to be made. This final problem involves the enterprise of theory construction itself.

Theory Construction

Along with the effort to effect the liberation, socially as well as spiritually, of their fellow citizens, liberation theologians have had to deal with the intellectual struggles of political theory construction that accompany any attempt to provide rational and coherent justification for the social realization of subjective values. The apparently simple move from accepting certain moral values to a commitment to political action may be deceptive, for the move is fraught with serious questions concerning the relationship between ethics and social science. Liberation theology provides a particular theoretical framework that claims the ability to offer moral justification for its particular political goals as well as for the means to attain those goals. But is liberation theology merely a variation of other social gospel movements that consist of an amalgam of two traditional disciplines? Or is it in itself a novel combination revealing unique explanations to important questions? And what are the implications either way for political ethics? In a sense, this is the problem of reconciling theology of human existence with sociology of religion, of finding the common ground between transcendental discourse on meaning and social analytical explanation.

This problem has not gone unnoticed among religious thinkers. For example, the theologian Brian Hebblethwaite points out that "the divine-human encounter takes place through the media of institutions and beliefs which have a discoverable history and intelligible interrelations with each other and with the rest of the social environment."[18] Consequently, he says, an incorporation of the human or social sciences should free the development of theology from "unknown causal processes." Still, the practical problem of uniting religious concerns and social science in any political theology consists of the difficulty of reconciling the absoluteness and transcendence of faith with the relativity and subjectivity of politics. Furthermore, according to the theologian Charles Davis, political theology must be concerned not only with "the mediation of the transcendent through the political, but with the preservation of the political as an intrinsically human value."[19] So what is the connection, the relationship, the nexus between the inward and vertical *being of faith* and the outward and horizontal *process of politics?*[20] This concern appears to be that of praxis.

Ethics and Social Theory

With regard to praxis, the religious individual must have some understanding of the context of his acts. Yet the parameters of this understanding are formed by a particular theoretical framework to give
it meaning. And this framework includes a particular understanding
of religion itself, which is different from that of the theology or
theory giving coherence to the values of religion. So, numerous problems may exist. But specifically with regard to social science and liberation theology, can radical theologians appropriate Marxist social
analysis and ignore Marxist sociology of religion? In fact, can one part
of any theory be retained while the rest is ignored and discarded
without doing harm to the essence of that which was appropriated?
If such a move is not legitimate, would any attempt to do so be assessed as a case of "theoretical imperialism"? Or is such a move in
fact legitimate, simply yielding a new theory in the process? And
could the latter be all that is really advocated by liberation theology?

Consider the result of theories being turned inside out and looking
back upon themselves, which appears to be the case here. The essence of one theory is simply the partial concern of the other; that
is, sociology explains the dynamics of religion in relation to other
facets of social life, and theology treats the importance of social relations among other facets of religious life. Assuming an objective reality, the appropriation by one theoretical perspective of an aspect of
another perspective simply yields a new perspective and a new essence. Destruction and reconstruction are *immanently* intertwined!

The realm of ideas can often be visualized as a universe filled with
Venn diagrams representing ideational structures that differ from
the intent of their neighbors while sharing common assumptions,
methods, or conclusions. The current plethora of social theories
evinces such a realm or universe. In this universe the overlap of
theories themselves often produces new theories that in turn merge
to generate more novel combinations. That theories about politics
differ is easy to see; that one theory is "more correct" than another
because of its place in time (abstractly) or space (applied) is less obvious objectively (and probably subjectively). The long history of
developments in Western political philosophy seems to indicate that
any contemporary claim to a pristine theory of society and politics
has long lost its innocence. At what point, then, is liberation theology's incorporation of radical social science legitimate? The criticism of liberation theology's use of Marxism highlights this problem.

169

Marxism

Liberation theologians want to involve themselves in liberating their oppressed fellow citizens. To do this they claim the need for incorporating social scientific analysis. But a number of questions arise in the attempt to merge theological assertions and speculations with social theoretical explanations: Primarily, will this process of modification or appropriation do harm to the essential character of either theology or social theory? Again, can an aspect of one worldview or framework be successfully incorporated into the framework of another without doing harm to the original intent of either, and thereby not lose the efficacy of both in the process?

A strong exception to liberation theology's methodology is Kirk's criticism of the use of Marxism by liberation theologians as a tool to liberate theology. He calls attention to Marxism's defense of values a priori to the process of liberation itself and maintains that indeed Marxism is more than an economic theory; it is a worldview that provides a philosophical defense of certain values, and these values provide the motive for revolutionary behavior that a mere explanatory theory of economics cannot do.[21] And in this same way, theology also maintains the existence of a priori values. So the problem, according to Kirk, is the obvious one of justifying the normative values of each worldview's claims and defending them against the claims of the other. Furthermore, theology has a superior claim to Marxism because of its acceptance of divine revelation, an acceptance discounted by Marxism and neglected by liberation theology; Kirk insists that liberation theologians would do well to reinvigorate their studies with fresh looks at biblical revelation.

Yet Kirk's criticism seems only partially accurate. Much serious exegetical work indeed needs to be done by liberation theologians to provide a deeper incorporation of the biblical heritage of revelation into their contemporarily focused theological enterprise. In fact, some liberation theologians, such as José Porfirio Miranda and Jon Sobrino, have produced studies of recognized erudition and scholarship on this very point.[22] Yet a more serious underlying assumption of Kirk's assessment is problematic: the implicit claim that theology and Marxism are competing for adherents. He implies that a "market place of ideas" exists where the careful "consumer" must compare philosophical systems before "buying" one or the other "product"; of course, that this has often been the case is a matter of historical record.[23] Liberation theologians argue, however, that this competition has itself resulted from a particular confusion in the philosophical development of both Christianity and Marxism, an errant development that pitted one against the other. In fact, as we have seen, they claim that the issue properly understood is not that of choosing one orthodox system over the other, but that of *orthopraxis*—of acting in a way that fulfills the individual's moral obligations. Whether political action is justified in terms of "historical materialism" or "biblical revelation" or both is of secondary importance, not primary, in liberation theology. Consequently, the concern posed by Kirk is irrelevant.

The theologian Robert T. Osborn poses a related question: Of the social problems theologians of liberation deal with, why should they be understood as theological problems in the first place?[24] Political theology can play an important role by addressing normative issues that transcend the ethical boundaries of the personal or privatized morality advocated by mainstream theology. Must the religious individual use theological categories and discourse to redefine a social problem as a theological problem? It would seem enough to address specific, personal moral crises as each is encountered in everyday life, without having to redefine broad social dynamics as to their moral merit. But on the other hand, even Davis maintains that theology need not always be thought of as "theoretical reflection upon permanent doctrines," but that its role as "the critical consciousness of Christian social practice" is acceptable as well.[25] Furthermore,

> For those not prepared to dismiss the changed outlook as simply a loss of faith, political theology may be seen as an attempt, with the use of the *Marxian* dialectic of theory and practice, to give systematic expression to the conviction that the identity and truth of the Christian faith can no longer be maintained by doctrinal assertion or theoretical interpretation, but only by the experience of that identity and truth as mediated in and through a social practice of liberation.[26]

Even though he also accepts Davis's attitude toward theology and Marxism, the European political theologian Jürgen Moltmann still questions whether Latin American liberation theology has anything specific to offer—that is, any novel insights from Latin America—that cannot be found in the political theologies of Europe and the North Atlantic community generally.[27] He claims that the same theological concerns and commitments can be found in other non-Latin American political theologies and that very little is learned about Latin America from Latin American liberation theology. But perhaps

Moltmann and others place too much emphasis on the abstract character of Latin American liberation theology and not enough on the *object* of the theology's abstraction: Latin America. Liberation theologians merely claim to utilize the theoretical tools and insights of others to comprehend, explain, and change a particular part of the world. The convergence of frameworks and insights from political theologies with Latin American social problems yields Latin American liberation theology. What this suggests, then, is that problems, social or otherwise, have no meaning apart from a theoretical perspective that interprets them in light of values that give meaning to existence. The "fact" of a social problem yields no meaning apart from a theoretical interpretation of the "fact." Liberation theology simply claims to offer one interpretation and thus "makes" social problems theological problems.

Liberation theologians are generally aware of these questions and deal with them in diverse ways. Unfortunately, they do not treat in systematic fashion the crucial moves necessary to link religiously motivated political ethics with Marxist social science. For, along with concern for human liberation, some *conceptual liberation* will be necessary if liberation theology's political theory is to make important contributions to deal with the moral shortcomings of society and the role of religion in dealing effectively with those shortcomings.

Critical Theory and Liberation Theology

To achieve its objectives of sorting out the moral ambiguities of social life and reestablishing society along lines more responsive to minimal requirements of respect for human dignity and rights, liberation theology is faced with at least two conceptual obstacles: the retention by the industrial state for its own purposes of the meaning, and hence existence, of religion, including religious symbols, beliefs, and institutions; and the narrow interpretation and use of class analysis that history has bestowed upon Marxist theoretical frameworks. Liberation theology must overcome these obstacles by conceptually liberating religion from the state and Marxism from history. Once this is done, religion has the potential of becoming a legitimate, viable, and effective agent of social change. And a freer adaptation of Marxist social analysis will permit liberation theology the ability to critique society and effect social change without undermining the radical potential of newly liberated religion. It appears, then, that some social theoretical claims are necessary for liberation theology to be critical and autonomous. Again, no comprehensive and systematic treatment of this problem in political and social theory is found in liberation theology.[28]

While Latin American liberation theology has emerged as an indigenous religious response to social injustice, it owes a great deal of its own methodological development to the antecedent emergence of European political theologies.[29] Several political theologians, concerned with the social and spiritual effects of modern industrialization, have borrowed many of the normative social analyses found in other areas of philosophy and social theory, particularly those from the Frankfurt School of *critical theory*. Influenced heavily by European writers, Latin American liberation theologians have also incorporated, usually indirectly, many of these same social theoretical insights into their own theological frameworks. In fact, according to the theologian Matthew L. Lamb, "this theological task [of political theology and liberation theology] goes to the very core of critical theory itself."[30] Yet Alfredo Fierro maintains that "the Latin American theology of liberation . . . is not filtered through the Frankfurt School of thinking, and is usually closer to orthodox Marxism."[31] To what extent, if at all, does critical theory have or could have a significant influence on the development of Latin American liberation theology? How can critical theory help solve the problem radical theologians face when attempting to incorporate Marxist social science while simultaneously retaining their religious faith?

Direct references by liberation theologians such as Hugo Assmann, Leonardo Boff, Gustavo Gutiérrez, Miranda, and Juan Luis Segundo, to those precursors of and thinkers frequently associated with the Frankfurt School, such as Antonio Gramsci, Erich Fromm, and Marcuse, are indeed sparse. Even so, these references can be broken down loosely into two basic categories: "political analysis" and "political ethics." The category of political analysis includes references to analytical concepts such as dialectical determinism, class structure and dynamics, and state hegemony, used in social theory construction. And the category of political ethics includes references to moral responses to social injustice such as demands for reform, revolution, and political leadership.

From the first category, for example, Miranda maintains that the concept of dialectical determinism for Marcuse need not be as narrowly construed as is done by orthodox Marxists and their conservative critics. He relies to a considerable degree on Marcuse as he develops his own discussion on dialectics and praxis within a theological framework.[32] Assmann also incorporates and develops at length Marcuse's critique of imperialism and technology as he analyzes the history and direction of Latin American socioeconomic development.[33] In his call for a new sociology of knowledge with regard to religious beliefs and practices, Segundo cites Fromm in support of his claim that individual values and behavior are imposed by society on citizens who blindly or unwittingly accept its dictates.[34] Furthermore, he quotes from Fromm's assessment of the political nature of the middle-class strata as support for his own claim that the middle class in Latin America is a potential source of revolutionary change.[35] With a similar concern, Boff refers to Gramsci's assessment of politics, noting the incomplete hegemony of the state as well as the role of the Church in providing legitimacy for the state.[36]

With regard to the second category of political ethics, for example, Gutiérrez frequently refers to Marcuse's "great refusal" as a morally legitimate response to the oppression of one-dimensional society.[37] Furthermore, he seizes upon the utopian vision of Marcuse as a motivating device to critique contemporary society and to urge action toward social reform or revolution. He also cites Gramsci in terms of justifying the radical theologian as the "organic intellectual" who exercises the prophetic function of denouncing social injustice.[38]

These representative references do not themselves prove the incorporation of critical theory as either a potential or a necessary epistemological element in the development of a Latin American theology of liberation. In fact, it is precisely at this point that the political theory of liberation theology encounters its weakest connection. However, a strong claim can be made, given liberation theology's insistence on the incorporation of Marxist social analysis, that its political theory *requires* some arguments from critical theory. Inasmuch as liberation theologians do not explicitly make this claim, the following section of this chapter attempts to construct the framework for an argument that seems to be implicit in their writings.[39] Again, this implicit framework is necessary to solve the primary problem in liberation theology's theory of politics: how to retain its tension between the religious commitment and the incorporation of Marxist social analysis.

From the various writings of liberation theologians, it appears that the analytical solution to its problem involves a four-stage process: (1) justification of the use of modern social science in general, (2) justification of the use of Marxist social science in particular, (3) conceptual liberation of Marxism from history, and (4) conceptual

liberation of religion from the state. Presumably, then, morally sensitive individuals will be able to find theological grounding for their use
of Marxist social analysis and their participation in political activities—reformist or revolutionary—without having to abandon their religious faith. Note that these stages are listed in the proposed order
of an analytically appropriate theory and not necessarily in the "real
world" order of emotional concern or haphazard development. In
fact, various theologians and religious activists often give more attention to the immediate concern of stopping violence in society than
engaging in formal, social theory construction. They find they must
first justify their presence in social conflict as religiously committed
individuals, whether clergy or laity, before elucidating the esoteric
realm of philosophical debate over subtle distinctions of classifications and categories. Of course, it is this immediate concern with social change that raises the question of the function of religion in the
first place.

Perhaps, then, it will be most appropriate to look at the analytical
four-stage development by first seeing where liberation theology
wants to go: the liberation of religion from the state. Hence, the
fourth stage will be pointed out first and then followed by a discussion of the first three stages to indicate the proper place of influence
for critical theory.

The Liberation of Religion from the State (Stage Four)

The sociological study of religion has repeatedly shown the close
relationship—often mechanical relationship—between religious ideas
and religious institutions as well as between religion and the rest of
society.[40] Typically, the institutionalization of religious beliefs has the
benefit of providing the conditions for the perpetuity of those ideas,
both as a pedagogical tool for current believers, and as a repository
for future generations. Quite often, however, religious institutions, as
with most bureaucracies, take on an existence independent of the validity or usefulness of the original ideas that gave them their birth.
To the extent that they are incapable of influencing completely the
surrounding community and as ideas and values of the surrounding
culture themselves evolve, religious institutions may find it necessary
to change their beliefs to maintain currency and legitimacy with the
community of believers and before secular authorities.[41] And as the
ideas and values about the world change and exercise greater importance in the lives of members of society, religious institutions and
ideas play a greater role in providing moral justification for the

changes in economic activity (both modes of production and patterns of distribution), politics (who rules), scientific discovery (human inquiry), and technology (application of new scientific discoveries). In the modern era, as the shift in the explanations if not origins of values away from religion to other sources becomes more complete, and as the state exercises more control over personal and social life, religious institutions and ideas generally metamorphose into, or become captured by and incorporated into, the ideological defense of the state.[42]

The rationalization of all apparently diverse aspects of the state—including religion—into one harmonious whole is the logical end of all social systems. This objective of extended longevity and, ultimately, immortality that encourages the use of reason for instrumental purposes—for example, bioengineering—finds little opposition in society; thus, barring any crisis of legitimacy, support for the state becomes unshakable. The status quo interests—economic, political, and religious—identify their individual goals of permanency with that of the state and their complementary roles with that of support for the state. The use of reason—technologically and biologically—is subordinated to the interests of the state, and the interests of the state are identified with the manipulation of reality itself. Reason, then, becomes merely an aspect of reality to be manipulated by it—not to critique it; reason and reality are fused together.

With regard to individual conscience (presuming the state has yet to rationalize and thereby subordinate all members of society and their interests to its imperatives), the human costs of rationalization may present a moral problem: the use and abuse of human life for ill-defined or unacceptable goals. The diminishing middle class and the expanding number of poor and homeless, the violation of human rights of suspects, and the disregard for civilians in war zones—all are timeless yet current problems. Given the likelihood of the rational success of the state, the primary problem for religion presently is the lack of any "negative dialectics," or in this case, "negative theology." That is, with the triumph of the rational state, the abstract Kingdom of God will have become thoroughly identified with the temporal Church; and the Church, of course, will have become completely an "ideological state apparatus."[43] Hence the Church, lacking any critique, will be part of the oppressive status quo.

But in their attempt to justify their political presence as religiously committed individuals in a society as yet incompletely rationalized, liberation theologians are faced with a social theoretical problem:

What social theoretical perspective explicates the dynamics that tend toward a complete rationalization of industrialized and industrializing states while recognizing the relative autonomy of religious thought and institutions? What social theoretical perspective recognizes the immoral nature of the alliance of technological and scientific rationality with industrial capitalism while recognizing religion as a potential agent of social change? Given the tradition of religion as a repository of transcendental values, what is the possibility of it being a source of negativity as well? As we have seen, liberation theologians find they must adopt a version of Marxist social analysis that admits the possibility of revolutionary change originating in at least one dimension of the social superstructure. After realizing the scholarly necessity of incorporating nontraditional theological studies, liberation theologians must now defend their use of modern social theory before they can deal with the question of religion as an agent of social change.

The Use of Modern Social Science (Stage One)

What an effective theology of liberation requires is the ability to distinguish reality from critical reason, to discover the potential of social reality evolving from its unjust predecessor by using reason not as a legitimating and instrumental factor for the status quo, but as a guide to unmasking the illegitimacy of contemporary social relationships. Liberation theology as methodology, especially with the hermeneutic circle,[44] already provides the justification for the incorporation of a critical theory of society that, along with its social critique, recognizes the autonomy and potentiality of the religious sphere.

As a result of using this circle, at least two important claims are found in liberation theology with respect to political theory. First, given the moral commitment to human liberation and the development of a new hermeneutic in light of this commitment and in conjunction with an assessment of current social conditions, religion emerges as a potential as well as an appropriate agent of social change. Religion need not act as a mere source of ideological support for status quo social policies nor remain quietistic. Secondly, the second step of the hermeneutic circle—"ideological suspicion"—in order to be effective, requires an appropriate understanding of the complexity of contemporary social problems. But not any theoretical perspective will suffice, since the first step of the circle requires an individual commitment to liberate the poor and oppressed. Not only must the religious individual be able to describe and explain social conditions, he must utilize a social theoretical perspective that itself takes social change into account as both objective reality and normative imperative.

The Use of Marxist Social Science and the Liberation of Marxism from History (Stages Two and Three)

Marxism and Christianity may well have an intellectual affinity for each other, given their eschatological concerns and moral denunciations of a "heartless" world.[45] Yet most Marxists, as well as Marx, have criticized the role of religion in society as well as Christianity's co-optation by the state.[46] As discussed earlier, however, liberation theology claims to be different, both normatively and methodologically, from more mainstream Christianity.

The theologian Alfred T. Hennelly has pointed out that a major theological distinction between the two approaches is the emphasis of the former on "a Jesus who administers to the needs of the impoverished masses" and the emphasis of the latter on "a Jesus who appeals to the abstract individual for a personal commitment of faith."[47] This suggests that, in attempting to apply religious values and solutions to problems of social injustice, liberation theologians prefer a mass-based social theoretical perspective, as opposed to a perspective that explains social change in terms of the heroic, at times admirable, efforts of elite personalities. In this regard, Marxist social science appears to them as more appropriate. Thus, this social concern moves liberation theology's methodological approach closer to Marxism than to mainstream Christianity.

Marxists generally claim that the use of their social science reveals at least three crucial characteristics about the class-based, social structure of capitalist society. First, they argue that class analysis reveals a direct linkage between economic arrangements and the arrangement of political power in the state. Both sets of arrangements, sharing the same point of origin, exhibit their own yet similar authoritarian social relationships. Relatedly, class analysis reveals a condition of alienation endemic in the social relationships of these arrangements. The worker is alienated from the product he has created through a wage system more interested in the pursuit of profits for a few rather than in fulfilling the creative potential of all. Profit oriented, market dynamics move the essence of human creativity to the periphery of moral and political concern. And finally, class analysis reveals that these relationships and conditions are enforced by the political and legal institutions of the state, institutions themselves influenced, if not controlled, by the wealthy few. Furthermore, powerful political actors confer legitimacy on other groups and interests in exchange for support by them for the status quo. Consequently, other institutions—for example, churches, schools, and unions— teach their members acquiescence to the state and maintenance of social stability as the highest moral end of politics.

With regard to the context of Latin America's social, political, and economic problems, liberation theologians, of course, find Marxist social science particularly appropriate. They maintain that the great disparity in the distribution of wealth, the social and political distance between rulers and ruled, and the congruity between wealth and political power, are tailor-made for class analysis.[48] Furthermore, both Marxism and liberation theology begin with an a priori condemnation of economic poverty and political oppression; both acknowledge the overwhelming presence of corporate capitalism in society; and both recognize the economic and political dependency of Third World countries on First World countries via international market arrangements dominated by powerful corporate interests. Thus, given the demands of the hermeneutic circle for a modern method of social scientific analysis, many liberation theologians incorporate Marxist social analysis to explain contemporary social conditions and to assist in clarifying the direction toward meaningful social change.[49]

A problem, however, with a mass-based theory that perceives the poor, the oppressed, or the proletariat as the social determinants of the future, is the place and role of religion in the process of social development. That is, how are we to understand the real and potential effect of religion on society? More specifically, how are we to understand *what* or *who* the Church is? Either the Church will be a church of the people (*la iglesia popular*), or the poor in fact will be identified literally as the Church, or the Church must be the vanguard of the revolution as advocated by some liberation theologians.[50] With the social analysis of orthodox Marxism and its deterministic explanations, the nature and possible autonomy of religion and the Church remain problematic.

One of the distinguishing characteristics, of course, of critical theorists has been their refusal to utilize a deterministic version of Marxist social analysis and in fact to criticize those who do. Furthermore, they have argued for and embraced the joint utilization and corresponding insights of other analytical social science paradigms, such as found in Freudian and Weberian approaches, alongside

Marxist paradigms. And, more importantly, these unique formulations have permitted them to reveal the potential for aspects of the social superstructure, including religious institutions, to act unilaterally on the material base.[51]

Max Horkheimer, for one, has recognized from his analyses the potential of Christianity, as a repository of certain values, to be a source for radical social change.[52] And with regard to religion and the critique of capitalist rationalization, Jürgen Habermas has also recognized and elaborated on the potential of the current "repoliticization of the biblical inheritance" to provide a novel source of humanistic critique of the one-dimensionality of modern technology and the oppression of administrative techniques.[53] In this regard, Habermas is particularly instructive.

Habermas argues that the logic of capitalism, including the dominant role of science and technology, continues to "rationalize" all aspects of social life. That is, it attempts to structure socioeconomic arrangements and relationships in a particular way to reduce the possibility of disruption of its activities from otherwise unforeseen, disturbing "contingencies" or events. The farther the system can "see," the more efficient it can function.[54] The problem for capitalist rationality, then, is the unpredictable occurrence of serious economic dislocations, due in part to internal contradictions of capitalism itself. The unexpected nature of these events will eventually outpace the ability of the social system to absorb and deal rationally with them. As the system faces increasing economic and social crises, its legitimacy will be called into question by members of society who seek, but do not receive, sufficient reassurances of stability. And eventually, the authoritarian character of the logic of the system will be recognized, along with the system's inability to achieve social justice, and, with the withdrawal of public legitimacy, the system will collapse. In an effort to deal with this logic, Habermas notices, European political theology has emerged to provide alternative sources of values for social criticism. But he is skeptical, and his skepticism has to do with theological claims concerning the moral values themselves and whether or not they are based on transcendental absolutes.

Recall that a major obstacle to effective social criticism for much of mainstream or academic theology has been its acceptance of an ontological dualism that recognizes the literal existence and separation of two worlds—the natural and supernatural—with the latter as the source of absolute values. Furthermore, this recognition has often led to an emphasis on inordinate concern for the latter and virtual abandonment of the former with a corresponding separation of, and disproportionate concern for, "religion" over "politics." Liberation theologians reject this dualism that consequently has allowed religion to play the uncomfortable role revealed and criticized by Marx and others.[55] Marx, too, rejected the existential claims for this dualism and thus the dualism itself. However, he denied the dualism's possibility because he rejected the existence of one of the worlds; he saw religion and its other-worldly, metaphysical explanations as merely the epiphenomenal manifestation of a flawed social order. Liberation theologians, on the other hand, reject this dualism, not by rejecting the existence of one of the worlds but by rejecting the line that demarcates the two; thus, they merge the two worlds and redefine the source and nature of moral values.

Critical theorists also tend to reject the ontological dualism of separate worlds, as with Marx. However, they do not reject the dualism of positivist and metaphysical questions; instead, they perceive it as representing semiautonomous spheres of intellectual concerns that are in legitimate tension with one another, as generally found in European political theology and Latin American liberation theology. But in a similar nature to the liberation theologians' criticisms of the ontological dualism of academic theology, Habermas also questions the potential of European political theology's effectiveness for social criticism. Ultimately, how can its approach be suitable when it, too, as with academic theology, accepts transcendental absolutes? He is doubtful that European political theology's absolutes are appropriate or sufficient to provide the necessary foundation for the development of a new society based on democratic decision making.

Similar, again, in many respects to the response of liberation theology and the emerging logic of Christian base communities in Latin America, Habermas has also developed a comprehensive theory of the "communication community" to yield a rationally and democratically constructed ethical theory. It is in this community where

> those affected, who as participants in a practical discourse test the validity claims of norms and, to the extent that they accept them with reasons, arrive at the conviction that in the given circumstances the proposed norms are "right."[56]

For Habermas, as for liberation theologians, the dynamics of social relationships ought to exist such that moral commitments and guidance are not imposed on the individual from "without" by political and ecclesiastical authorities, who rule with absolute certitudes, but evolve from "within" as a result of individual moral commitments and democratic discussion.

Moreover, with regard to proper ethical arrangements that can be found in society, between purely sacred or religious rituals and profane or nonreligious oriented activities, Habermas admits that frequently "[religious] myth bridges over the two domains of action."[57] Yet, with his Marxist suspicions, he continues to question the overall merit of theological discourse as anything more than "false consciousness" or "systematically distorted communication."[58] That is, to what extent can liberation oriented religious assessments be more than practically useful, but nontranscendentally oriented, critiques of social conditions of poverty and oppression? And, if this is the case, how can any radical theology such as liberation theology be anything more than another ideology? Nevertheless, Habermas admits that the revolutionary potential of religion must be investigated further for the possibility of its occupying an acceptable "quasi-transcendental" status.[59]

So the possibility of religion with values subversive of the status quo has long been recognized by theologians and more recently given limited acknowledgment by critical theorists. The practical as well as theoretical problem, however, has been one of bringing these subversive values into dialogue and alliance with critical social science in a way that retains the essence of religion while having practical political outcomes.[60] It is precisely at this point of adopting a "more flexible Marxism" as the appropriate critical social science—via the reformulations of critical theory—that liberation theology may develop a political praxis to act on its values and thus sustain its theoretical claim to the revolutionary viability of religion. Indeed, Marxism's emphasis on praxis coincides with liberation theology's emphasis on describing and explaining as well as changing society.[61] Furthermore, this emphasis on praxis as consisting of more than a dialectical relationship between theory and reality, but also between the superstructure of ideas and the political economic base of society, has allowed for what Lamb has referred to as a "creative tension" between Marxism and theology to be found in critical theory itself.[62]

Critical theorists have pointed out that Marx did not give sufficient credit to theology as representing the spiritual dimension of praxis. Liberation theologians argue that they represent the expression of the creative tension missed by Marx, with their emphasis on the values of their religious tradition as a source of subversion, while calling for the radical transformation of society toward a socialist state.[63] Nevertheless, theologians of liberation must now develop the theoretical justifications for this creative tension if the political theory of liberation theology is to be perceived as a complete and proper foundation for a prophetic movement attempting to break the hegemony of the capitalist state.[64]

Conclusion

As we have seen, the political theory of liberation theology arises in response to concern over distressing social issues. It utilizes modern social scientific analyses to explain the nature of unjust socio-economic conditions in Latin America. And with this theory, liberation theologians call for systemic changes in society to conform to their own conception of justice. How can their explanation for political theorizing and political activism be justified? How should these aspects of their explanation be assessed? We should understand that speculation and action are two interrelated concerns.

Our personal ethics are dependent on our understanding of existence or reality, and of society as part of reality. Our understanding of reality is given coherency and consistency by reference to a particular theoretical framework, which includes the potential to develop a theory of politics with an attendant social science to explain social reality.[65] Of course, some theoretical frameworks are more comprehensive than others, and all may be flawed to some extent, at least when evaluated from another perspective. More importantly, though, within any given framework, several theories of politics may be possible to explain and justify a particular relationship between social science and political ethics. Consequently, we cannot fully assess the merits of a particular social scientific analysis without taking into account the moral commitments that may well have influenced the selection of that method of analysis over another. We must consider not only the logic of the social science in the "superstructure" of our political theory, but the value "base" of morality that provides the foundation for the entire system as well.

We should also keep in mind that political theories are not developed in a vacuum; they emerge out of real-life considerations, including empirical and evaluative reflection upon the meaning of, and possibility for, social justice. The history of Western political thought

183

is replete with examples of the development of theoretical arguments, often with universal application. For example, in many of his dialogues, Plato dealt with several epistemological and moral arguments, including the nature of the best political regime. His concern for justice and how it might be achieved arose in part from his dissatisfaction with the political regime in Athens. John Locke also struggled with delineating an accurate explanation of the state and an argument for its subordination to and delimitation by individual rights. And the framers of the American Constitution attempted to construct and defend a political economic arrangement that would protect individual rights and the emerging propertied classes. This is not to say that theories about epistemology, morality, and politics are determined by their historical context, but only to say that the context often conditions the response of thinkers to social situations and poses certain questions with more urgency than others.[66]

Now, the influence of the value base on the development of political theories may vary. Locke, John Stuart Mill, and other intellectual heirs of classical liberalism, for example, have been concerned primarily with discovering the best political regime that retains and promotes individual liberty;[67] thus, their arguments are constructed so as to defend and promote their valued interests. Jean-Jacques Rousseau and the intellectual heirs of the democratic tradition, while also interested in individual liberty, have been concerned with the effects that unbridled individualism has on the body politic and in turn the beneficial effects political life can have for the individual;[68] thus, they have emphasized the importance of preserving individual autonomy and its crucial relationship with democratic institutions. And Marx, writing during a period of virtually unrestrained industrial growth, concerned himself with the effects that a particular form of socioeconomic organization—capitalism—had on workers and the development of individual creativity, hence his and his intellectual heirs' concern for the attainment of a just political economic order.[69]

With regard to the superstructure of social science, the intellectual roots of most contemporary approaches extend deep into the soil of the Enlightenment. Reliance on the scientific method, historical evidence, and critical acceptance of the fact-value relationship remain the hallmarks of the Enlightenment that have resonated throughout the modern era. They reveal themselves today in various social forms and political arrangements as the primary elements of modern, rational theories of society and politics. For example, many modern thinkers have drawn on the thoughts of Thomas Hobbes who set the theoretical foundation for a comprehensive analysis of social behavior, from individual psychology to the structure of the liberal state.[70] The development of a positivist political theory based on Hobbesian assumptions concerning human behavior must limit itself to conditions that can be empirically examined. Although other theorists, such as Marx, have also offered materialist explanations, they have modified these by replacing significant assumptions about the nature of logic itself, from formal to dialectical logic. As a result, Marxist explanations of the nature and development of societies tend to differ markedly from those of the liberal, epistemological tradition;[71] thus, despite many of their common theoretical assumptions, modern liberals will often differ considerably with Marxists in both their analyses of the conditions of modern societies, and in their prescriptions for social change.

At this point in our thinking about the relationship between social science and political ethics in political theory, we face a necessary question: Which political theory is superior? Of course, this depends to some extent on the theoretical framework itself. Even so, if we want to be objective in our identification of the best framework, what should we look for and how should we handle what we find? In the name of objectivity, authoritative responses to questions concerning both frameworks and theories often assume that an inability exists to achieve any consensus on subjective values. Then they attempt to identify the subjective claims of each and proscribe them as inappropriate for comparative consideration. For example, A.J. Ayer, as one of the leading proponents of logical positivism, has ruled out metaphysical statements in both science and ethics as inappropriate for serious consideration, since they cannot be subject to empirical verification.[72] In this way, the search for theoretical grounding is limited to those explanations that presumably can be shown to be true or false. Other contemporary thinkers, however, are willing to admit transcendental explanations as appropriate themes for analysis. Certain critical rationalists, such as Karl Popper, allow for metaphysical explanations to be subject to the same objective falsifying procedures as any other explanation.[73] Furthermore, Habermas and other critical theorists actually maintain the objective existence of a "rational logic" that guides the development of industrial societies, and they often refer to a "dialectic of history" to explain its movement.[74] These and other individuals have attempted to devise various ways to deal with the issue of the objective superiority of one framework or theory over another.

The Political Theory of Liberation Theology

Nevertheless, these different approaches will ultimately fall short in their attempts to provide any objective defense of the best framework or theory to explain reality. For example, logical positivists suffer from an inability to recognize the limits of their own position; in fact, they are blind to their own inability to proscribe metaphysical claims. Critical rationalists, while claiming to include metaphysical questions as legitimate, overlook the inadequacy of scientific methods derived from the natural sciences to disprove social hypotheses. This inadequacy results from the lack of a universally acceptable set of standards by which results can be judged, as well as the inability to replicate conditions and control social experiments.[75] And those from other critical traditions bring concepts to bear that must be justified before admitting to the applicability of their social theories— for example, Locke's and Marx's labor theory of value—upon which moral foundation their ethical systems rest.

These attempts miss the mark not because they are in error, but precisely because they are correct. They are correct in asserting that value-laden assumptions must be purged to construct an objective social science. But values cannot be purged; and because they cannot be purged, all social science approaches must necessarily be found wanting and hence open to doubt. And it is this doubt, as a result of the inability to achieve a consensus on values, which ultimately dooms the universal recognizability of a particular social science methodology.[76] And this raises the ultimate doubt as to whether an objective social science is possible at all.

This discussion suggests that values comprise an inescapable aspect of theories about politics and political activities. An individual's justification for his political ethics, then, relies in part on his particular understanding of society. It also relies in part on the values and commitments he brings to the situation. A comprehensive explanation taking into account both sets of concerns provides the moral legitimacy for the individual's political assessment and political behavior. Hence, any critique of an explanation for the legitimacy of particular political ethics must include an evaluation of epistemological problems, with regard to the use of social science, and logical problems, with regard to the relationship between personal moral commitments and social science.

For liberation theologians, too, the legitimacy of their political ethics cannot be discussed separately from the legitimacy of their social scientific assessment of Latin American society in conjunction with their moral commitments. At a minimum, the discussions in the previous chapters suggest the following interpretive implications of the political theory of liberation theology.

Interpretive Implications of the Political Theory of Liberation Theology

With the peculiar methodology of liberation theology, knowledge about God and the world is not derived from set propositions, but from the interactive process of tentative theoretical explanations and the theoretician's efforts to change that which he is attempting to explain. The process yields "knowledge" about a changing world; and since knowledge itself continually undergoes change as theories are modified to interpret the fluid world of "facts," the ultimate realization for the theologian must be that God changes in some fashion as well. Yet out of this seemingly chaotic world of matter and ideas in motion emerges the constancy of God's intervention in the world out of concern for human well-being, despite the limitations of his own existence. In fact, it is the limitations themselves that force God and man to act together, complementing each other in a way that provides for unity of purpose while recognizing diversity of perspectives in the common attempt to achieve the noble end of existence (the eschatological promise).

This interpretive claim, then, suggests that man's use of social science to explain social reality complements the development of religious belief that explains the nature of God and the relationship between God and man. Furthermore, this claim suggests that not only does social science complement religious belief, but that each requires the other in the common search for an explanation of the totality of existence. And given the changing nature of reality, a dialectical relationship exists between political theory and theology. This ideational dialectic transcends other artificial classifications that attempt to sever the relationship between social science and religion and to compartmentalize them into separate, academic pursuits.

The necessity of this complementary relationship between social theory and theology becomes apparent with regard to political ethics. Any set of ethics that is derived strictly from personally or individually determined values and that utilizes social scientific insights, may provide for the justification of morally limitless behavior. Yet without limits, no standard of ethics can exist. For to know what is ethical implies minimally a concept of unethical behavior; without limits, standards are impossible to set. In other words, a logically impossible or contradictory condition obtains.

Similarly, a set of ethics based on purported theological insight into the will of God with no complementary grasp of the social context in which ethical behavior is to take place, results in the absurd attempt to apply an absolute standard of moral behavior to society, oblivious to the myriad exigencies of changing and shifting social settings. And this in turn usually results in the failure to apply any ethical standard whatsoever to the world; for example, consider the support given to Latin American dictatorships by fundamentalist Christian sects.

Hence, in the existential condition of individualist ethics, all manner of political activism and behavior may be legitimated; in the privatized world of selective withdrawal, quietism prevails. And in neither does human responsibility for oneself or others exert itself. A proper balance must be discovered between subjective politics and transcendent values that reveals the complementary as well as necessary relationship between social theory and theology.

An initial drawback of liberation theology as a viable political movement for many skeptics concerns elements of its theoretical or theological framework, the substance and truthfulness of which cannot be definitively ascertained—such as, the existence of God, the historicity of the Incarnation, or the eschatological component of Christianity. They maintain that one understanding of religious belief influences social behavior in one direction while another influences in another direction; the causal connection between unsubstantiated belief and behavior seems problematic. Yet the skeptics should pause for a moment. Given the beliefs that comprise the framework for grounding a particular theoretical approach to explaining and judging social conditions, one can still critically evaluate that movement's comprehension of social reality as well as the internal logical consistency of its explanations. For example, arguments for the existence of God need not be accepted or understood literally as proofs of God's existence, but only as justifications for religious beliefs.[77] And then it is these religious beliefs, regardless of origin or purported authenticity, that can be recognized as providing the basic normative foundation for social, if theologically based, critiques. And how these critiques are applied, then, becomes a a proper focal point for evaluating the overall theological approach to political ethics.

The political theory of liberation theology must deal with a host of complex issues from abstract epistemological problems of theory construction, to practical problems of applied social ethics. The study of liberation theology, however, yields more than its normative critique of, and political challenge to, ideological justifications and social institutions that defend and maintain poverty and oppression in Latin America. Closer inspection reveals liberation theology to be a genuine philosophical movement whose political theory, if fully developed, has the potential to resist the usual, disciplinary dichotomy between the studies of religion and politics, to speak to the limitations of traditional ethical arguments on political behavior, and to contribute significantly to contemporary debates on epistemology.

Appendix

Brief Biographies of Selected Liberation Theologians

The following biographical sketches provide educational, national, religious, and other background information on the most prominent theologians of liberation in Latin America discussed in this book.

Hugo Assmann was born in Brazil in 1933. He holds a licentiate in the Social Sciences, a doctorate in Theology, and a special diploma in Mass Communications. He studied philosophy and sociology in Brazil and theology in Rome as well as other subjects at various universities throughout Latin America. Assmann has taught at the Jesuit theologate in São Leopoldo and at the pontifical Catholic University of Pôrto Alegre, both in Brazil. From 1966 to 1968 he was Coordinator of Studies at the São Paulo Institute of Philosophy and Theology. In response to his radical theological positions, the Brazilian military government forced him into exile. After his expulsion for similar reasons by the governments of Uruguay, Bolivia, and Chile, Assmann was a visiting member of the theology faculty of the University of Münster, West Germany. Since 1974, he has been serving as a Professor of Journalism and Theology, as well as a member of the Social Science Research Institute, at the National University of Costa Rica in San José.

Appendix

Clodovis Boff, brother of Leonardo Boff, was born in Concordia, Brazil, in 1944. He is a Servite priest and a Professor of Theology at the Catholic University of São Paulo. Boff also works with the Christian base communities and provides theological assistance to clergy.

Leonardo Boff was born in Concordia, Brazil, in 1938. He is a Franciscan priest, educated first in philosophy and theology in Brazil, with later studies in Europe at Wurzburg, Louvain, and Oxford. He gained his doctorate in Theology from Ludwig-Maximilian University in Munich. Boff is currently a Professor of Systematic Theology at the Institute for Philosophy and Theology in Petrópolis, Brazil. He edits the theological journal, *Revista Eclesiástica Brasileira,* as well as serving as an advisor to the Brazilian National Conference of Bishops, the Brazilian Religious Conference, and the Latin American Confederation of Religious. Summoned to the Vatican in September 1984, Boff was "silenced" for one year in response to his writings on liberation theology.

José Comblin, born in Belgium in 1923, has lived and worked in Latin America since 1958. Holding a doctorate in Theology, Comblin was also expelled for his social criticism from Brazil by the military government in 1972, after having taught theology for seven years at the Theological Institute in Recife. He is currently teaching at the Catholic University of Chile in Talca, and is also a professor at the Catholic University of Louvain.

José Severino Croatto studied Semitic languages and biblical archaeology at the Biblical Institute in Rome and at the Hebrew University in Jerusalem. Croatto is a Professor of Old Testament Studies and of Hebrew at the Instituto Superior Evangélico de Estudios Teológicos in Buenos Aires, Argentina. He is the first Catholic professor in the history of this evangelical seminary.

Enrique Dussel was born in Mendoza, Argentina, in 1934. Dussel holds a licentiate in Philosophy from the University of Mendoza, a doctorate in Philosophy from the University of Madrid, a doctorate in History from the Sorbonne, and a licentiate in Theology from the Catholic Institute of Paris. As a result of his radical theological positions, the military government of Argentina forced him into exile from his teaching position at the Cuyo University of Mendoza; he currently teaches at the University of Mexico City. He is also a committee member for the theological journal, *Concilium,* as well as President of the Commission on Historical Studies of the Church in Latin America.

191

Appendix

Ignacio Ellacuría is a Jesuit priest from the Basque region of Spain, but has lived and worked in Central America for over twenty-five years. He holds a licentiate in Theology and Philosophy and a doctorate in Theology. Ellacuría studied philosophy in Quito, Ecuador, and Madrid, and theology in Innsbruck, Austria. At the José Simeón Cañas University of Central America in San Salvador, El Salvador, Ellacuría was a Professor of Theology, head of the department of philosophy, Director of the Center for Theological Reflection, and a member of the Board of Directors. Presently, he is on the editorial board of the regional journal, *Estudios Centroamericanos,* and teaches at the University of Central America in Managua, Nicaragua.

Gustavo Gutiérrez was born in Lima, Peru, in 1928. After initiating studies in medicine, philosophy, and theology at the National University in Lima, Gutiérrez traveled to Europe where he continued and completed studies in philosophy at the University of Louvain. He also studied theology in Lyon, and at the Gregorian University in Rome. Gutiérrez was ordained a priest in 1959. Currently he is a Professor of Theology at the Catholic University in Lima. He also devotes considerable time and effort to involvement with the people of Rimac, a slum area of Lima.

José Míguez Bonino was born in Santa Fé, Argentina, in 1924. He studied at the Evangelical theologate in Buenos, Aires, as well as at Emory University and Union Theological Seminary in the United States. Míguez Bonino was ordained a Methodist minister in Argentina and assigned to pastoral duties in both Bolivia and Argentina. He also served as an observer of the Methodist church at the Second Vatican Council. Míguez Bonino has taught at the Union Theological Seminary in New York, the Waldensian theologate in Rome, and the Selly Colleges in Birmingham, England. He has also served as Rector of the Evangelical theologate from 1960 to 1969, and currently is a Professor of Systematic Theology at the Evangelical Institute of Advanced Theological Studies in Buenos Aires. Míguez Bonino is also a member of the Presidium of the World Council of Churches.

José Porfirio Miranda studied economics at the Universities of Munich and Münster, and received his licentiate in Biblical Sciences from the Biblical Institute in Rome. Miranda has been a Professor of Mathematics at the Institute of Science and Professor of Economic Theory at the Institute of Technology in Guadalajara, Mexico, Professor of Philosophy at the Regional Institute in Chihuahua, Mexico, and

Professor of Philosophy of Law at the National University, as well as Professor of Exegesis at the Free Institute of Philosophy, both in Mexico City. He currently teaches at the Metropolitan Tztapalapa University in Mexico City, and is an advisor and lecturer for workers' and student groups throughout Mexico.

Juan Luis Segundo was born in Montevideo, Uruguay, in 1925. He completed his philosophical studies in Argentina and his theological studies at the University of Louvain. He received his licentiate in Theology and obtained a doctorate in Literature from the Sorbonne. He has taught theology at the universities of Harvard, Chicago, Toronto, Montreal, Birmingham, and São Paulo, Brazil. Segundo is a Jesuit priest and also serves as a chaplain to various groups in Uruguay. He is currently Director of the Peter Faber Pastoral Center in Montevideo.

Jon Sobrino was born into a Basque family in Barcelona during the Spanish Civil War. He earned his masters in Engineering Mechanics at St. Louis University and his doctorate in Theology from the Hochschule Sankt Georgen in Frankfurt. Sobrino is a Jesuit priest and a Professor of Philosophy and Theology at José Simeón Cañas University of Central America and at the Center for Theological Reflection, both in San Salvador, El Salvador.

Raúl Vidales was born in Monterrey, Mexico, in 1943, and ordained to the priesthood in 1967. Vidales holds a licentiate in Theology and Sociology, and has taught at the Latin American Pastoral Institute and the Catholic University both in Quito, Ecuador, the University of Monterrey, and the Catholic University in Lima, Peru. He has also worked extensively with pastoral reflection groups at the Regional Institute of Higher Theological Studies in Mexico, the Missionary Training Institute in Guatemala, and the Latin American Catechetical Institute in Colombia. Presently Vidales is working with Gustavo Gutiérrez at the Bartolomé de las Casas Research Center in Lima.

Notes

Introduction

    1. For representative examples with regard to the history, dynamics, and impact of religious involvement in Latin American politics, see Phillip Berryman, *The Religious Roots of Rebellion: Christians in Central American Revolutions* (Maryknoll, N.Y.: Orbis Books, 1984); Daniel H. Levine, *Religion and Politics in Latin America: The Catholic Church in Venezuela and Colombia* (Princeton: Princeton University Press, 1981); and Brian H. Smith, *Church and Politics in Chile: Challenges to Modern Catholicism* (Princeton: Princeton University Press, 1982). A representative sample with regard to theological critiques would include Harvey Cox, *Religion in the Secular City: Toward a Postmodern Theology* (New York: Simon & Schuster, 1984), Alfredo Fierro, *The Militant Gospel: A Critical Introduction to Political Theologies* (Maryknoll, N.Y.: Orbis Books, 1977), Dennis P. McCann, *Christian Realism and Liberation Theology: Practical Theologies in Conflict* (Maryknoll, N.Y.: Orbis Books, 1981); and Michael Novak, *Will It Liberate? Questions about Liberation Theology* (Mahwah, N.J.: Paulist Press, 1987). And with regard to examples of treatment from other disciplines, see Otto Maduro, *Religion and Social Conflicts* (Maryknoll, N.Y.: Orbis Books, 1982); and Wolfhart Pannenberg, *Theology and the Philosophy of Science* (Philadelphia: Westminster Press, 1976).

    2. Those who offer primary insights into this political theory and upon whose writings this study relies, include Hugo Assmann, Leonardo Boff, José Comblin, Enrique Dussel, Ignacio Ellacuría, Gustavo Gutiérrez, José Míguez Bonino, José Porfirio Miranda, Juan Luis Segundo, and Raúl Vidales. While many other Latin American thinkers are also writing on liberation theology and will at times be cited, this select group provides collectively the source for the basic arguments that comprise the political theory of liberation theology.

Chapter 1

1. With regard to Acts 5:19, as reported by Carlos Mesters, "The Use of the Bible in Christian Communities of the Common People," in *The Challenge of Basic Christian Communities: Papers from the International Ecumenical Congress of Theology, February 20 - March 2, 1980, São Paulo, Brazil,* eds. Sergio Torres and John Eagleson (Maryknoll, N.Y.: Orbis Books, 1981), pp. 206–7.

2. From the data set compiled by Robert Summers and Alan Heston, "Improved International Comparisons of Real Product and Its Composition: 1950–1980," *The Review of Income and Wealth* 30 (June 1984): 242–43. The averages calculated cover the Latin American countries of Costa Rica, El Salvador, Guatemala, Honduras, Nicaragua, and Panama in Central America, and Argentina, Bolivia, Brazil, Chile, Colombia, Ecuador, Guyana, Paraguay, Peru, Surinam, Uruguay, and Venezuela in South America.

3. Juan Luis Segundo, "Christianity and Violence in Latin America," *Christianity and Crisis* 4 (March 1968): 32–35.

4. José Porfirio Miranda, *Marx y la biblia, Crítica de la filosofía de la opresión* [*Marx and the Bible: a critique of the philosophy of oppression*] (Salamanca: Ediciones Sígueme, 1971).

5. Gustavo Gutiérrez, *Teología de la liberación: perspectivas* [*A theology of liberation: perspectives*] (Lima, Peru: CEP, 1971).

6. "*Gaudium et Spes*: Vatican II, 7 December 1965," *Vatican Council II: The Conciliar and Post Conciliar Documents,* gen. ed. Austin Flannery (Northport, New York: Costello Publishing Co., 1975), pp. 968–73, pars. 63, 65, 67.

7. Ibid., pp. 975–77, pars. 69, 71.

8. Ibid., pp. 918–22, pars. 19–22.

9. Ibid., p. 981, par. 74.

10. For an overview, see Michael Dodson, "Prophetic Politics and Political Theory in Latin America," *Polity* 12 (Spring 1980): 388–408.

11. Arthur F. McGovern, *Marxism: An American Christian Perspective* (Maryknoll, N.Y.: Orbis Books, 1980), p. 176.

12. See, for example, "*Mater et Magistra:* Encyclical of Pope John XXIII on Christianity and Social Progress, May 15, 1961," *The Papal Encyclicals,* vol. 5, pp. 59–90. The pope expressed optimism with regard to the value of non-religiously oriented social perspectives and appreciation for the need for long-range planning with regard to the Church's social teachings. Instead of condemning false ideologies, he called for creative and practical solutions to socioeconomic problems. This document as with other official statements that immediately followed—for example, *Pacem in Terris* (1963) and *Gaudium et Spes* (1965)—broke away from traditional reliance on natural law principles that had been used to fashion deductive arguments with regard to

social issues. Instead, the pope proceeded in a more inductive fashion implementing contemporary social science methodologies and claims. Cf. Donal Dorr, *Option for the Poor: A Hundred Years of Vatican Social Teachings* (Maryknoll, N.Y.: Orbis Books, 1983).

13. McGovern, *Marxism*, p. 177. The Medellín documents can be found in Joseph Gremillion, ed., *The Gospel of Peace and Justice: Catholic Social Teaching Since Pope John* (Maryknoll, N.Y.: Orbis Books, 1976), pp. 445–76 (hereafter referred to as "Medellín Documents"). The set of documents consists of four treatises each reflecting upon a particular theme: "Justice," "Peace," "Family and Demography," and "Poverty of the Church."

14. "Medellín Documents," p. 455.

15. Ibid., p. 472.

16. Ibid., p. 446.

17. Ibid., p. 460.

18. Ibid., pp. 446, 455.

19. Ibid., p. 449.

20. Ibid., p. 447.

21. Ibid., pp. 473–74. According to the bishops,

Peace is, above all, a work of justice. It presupposes and requires the establishment of a just order in which men fulfill themselves as men, where their dignity is respected, their legitimate aspirations satisfied, their access to truth recognized, their personal freedom guaranteed; an order where man is not an object, but an agent of his own history (pp. 458–59).

22. Cf. Penny Lernoux, *Cry of the People: The Struggle for Human Rights in Latin America - The Catholic Church in Conflict with U.S. Policy* (New York: Penguin Books, 1982), p. 38.

23. "Medellín Documents," p. 452. Emphasis on the political sphere is a constant theme throughout liberation theology.

24. For an example of Paulo Freire's approach, see his book, *Pedagogy of the Oppressed* (New York: Seabury Press, 1970); for a critique of how Freire's methodology has been used, see Peter L. Berger, *Pyramids of Sacrifice: Political Ethics and Social Change* (Garden City, N.Y.: Anchor Books, 1976), chap. 4.

25. "Medellín Documents," p. 475; cf. p. 476.

26. Ibid., p. 447; cf. pp. 448, 450.

27. Ibid., p. 462; cf. pp. 451, 458.

28. Lernoux, *Cry of the People*, p. 40. See chap. 5. Also see Thomas C. Bruneau, "Basic Christian Communities in Latin America: Their Nature and Significance (especially in Brazil)," in *Churches and Politics in Latin America*,

ed. Daniel H. Levine (Beverly Hills: Sage Publications, 1980), pp. 225–37; cf. Alvaro Barreiro, *Basic Ecclesial Communities: The Evangelization of the Poor* (Maryknoll, N.Y.: Orbis Books, 1982), chap. 2. For a theological defense of CEBs, see Leonardo Boff, *Ecclesiogenesis: The Base Communities Reinvent the Church* (Maryknoll, N.Y.: Orbis Books, 1986).

29. Lernoux, *Cry of the People,* p. 41.

30. According to Lernoux, many who signed the final documents did not realize the full impact of their positions.

> Most missed the heart of the matter: that the Medellín documents were a revolutionary call to work for social justice, placing the Church in open conflict with the moneyed classes that for centuries had been its political and economic mainstay. There were no platitudes or concessions—the gates were wide open.

(*Cry of the People,* p. 42). Cf. Louis Althusser, "Ideology and Ideological State Apparatuses," in *Lenin and Philosophy and other Essays,* Althusser (New York: Monthly Review Press, 1971), pp. 127–86.

31. "Medellín Documents," p. 475.

32. Ibid., p. 459.

33. Ibid., pp. 456, 460; cf. Lernoux, *Cry of the People,* chaps. 3, 5.

34. Ibid., pp. 460–61; cf. Oscar Arnulfo Romero and Arturo Rivera Damos [Rivera y Damas], "The Church, Political Organization and Violence," *Cross Currents* 29 (Winter 1979–80): 385–408. Also, see chap. 5.

35. Daniel H. Levine, *Religion and Politics in Latin America: The Catholic Church in Venezuela and Colombia* (Princeton: Princeton University Press, 1981), p. 39.

36. "Medellín Documents," p. 460.

37. Ibid., p. 461; cf. Paul VI, *"Populorum Progressio,"* in *The Papal Encyclicals,* ed. Claudia Carlen (Raleigh, N.C.: McGrath Publishing Co., 1981), vol. 5, pp. 188–89, par. 31. Also of importance in this document for the Latin American bishops was the pope's denunciation of affluent nations for implementing foreign economic policies that contributed to conditions of hunger and misery in much of the Third World. He argued that policies of colonialism have left the colonized countries with a single-crop economy and an authoritarian political system dominated by an elite group. Furthermore, the introduction of modernization and industrialization has led to serious breakdown in traditional values and concern for the community. Capitalism has itself constructed an economic arrangement with a pernicious ideology for its moral justification; it "presents profit as the chief spur to economic progress, free competition as the guiding norm of economics, and private ownership of the means of production as an absolute right, having no limits nor concomitant social obligations." (p. 188, par. 26) Conversely, Paul argued that the "right to private property" and the "right to free trade" were subor-

dinate to "the right to glean what [an individual] needs from the earth for growth and development." (p. 187, par. 22) He supported the expropriation for the common good of landed estates that either were not being used or were poorly used, and condemned the transfer abroad of income by the wealthy citizens of poor nations. Paul called for foreign aid to rectify the wrongs of inequitable trade relations, and the adoption of a global strategy that would bring about "the common development of mankind." (pp. 186, 191, pars. 18, 43–46)

38. Ibid., p. 460.

39. J. Andrew Kirk, *Theology Encounters Revolution* (Downers Grove, Ill.: InterVarsity Press, 1980), p. 55.

40. Levine, *Religion and Politics in Latin America,* p. 39.

41. Ibid., p. 40.

42. See, for example, John Gerassi, ed. *Revolutionary Priest: The Complete Writings and Messages of Camilo Torres* (New York: Random, 1971).

43. For a discussion on "theologies of revolution," see José Comblin, *The Church and the National Security State* (Maryknoll, N.Y. Orbis Books, 1979), chap. 2. Cf. Denis Goulet, *A New Moral Order: Development Ethics and Liberation Theology* (Maryknoll, N.Y.: Orbis Books, 1974).

44. For criticisms of liberation theology by other Latin American clergy, see, for example, Alfonso López Trujillo, *Liberation or Revolution? An Examination of the Priest's Role in the Socioeconomic Class Struggle in Latin America* (Huntington, Ind.: Our Sunday Visitor, 1977); and Roger Vekemans, *Caesar and God: The Priesthood and Politics* (Maryknoll, N.Y.: Orbis Books, 1972). Cf. Michael Novak, ed., *Liberation South, Liberation North* (Washington, D.C.: American Enterprise Institute, 1981).

45. This simultaneous occurrence of theological development and criticism became apparent at the subsequent third meeting of CELAM held in Puebla, Mexico, in 1979. On the Puebla meeting, see John Eagleson and Philip Scharper, eds., *Puebla and Beyond: Documentation and Commentary* (Maryknoll, N.Y.: Orbis Books, 1979), pp. 116–21.

46. Kirk, *Theology Encounters Revolution,* pp. 114–16.

47. For a selection of traditional opposing views on which is prior—political philosophy or political theology—see Ralph Lerner and Muhsin Mahdi, eds., *Medieval Political Philosophy: A Sourcebook* (Ithaca, N.Y.: Cornell University Press, 1963); selections include writings from Alfarabi, Avicenna, Averroes, Maimonides, and Aquinas.

48. Many scholars have recognized the special problems that Christianity, as well as other religious perspectives, has in taking these issues into account. See, for example, Charles Davis, *Theology and Political Society* (Cambridge: Cambridge University Press, 1980), pp. 58–59.

49. Cf. Plato, *Republic*, 427d–434d; Aristotle, *Politics*, 1280a7–35, 1280b39–1281a7; Cicero, *On the Commonwealth*, trans. George H. Sabine and Stanley B. Smith (Indianapolis: Bobbs-Merrill, 1976), pp. 122, 129, 138; Alfarabi, "The Political Regime," in *Medieval Political Philosophy*, pp. 34–38, 46; Avicenna, "Healing: Metaphysics X," in *Medieval Political Philosophy*, p. 99; Aquinas, *Summa Theologica*, question 92. Also, cf. J. Peter Euben, "The Battle of Salamis and the Origins of Political Theory," *Political Theory* 14 (August 1986): 359–90; and Jürgen Gebhardt, "The Origins of Politics in Ancient Hellas: Old Interpretations and New Perspectives," in *Sophia and Praxis: The Boundaries of Politics*, ed. J. M. Porter (Chatham, N.J.: Chatham House, 1984), pp. 1–31.

50. Francis Fox Piven and Richard A. Cloward, *The New Class War* (New York: Pantheon Books, 1982), p. 45; cf. Henry Shue, *Basic Rights: Subsistence, Affluence, and U.S. Foreign Policy* (Princeton: Princeton University Press, 1980), pt. 1.

51. John Stuart Mill, *Essay on Liberty* (1859), chap. 1.

52. Cf. Niccolò Machiavelli, *The Prince* (1513); but also cf. Mary Dietz, "Trapping the Prince: Machiavelli and the Political Regime," *American Political Science Review* 80 (September 1986): 777–99.

53. For an example of Hobbes's psychology of human behavior, see *Leviathan* (1651), chaps. 1–3, 6, 8, 10, 11, 13.

54. On Locke's theory of acquisition and labor theory of value, see *Two Treatises of Government* (c. 1681), "Second Treatise," chap. 5, esp. secs. 26–29, 33, 37, 39, 40, 42, 44.

55. D. M. Turner, *The Book of Scientific Discovery: How Science Has Aided Human Welfare* (New York: Barnes & Noble, 1933).

56. Cf. John C. Greene, *Science, Ideology, and World View: Essays in the History of Evolutionary Ideas* (Berkeley: University of California Press, 1981).

57. Frank Coleman, *Hobbes and America: Exploring the Constitutional Foundations* (Toronto: University of Toronto Press, 1977); Robert Nozick, *Anarchy, State and Utopia* (New York: Basic Books, 1974); and C. B. Macpherson, *The Political Theory of Possessive Individualism: Hobbes to Locke* (London: Oxford University Press, 1962).

58. Kai Nielson, "Capitalism, Socialism and Justice," in *And Justice for All: New Introductory Essays in Ethics and Public Policy*, eds. Tom Regan and Donald VanDeVeer (Totowa, N.J.: Rowman and Littlefield, 1982), pp. 264–86.

59. Adam Smith, *Wealth of Nations* (1776).

60. Allen Buchanan, *Ethics, Efficiency, and the Market* (Totowa, N.J.: Rowman & Allanheld, 1985), chap. 2.

61. Cf. Nozick, *Anarchy, State and Utopia*, chap. 7.

62. Herbert Butterfield, *The Origins of Modern Science*, ed. rev. (New York: Free Press, 1965).

Notes to Chapter 1

63. T. S. Ashton, *The Industrial Revolution: 1760–1830* (London: Oxford University Press, 1948).

64. Theodore J. Lowi, *The End of Liberalism,* 2d ed. rev. (New York: Norton, 1979), chap. 2.

65. Ibid., chap. 3; cf. Robert A. Dahl, *Dilemmas of Pluralist Democracy: Autonomy vs. Control* (New Haven: Yale University Press, 1982), pp. 176–81; and Lawrence J. R. Herson, *The Politics of Ideas: Political Theory and American Public Policy* (Homewood, Ill.: Dorsey Press, 1984), chap. 9.

66. Ibid., pp. 7–14.

67. John Stuart Mill, *Principles of Political Economy* (1867), bk. II, chap. 1.

68. For a more comprehensive account of the development of the Western intellectual tradition in Latin America, see Leopoldo Zea, *The Latin American Mind* (Norman: Oklahoma University Press, 1963).

69. For a classic analysis of the relationship among the Protestant Reformation, liberalism, and the development of capitalism, see Max Weber, *The Protestant Ethic and the Spirit of Capitalism* (New York: Scribner, 1958).

70. Cf. papal encyclical *Rerum Novarum* (1891). In this encyclical, Pope Leo XIII confronted the twin problems of working-class conditions and class conflict, both perceived as resulting from the capitalist Industrial Revolution. Leo claimed that, while a natural social division exists between owners and workers, mutual obligations also exist. Workers must complete agreements and never sabotage machinery or engage in any form of violence, especially riots and other civil disorders. And the wealthy class and employers should not treat workers as slaves, but must pay them a just wage.

71. Cf. L. S. Stavrianos, *Global Rift: The Third World Comes of Age* (New York: Morrow, 1981), pp. 95–98.

72. Peter DeWitt and James F. Petras, "The Political Economy of International Debt," in *Class, State and Power in the Third World: With Case Studies on Class Conflict in Latin America,* ed. Petras (Montclair, N.J.: Allanheld, Osmun, 1981), pp. 96–117; David Collier and Ruth Berins Collier, "Who Does What to Whom, and How: Toward a Comparative Analysis of Latin American Corporatism," in *Authoritarianism and Corporatism in Latin America,* ed. James M. Malloy (Pittsburgh: University of Pittsburgh Press, 1977), pp. 489–512. Also cf. Guillermo O'Donnell, *Modernization and Bureaucratic-Authoritarianism: Studies in South American Politics* (Berkeley: Institute of International Studies, 1973).

73. Lernoux, *Cry of the People,* chap. 7.

74. See, for example, the discussion in Alain de Janvry, *The Agrarian Question and Reformism in Latin America* (Baltimore: Johns Hopkins, 1981).

75. Cf. Brian H. Smith, "Churches and Human Rights in Latin America: Recent Trends on the Subcontinent," in *Churches and Politics in Latin America,* ed. Daniel H. Levine (Beverly Hills, Sage Publications, 1980), pp. 162–67.

76. For an early discussion of the problems of development for religious individuals, see René Laurentin, *Liberation, Development and Salvation* (Maryknoll, N.Y.: Orbis Books, 1972).

Chapter 2

1. Isaiah Berlin, "Two Concepts of Liberty," in *Four Essays on Liberty,* Berlin (London: Oxford University Press, 1977), p. 119. Berlin continues in his reference to Heine,

> He spoke of Kant's *Critique of Pure Reason* as the sword with which European deism had been decapitated, and described the works of Rousseau as the blood-stained weapon which, in the hands of Robespierre, had destroyed the old regime; and prophesied that the romantic faith of Fichte and Schelling would one day be turned, with terrible effect, by their fanatical German followers, against the liberal culture of the West.

While Heine's interpretation as portrayed by Berlin may be open to challenge, the importance of ideas moving the world must not be ignored.

2. For example, Augustine incorporated neo-Platonism to give consistent structure and rationality to Christian beliefs; see, for example, *The City of God* (413–26). Later, Aquinas utilized Aristotelian categories for the same purpose; see, for example, *Summa Theologica* (1265). And in the modern era, efforts to incorporate Kantian categories are well underway; see, for example, Karl Rahner, *Foundations of Christian Faith* (New York: Seabury Press, 1978).

3. For a more comprehensive treatment of this development, see Alexa Suelzer, "Modern Old Testament Criticism," in *The Jerome Biblical Commentary,* eds. Joseph A. Fitzmyer and Raymond E. Brown (Englewood Cliffs, N.J.: Prentice-Hall, 1968), vol. 2, pp. 590–604.

4. David Tracy, *Blessed Rage for Order: The New Pluralism in Theology* (New York: Seabury Press, 1975), p. 6.

5. Ibid., p. 26.

6. Ibid., pp. 6–10.

7. Ibid., pp. 12–13.

8. In fact, Tracy discusses five models of theology vying for attention in response to the crisis of modernity. He uses the following labels:

Notes to Chapter 2

orthodox, liberal, neo-orthodox, radical, and revisionist; see ibid., primarily chap. 2. He characterizes liberation theology generally as a neo-orthodox model of theology; see ibid., pp. 242, 244–45.

9. For a brief biography of Gustavo Gutiérrez, see Robert McAfee Brown, *Gustavo Gutiérrez* (Atlanta: John Knox Press, 1980).

10. This protest consists of three main thrusts discussed later; for a brief overview, see J. Andrew Kirk, *Theology Encounters Revolution* (Downers Grove, Ill.: InterVarsity Press, 1980), pp. 116–17.

11. José Comblin, *The Church and the National Security State* (Maryknoll, N.Y.: Orbis Books, 1979), chap. 1.

12. Ibid., p. 4.

13. Ibid. Cf. José Míguez Bonino, "Popular Piety in Latin America," in *The Mystical and Political Dimension of the Christian Faith,* eds. Claude Geffré and Gustavo Gutiérrez (New York: Herder and Herder, 1974), pp. 148–57.

14. Ignacio Ellacuría, *Freedom Made Flesh: The Mission of Christ and His Church* (Maryknoll, N.Y.: Orbis Books, 1976), p. 8.

15. Ibid., p. 9; cf. Dennis P. McCann, *Christian Realism and Liberation Theology: Practical Theologies in Conflict* (Maryknoll, N.Y.: Orbis Books, 1981).

16. Ibid. Cf. Kirk, *Theology Encounters Revolution,* p. 180; Kirk also laments

the division of theology into self-contained areas of specialization, which has effectively divorced ethics, systematic theology and biblical studies, from each other, and an approach to the Bible which implies that it can be "scientifically" studied without consideration of the interpreter's historical and cultural situation.

17. Comblin, *Church and the National Security State,* p. 5.

18. Ibid., p. 6.

19. Ibid., p. 3.

20. Ibid., p. 6.

21. Ibid., p. 2.

22. Gustavo Gutiérrez, *A Theology of Liberation: History, Politics and Salvation* (Maryknoll, N.Y.: Orbis Books, 1973), p. 4.

23. Ibid.

24. Ibid., p. 5.

25. See, for example, Juan Gutiérrez, *The New Libertarian Gospel: Pitfalls of the Theology of Liberation* (Chicago: Franciscan Herald Press, 1977), pp. 21–35.

26. Comblin, *Church and the National Security State,* p. 2.

27. Included are political theologians from Europe and North America as well as the Third World; see, for example, Jürgen Moltmann, *A Theology*

of Hope: On the Ground and the Implications of a Christian Eschatology (New York: Harper, 1967), and James Cone, *God of the Oppressed* (New York: Seabury Press, 1975). For an introduction to these and other radical theological perspectives, see Kirk, *Theology Encounters Revolution,* esp. chaps. 4–7.

28. Comblin, *Church and the National Security State,* p. 7.

29. Examples of more critical, biblical exegetical work can be found in Norman K. Gottwald, ed., *The Bible and Liberation: Political and Social Hermeneutics* (Maryknoll, N.Y.: Orbis Books, 1983).

30. Juan Luis Segundo, *The Liberation of Theology* (Maryknoll, N.Y.: Orbis Books, 1976), p. 75.

31. Ibid.

32. Ibid., p. 76.

33. Ibid.

34. Gutiérrez, *Theology of Liberation,* p. 11.

35. Segundo, *Liberation of Theology,* p. 77.

36. Ibid.

37. Ibid., pp. 77–78.

38. Ibid., p. 78.

39. Currently, such criticisms have been made by social theorists of radical theologies that deduce judgments on contemporary social conditions from theological certitudes; see, for example, Jürgen Habermas, *Legitimation Crisis* (Boston: Beacon, 1975), p. 121, wherein he criticizes European political theologians who call for revolution in a way that bypasses the human element by relying solely on God's intervention.

40. Segundo, *Liberation of Theology,* p. 80.

41. Ibid., p. 80.

42. Ibid., p. 81.

43. See, for example, Augustine, *City of God,* (413–426) and John B. Cobb, Jr., and David Ray Griffin, *Process Theology: An Introductory Exposition* (Philadelphia: Westminster Press, 1976); cf. John B. Cobb, Jr., *Process Theology as Political Theology* (Philadelphia: Westminster Press, 1982) ; and John B. Cobb, Jr., and W. Widick Schroeder, eds., *Process Philosophy and Social Thought* (Chicago: Center for the Scientific Study of Religion, 1981), esp. pt. 3, "Process Thought and Liberation Theology."

44. José Míguez Bonino, *Doing Theology in a Revolutionary Situation* (Philadelphia: Fortress Press, 1975), pp. 89–90.

45. José Porfirio Miranda, *Marx and the Bible: A Critique of the Philosophy of Oppression* (Maryknoll, N.Y.: Orbis Books, 1974), p. 44.

46. Ibid., pp. 45–46.

47. Ibid., pp. 46–47.

48. Ibid., p. 47.

49. Ibid., p. 47.

50. Ibid., p. 48.

51. Míguez Bonino, *Doing Theology in a Revolutionary Situation,* p. 90.

52. Gustavo Gutiérrez, "Talking About God," *Sojourners* 12 (February 1983): 29. (Reprinted with permission from *Sojourners,* Box 29272, Washington, D.C. 20017.)

53. Gustavo Gutiérrez, "Latin America's Pain is Bearing Fruit," in *A New Way of Being Church: Interviews and Testimonies* (Lima, Peru: Latinamerica Press, 1984), p. 3.

54. Raúl Vidales, "Methodological Issues in Liberation Theology," *Frontiers of Theology in Latin America,* ed. Rosino Gibellini (Maryknoll, N.Y.: Orbis Books, 1979), pp. 43–53.

55. Ibid., pp. 43–44; cf. T. Howland Sanks and Brian H. Smith, "Liberation Ecclesiology: Praxis, Theory, Praxis," *Theological Studies* 38 (March 1977): 3–38.

56. Cf. Míguez Bonino, *Doing Theology in a Revolutionary Situation,* pt. 1; and Gutiérrez, *Theology of Liberation,* pp. 123–24.

57. Ellacuría, *Freedom Made Flesh,* chap. 1.

58. Vidales, "Methodological Issues," p. 44.

59. Ibid., p. 45; cf. Gustavo Gutiérrez, "Liberation Praxis and Christian Faith," in *Frontiers of Theology in Latin America,* ed. Rosino Gibellini (Maryknoll, N.Y.: Orbis Books, 1979), pp. 1–33.

60. Ibid.

61. Ibid., p. 46.

62. Kirk, *Theology Encounters Revolution,* p. 12.

63. Vidales, "Methodological Issues," p. 47.

64. Consider the official Catholic church's usage of "liberation" language as an attempt to forestall the radical social implications of liberation theology in recent documents on social justice; see, for example, *Instructions on Certain Aspects of the "Theology of Liberation",* Sacred Congregation for the Doctrine of the Faith (Rome, 6 August 1984).

65. Vidales, "Methodological Issues," p. 47; cf. J. Severino Croatto, "Biblical Hermeneutics in the Theologies of Liberation," in *Irruption of the Third World: Challenge to Theology,* eds. Virginia Fabella and Sergio Torres (Maryknoll, N.Y.: Orbis Books, 1983), pp. 140–68.

66. Ibid., p. 48.

67. Ibid.

68. Ibid.

69. Ibid., p. 49.

70. Ibid., p. 50.
71. Ibid.
72. Ibid.
73. Ibid., p. 51.
74. Segundo, *Liberation of Theology*, p. 8; chap. 1 deals with the dynamics of the circle. Cf. Alfred T. Hennelly, *Theologies in Conflict: The Challenge of Juan Luis Segundo* (Maryknoll, N.Y.: Orbis Books, 1979), pp. 108–15.
75. See, for example, Gutiérrez's list: fraudulent commerce and exploitation: Hos. 12:8, Amos 8:5, Mic. 6:10–11, Isa. 3:14, Jer. 5:27, 6:12; hoarding of lands: Mic. 2:1–3, Ezek. 22:29, Hab. 2:5–6; dishonest courts: Amos 5:7, Jer. 22:13–17, Mic. 3:9–11, Isa. 5:23, 10:1–2; the violence of the ruling classes: 2 Kings 23:30, 35, Amos 4:1, Mic. 3:1–2, 6:12, Jer. 22:13–17; slavery: Neh. 5:1–5, Amos 2:6, 8:6; unjust taxes: Amos 4:1, 5:11–12; unjust functionaries: Amos 5:7, Jer. 5:28; oppression by the rich: Luke 6:24–25, 12:13–21, 16:19–31, 18:18–26, James 2:5–9, 4:13–17, 5:16; *Theology of Liberation,* p. 293. For usage of the biblical account of the Great Exodus as a paradigm for politics by liberation theologians, see J. Severino Croatto, *Exodus: A Hermeneutics of Freedom* (Maryknoll, N.Y.: Orbis Books, 1981); and for a general assessment of this usage, see William K. McElvaney, *Good News Is Bad News Is Good News* (Maryknoll, N.Y.: Orbis Books, 1980).
76. For further discussion on "Christian base communities" or CEBs, see chap. 5.
77. On political ethics, see chap. 5.

Chapter 3

1. Gustavo Gutiérrez, *Teología de la liberación: perspectivas* [*A Theology of liberation: perspectives*] (Lima: CEP, 1971).
2. Michael Dodson, "Prophetic Politics and Political Theory in Latin America," *Polity* 12 (Spring 1980): 391; cf. Michael Dodson, "Liberation Theology and Christian Radicalism in Contemporary Latin America," *Journal of Latin American Studies* 2 (May 1979): 203–22.
3. For a brief account of this conflict, see Arthur F. McGovern, *Marxism: An American Christian Perspective* (Maryknoll, N.Y.: Orbis Books, 1980), pp. 90–109. However, the attitude of the Catholic church, for one, toward Marxism has shifted over time. In *Quadragesimo Anno* (1931), Pope Pius XI condemned those socialists who were openly hostile to the Church. (See "*Quadragesimo Anno:* Encyclical of Pope Pius XI on Reconstruction of the Social Order, May 15, 1931," in *The Papal Encyclicals,* 5 vols., ed. Claudia Carlen [Raleigh, North Carolina: McGrath Publishing Co., 1981], vol. 3, pp. 415–43.) And in *Divini Redemptoris* (1937), he condemned atheistic communism in

response to the exposed brutality of Stalin's regime, the Civil War in Spain, and the revolution in Mexico, all of which had involved the violent repression of the clergy by communists. (See "*Divini Redemptoris:* Encyclical of Pope Pius XI on Atheistic Communism, March 19, 1937," in *The Papal Encyclicals,* vol. 3, pp. 537–54.) But by 1971, the Church's position had mollified. In *Octogesima Adveniens,* Pope Paul VI officially recognized distinctions regarding Marxism and socialism, and set forth guidelines for distinguishing between those Marxist positions unacceptable for Christians and those of legitimate use. (See *Octogesima Adveniens,* in *The Gospel of Peace and Justice: Catholic Social Teaching since Pope John,* ed. Joseph Gremillion (Maryknoll, N.Y.: Orbis Books, 1976].) Consequently, for those religious individuals who had a predisposition toward utilizing Marxist social analysis, Paul's position seemed to offer support. Likewise for those who disdained any use of Marxist theory, Paul also appeared to offer support.

4. For an earlier discussion on this topic, see Reinhold Niebuhr, "Social Justice," in *Christianity and Communism,* ed. H. Wilson Harris (Boston: Marshall Jones Co., 1937), pp. 62–69.

5. Hugo Assmann, *Theology for a Nomad Church* (Maryknoll, N.Y.: Orbis Books, 1976), pp. 116, 132; cf. José Míguez Bonino, *Doing Theology in a Revolutionary Situation* (Philadelphia: Fortress Press, 1975), p. 36. Also see J. Andrew Kirk, *Theology Encounters Revolution* (Downers Grove, Ill.: Inter-Varsity Press, 1980), p. 118.

6. See, for example, Karl Marx, "Economic and Philosophic Manuscripts of 1844," and Míguez Bonino, *Doing Theology in a Revolutionary Situation,* pt. 1, esp. pp. 26–27.

7. This has been a perplexing problem for liberals for some time. The emergence of the welfare state is an attempt to address problems of social inequities while maintaining a capitalist economy. See, for example, John Stuart Mill, *The Principles of Political Economy* (1948). For a contemporary attempt to imbue liberalism with a concept of justice, see John Rawls, *A Theory of Justice* (Cambridge: Harvard University Press, 1971); for right and left criticisms of a Rawlsian approach, cf. Robert Nozick, *Anarchy, State and Utopia* (New York: Basic Books, 1974), pp. 183–231, and Arthur DiQuattro, "Rawls and Left Criticism," *Political Theory* 11 (February 1983): 53–78, respectively. However, for a dialogic defense of liberalism see Bruce A. Ackerman, *Social Justice in the Liberal State* (New Haven: Yale University Press, 1980). And for other significant attempts to maintain liberal democracy, see Michael Margolis, *Viable Democracy* (New York: Penguin Books, 1979), and Robert A. Dahl, *Dilemmas of Pluralist Democracy* (New Haven: Yale University Press, 1982). Also see Roger Benjamin and Stephen L. Elkin, eds., *The Democratic State* (Lawrence: University of Kansas Press, 1985).

8. José Porfirio Miranda, *Communism in the Bible* (Maryknoll, N.Y.: Orbis Books, 1982), esp. chaps. 1, 2.

Notes to Chapter 3

9. Ibid., pp. 12–20; cf. chap. 2.

10. For an indepth treatment of the humanism of Karl Marx, see José Porfirio Miranda, *Marx Against the Marxists: The Christian Humanism of Karl Marx* (Maryknoll, N.Y.: Orbis Books, 1980).

11. Cf. Alasdair MacIntyre, *Marxism and Christianity* (New York: Schocken Books, 1968).

12. See, for example, Juan Luis Segundo, "Capitalism—Socialism: A Theoretical Crux," in *The Mystical and Political Dimension of the Christian Faith,* eds. Claude Geffré and Gustavo Gutiérrez (New York: Herder and Herder, 1974), pp. 105–23, and Karl Marx and Friedrich Engels, "Manifesto of the Communist Party" (1836).

13. Gutiérrez, *Theology of Liberation,* p. 274; cf. Miranda, *Communism in the Bible,* chap. 1; McGovern, *Marxism,* pp. 199–200; and Peter L. Berger, *Pyramids of Sacrifice: Political Ethics and Social Change* (Garden City, N.Y.: Anchor Books, 1974), pp. 26–27.

14. Non-Latin American political theologians include Johannes B. Metz, *Faith in History and Society* (New York: Seabury Press, 1980); Jürgen Moltmann, *Theology of Hope: On the Ground and the Implications of a Christian Eschatology* (New York: Harper, 1967); Wolfhart Pannenburg, *Theology and the Philosophy of Science* (Philadelphia: Westminster Press, 1976); and Dorothee Soelle, *Political Theology* (Philadelphia: Fortress Press, 1974).

15. Alfredo Fierro, *The Militant Gospel: A Critical Introduction to Political Theologies* (Maryknoll, N.Y.: Orbis Books, 1977), p. 77.

16. Ibid., p. 78.

17. Fierro's understanding of the origins of political theology, including its adoption of Marxism, comes from *Militant Gospel,* chap. 3, "The Era of Dialectical Thinking."

18. For a comprehensive analysis of the evolution of attempts to ground moral theories, see Alasdair MacIntyre, *After Virtue: A Study in Moral Theory* (Notre Dame: University of Notre Dame Press, 1981).

19. Fierro, *Militant Gospel,* p. 81.

20. Ibid., p. 82.

21. For one of many discussions on the strengths and weaknesses of this change, see Richard Bernstein, *The Restructuring of Social and Political Theory* (Philadelphia: University of Pennsylvania Press, 1978).

22. Cf. Scott Warren, *The Emergence of Dialectical Theory: Philosophy and Political Inquiry* (Chicago: University of Chicago Press, 1984). The Enlightenment has produced paradoxical results. The development of modern notions of scientific thought has yielded vast social changes as a result of "advances" in technology, especially medicine and mechanical engineering. Cf. Francis Bacon, *Novum Organum* (1620), Herbert Marcuse, *One-Dimensional Man: Studies in the Ideology of Advanced Industrial Society* (Boston:

Notes to Chapter 3

Beacon, 1964), and Jürgen Habermas, *Toward a Rational Society* (Boston: Beacon, 1970). This emphasis on the transformation of nature as the only legitimate approach to organized human activity has also resulted from "positivist" attitudes toward science and theology, effectively proscribing intellectual pursuits containing metaphysical and transcendental categories of speculation. See, for example, A.J. Ayer, *Language, Truth and Logic* (New York: Dover, 1952), and Ayer, ed., *Logical Positivism* (New York: Free Press, 1959).

23. Fierro, *Militant Gospel*, pp. 78–79

24. From Jean-Paul Sartre, *Critique de la raison dialectique* (Paris: Gallimard, 1960), pp. 9–10, quoted by Fierro, *Militant Gospel*, p. 79; English trans., *Critique of Dialectical Reason* (New York: Schocken, 1976).

25. Fierro, *Militant Gospel*, p. 82.

26. Ibid., p. 80. According to Fierro, "Political theology is a theology operating under the sign of Marx, just as truly as scholasticism was a theology operating under the sign of Aristotle and liberal Protestant theology was one operating under the sign of Kant."

27. Ibid., pp. 88–89.

28. Ibid., pp. 92–93.

29. For a general discussion of this distinction, see William K. Frankena, "The Naturalistic Fallacy," in *Perspectives on Morality: Essays of William K. Frankena*, ed. Kenneth K. Goodpaster (Notre Dame: University of Notre Dame, 1976), pp. 1–11.

30. Fierro, *Militant Gospel*, pp. 94–95.

31. Approved 6 August 1984; see Sagrada Congregação para a Doutrina da Fé, *Instrução sobre alguns aspectos da "teología da libertação,"* ed. Joseph Cardinal Ratzinger (São Paulo: Edições Paulinas, 1984). This document is the first part of a two-part, comprehensive statement on liberation theology promulgated by the Congregation for the Doctrine of the Faith under Ratzinger. The second document, "Instruction on Christian Freedom and Liberation," was approved on 22 March 1986; see *Origins: NC Documentary Service* 15 (17 April 1986): 713, 715–28. In the second Instruction, Ratzinger indicates that "between the two documents there exists an organic relationship. They are to be read in the light of each other." (p. 715, par. 2) The first document deals critically and directly with the question of the incorporation of Marxist analysis and theory in Christian theology; the second document is more conciliatory toward liberation theology and does not deal directly with Marxism per se, but instead focuses more broadly on moral problems associated with economic and political development in the Third World, such as the question of "sinful [social] structures," Christian base communities, civil law and freedom, hatred of enemies, revolution, and totalitarianism. (esp. pp. 723-25, pars. 67–70, 72–80)

32. Ibid., pp. 27–28. (translation mine)

33. Ibid., p. 29. (translation mine)
34. Discussion of these themes is found primarily in ibid., chaps. 7–9.
35. Ibid., p. 31.
36. Ibid., p. 30.
37. Ibid., p. 34.
38. Ibid., pp. 29–30. (translation mine)
39. Ibid., p. 33.
40. Ibid., p. 35. (translation mine) For a similar point of view to that of Ratzinger, see Ronald H. Nash, *Poverty and Wealth: The Christian Debate Over Capitalism* (Westchester, Ill.: Crossway Books, 1986), pp. 89–102.
41. Bishop Alfonso López Trujillo, *Liberation or Revolution? An Examination of the Priest's Role in the Socioeconomic Class Struggle in Latin America* (1975; reprint ed., Huntington, Ind.: Our Sunday Visitor, 1977).
42. On Medellín, see chap 1.
43. López Trujillo, *Liberation or Revolution?* pp. 37–38.
44. Ibid., p. 35.
45. Ibid., p. 92.
46. Ibid., p. 94.
47. Father Juan Gutiérrez, *The New Libertarian Gospel: Pitfalls of the Theology of Liberation* (1975; reprint ed., Chicago: Franciscan Herald Press, 1977), pp. 63–66.
48. Ibid., p. 65.
49. Ibid., p. 66.
50. Ibid., p. 66–69.
51. Ibid., p. 69.
52. For a nice introduction to this area of controversy, see McGovern, *Marxism,* chaps. 1, 2.
53. See, for example, David Held, *Introduction to Critical Theory: Horkheimer to Habermas* (Berkeley: University of California Press, 1980).
54. Juan Luis Segundo, *Theology and the Church: A Response to Cardinal Ratzinger and a Warning to the Whole Church* (Minneapolis: Winston Press, 1985), esp. pp. 92–105.
55. Ibid., pp. 96–97.
56. Ibid., pp. 98ff.
57. Ibid., pp. 103ff.
58. Joseph Kroger, "Prophetic-Critical and Practical-Strategic Tasks of Theology: Habermas and Liberation Theology," *Theological Studies* 46 (March 1985): 3–20.
59. Ibid., pp. 16–20.

Notes to Chapter 3

60. MacIntyre, *Marxism and Christianity*, p. 6.

61. Dennis P. McCann, *Christian Realism and Liberation Theology: Practical Theories in Creative Conflict* (Maryknoll, N.Y.: Orbis Books, 1981), p. 160.

62. Karl Marx, "On the Jewish Question" in *Karl Marx: Early Writings*, trans. and ed. T.B. Bottomore (New York: McGraw-Hill, 1964), pp. 1–40.

63. Ibid., p. 7. (emphasis original)

64. Ibid., p. 8. (emphasis original)

65. Ibid., p. 12. (emphasis original)

66. Ibid., p. 15. (emphasis original)

67. Ibid., pp. 15–16. (emphasis original)

68. Ibid., p. 16.

69. Ibid., p. 24. (emphasis original)

70. Ibid., p. 29.

71. Ibid., pp. 30–31.

72. Ibid., p. 34.

73. Ibid.

74. Ibid., p. 39.

75. Ibid., p. 40. Cf. Jean-Paul Sartre, *Anti-Semite and Jew* (New York; Schocken, 1965).

76. According to Delos B. McKown, Marx made no contribution to the scientific study of religion by identifying Judaism with egoism since ordinary people concerned with the practicality of daily living, would possess a religion that is compatible with those practicalities; see *Classical Marxist Critiques of Religion: Marx, Engels, Lenin, Kautsky* (The Hague: Martinus Nijhoff, 1975), pp. 39–40.

77. See, for example, Ian G. Barbour, *Issues in Science and Religion* (New York: Harper Torchbooks, 1966).

78. See Leo Strauss, *Jerusalem and Athens* (New York: The City College, 1967), for a defense of this dichotomy from a nonpositivist perspective. For a counterargument to Strauss, also from a nonpositivist perspective, see Frederick D. Wilhelmsen, *Christianity and Political Philosophy* (Athens, Georgia: The University of Georgia Press, 1978). Cf. Kirk, *Theology Encounters Revolution*, pp. 83–84.

79. Marx, "Introduction to the Contribution to the Critique of Hegel's Philosophy of Right," in *Karl Marx: Early Writings*, p. 43. (emphasis original)

80. Marx, "Introduction," pp. 43–44 (emphasis original); cf. McKown, *Classical Marxist Critiques*, p. 52.

81. Ibid., p. 44. (emphasis original)

Notes to Chapter 3

82. Fierro, *Militant Gospel,* pp. 114–15. Yet this position has been attacked as an incorrect reading both by and of Marx; see McGovern, *Marxism,* chaps. 1, 2.

83. Ibid., p. 117.

84. Cf. Brian H. Smith's discussion of the Catholic church as an agent of social change in *Church and Politics in Chile: Challenges to Modern Catholicism* (Princeton: Princeton University Press, 1982).

85. The following are some examples of writings in this regard: Assmann, *Theology for a Nomad Church*; Ignacio Ellacuría, *Freedom Made Flesh* (Maryknoll, N.Y.: Orbis Books, 1976); Leonardo Boff, *A vida religiosa e a igreja no processo de libertação* (Petrópolis: Editora Vozes, 1975); Leonardo and Clodovis Boff, *Introducing Liberation Theology* (Maryknoll, N.Y.: Orbis Books, 1987); Gutiérrez, *Theology of Liberation; The Power of the Poor in History* (Maryknoll, N.Y.: Orbis Books, 1983); Míguez Bonino, *Christians and Marxists: The Mutual Challenge to Revolution* (Grand Rapids, Mich.: William B. Eerdmans, 1976); *Doing Theology in a Revolutionary Situation*; Miranda, *Communism and the Bible; Marx Against the Marxists; Marx and the Bible: A Critique of the Philosophy of Oppression* (Maryknoll, N.Y.: Orbis Books, 1974); Segundo, *Faith and Ideologies* (Maryknoll, N.Y.: Orbis Books, 1984); *The Liberation of Theology* (Maryknoll, N.Y.: Orbis Books, 1976); and *Theology and the Church.*

86. Segundo, *Liberation of Theology,* chap. 1. He also assesses the thought of Harvey Cox, Max Weber, and James Cone with respect to the hermeneutic circle. With regard to Marx, cf. McKown, *Classical Marxist Critiques,* pp. 59–60. With regard to liberation theology, see Kirk, *Theology Encounters Revolution,* p. 120.

87. Ibid., p. 16.

88. Ibid.

89. Ibid., p. 17; cf. McKown, *Classical Marxist Critiques,* p. 29.

90. Cf. Khomeini's revolution in Iran in 1979, the Sandinista revolution in Nicaragua in 1979, and the various successes of the New Right in elections in the United States in 1980. Leaders in these movements understood the potential of tapping into prevailing religious and cultural values to effect political and economic change.

91. Friedrich Engels to Joseph Bloch, 21–22 September 1890, in *The Marx-Engels Reader,* ed. Robert C. Tucker (New York: Norton, 1972), pp. 640–42. Engels goes on to admit that he and Marx were partially responsible for the misunderstanding as a result of their rush to emphasize the importance of economics in any study of social relations. (emphasis original)

92. McKown, *Classical Marxist Critiques,* p. 24.

93. Fierro, *Militant Gospel,* p. 118.

Notes to Chapter 4

94. See, for example, Jürgen Habermas, *Legitimation Crisis* (Boston: Beacon, 1975), p. 121.

95. Fierro, *Militant Gospel,* pp. 119–20.

96. Douglas Sturm, "Praxis and Promise: On the Ethics of Political Theology," *Ethics* 92 (July 1982): 733–50.

97. Assmann, *Theology for a Nomad Church,* pp. 139–40.

98. Ibid., pp. 140–43.

99. Ibid., p. 143. For a discussion of the role of "prophetic movements" within the Church, see Otto Maduro, *Religion and Social Conflicts* (Maryknoll, N.Y.: Orbis Books, 1982), chap. 25.

100. Ibid., p. 144.

101. Leonardo Boff, "Christians Called to Transform Marxism into Tool for Liberation," in *A New Way of Being Church* (Lima: Latinamerica Press, 1984), p. 7.

102. The eleventh of Marx's "Theses on Feuerbach" (1845).

103. For further discussion on this issue, see chap. 6.

104. MacIntyre, *Marxism and Christianity,* p. 112.

105. Ibid., pp. 115–16.

106. See Herber Aptheker, *The Urgency of Marxist-Christian Dialogue* (New York: Harper, 1970); Roger Garaudy, *The Alternative Future: A Vision of Christian Marxism* (New York: Simon & Schuster, 1974); *From Anathema to Dialogue: A Marxist Challenge to the Christian Churches* (New York: Vintage Books, 1968); Guido Girardi, *Marxism and Christianity* (New York: MacMillan, 1968); Paul Oestreicher, *The Christian Marxist Dialogue: An International Symposium* (London: Collier-Macmillan, 1969); and Nicholas Piediscalzi and Robert G. Thobaben, eds., *From Hope to Liberation: Towards a New Marxist-Christian Dialogue* (Philadelphia: Fortress Press, 1974).

107. Cf. Míguez Bonino, *Christians and Marxists,* chap. 3.

108. Cited in Sergio Arce Martínez, *Cristo vivo en Cuba* (San José: DEI, 1978), p. 27.

Chapter 4

1. Hugo Assmann, *Theology for a Nomad Church* (Maryknoll, N.Y.: Orbis Books, 1976), p. 94.

2. See chaps. 2 and 3.

3. See, for example, *A Theology of Liberation: History, Politics and Salvation* (Maryknoll, N.Y.: Orbis Books, 1973); and *The Power of the Poor in History* (Maryknoll, N.Y.: Orbis Books, 1983). Cf. Juan Luis Segundo, *The Liberation of Theology* (Maryknoll, N.Y.: Orbis Books, 1976); Enrique Dussel,

Ethics and the Theology of Liberation (Maryknoll, N.Y.: Orbis Books, 1978); and José Míguez Bonino, *Doing Theology in a Revolutionary Situation* (Philadelphia: Fortress Press, 1975).

4. See chap. 3. According to Assmann, the very language of liberation theology invites the use of Marxist sociology; see *Theology for a Nomad Church*, p. 116.

5. Gustavo Gutiérrez, "Freedom and Salvation: A Political Problem," in *Liberation and Change*, ed. Ronald H. Stone (Atlanta: John Knox Press, 1977), pp. 27–32.

6. Ibid., pp. 28–30; cf. Gutiérrez, *Power of the Poor in History*, pp. 171–76.

7. Ibid., p. 30.

8. Gutiérrez, *Theology of Liberation*, p. 82.

9. Ibid.

10. Ibid., p. 83.

11. Ibid.

12. Early important discussions of economic stages can be found in W. W. Rostow, ed., *The Economics of Take-Off into Sustained Growth* (New York: St. Martin's, 1963); cf. Samuel P. Huntington, *Political Order in Changing Societies* (New Haven: Yale University Press, 1968).

13. Gutiérrez, *Theology of Liberation*, p. 84.

14. Ibid.

15. According to Dussel, in fact there are three levels of domination: political, sexual, and educational. See his article, "Domination-Liberation: A New Approach," in *The Mystical and Political Dimension of the Christian Faith*, eds. Claude Gerré and Gustavo Gutiérrez (New York: Herder and Herder, 1974), pp. 34–56.

16. Ibid., p. 41.

17. Enrique D. Dussel, "Historical and Philosophical Presuppositions for Latin American Theology," in *Frontiers of Theology in Latin America*, ed. Rosino Gibellini (Maryknoll, N.Y.: Orbis Books, 1979), pp. 195–96.

18. Ibid., pp. 209–10. For further discussion of the dynamics itself of sexual politics or "erotics," see Enrique Dussel, *Philosophy of Liberation* (Maryknoll, N.Y.: Orbis Books, 1985), pp. 78–87.

19. Dussel, *Philosophy of Liberation*, p. 147.

20. Ibid., pp. 147, 171.

21. Ibid., p. 150.

22. Dussel, "Domination-Liberation," p. 41.

23. Gutiérrez, *Theology of Liberation*, p. 84; with regard to the dependent status of Cuba and Nicaragua on the United States, see Herbert L. Matthews, *Revolution in Cuba: An Essay in Understanding* (New York: Scribner,

Notes to Chapter 4

1975), pp. 34–48; and John A. Booth, *The End and the Beginning: The Nicaraguan Revolution* (Boulder, Colo.: Westview Press, 1982), chaps. 1–5, respectively.

24. Ibid., p. 85.

25. Ibid., p. 86; cf. Fernando Henrique Cardoso and Enzo Faletto, *Dependency and Development in Latin America* (Berkeley: University of California Press, 1979).

26. Michael Novak, *Will It Liberate? Questions About Liberation Theology* (New York: Paulist Press, 1986), pp. 127–42. Novak writes here in response to an article defending liberation theology's use of dependency theory by Arthur F. McGovern, "Latin America and Dependency Theory," *This World* (Spring-Summer 1986): 104–23; cf. Hugo Assmann, "Democracy and the Debt Crisis," *This World* (Spring-Summer 1986): 83–103. Interestingly, McGovern's article was written in response to an earlier article by Novak, "The Case Against Liberation Theology," *New York Times Sunday Magazine* (21 October 1984): 51, 82–87, 93–95.

27. Ibid., p. 128; cf. Novak, "The Case Against Liberation Theology," p. 86.

28. Novak, "The Case Against Liberation Theology," pp. 85, 93.

29. Ibid., p. 84; and Novak, *Will It Liberate?* p. 139.

30. Novak, *Will It Liberate?* p. 130.

31. Ibid., p. 138. (emphasis added)

32. Ibid., p. 140.

33. Cf. Official Catholic church documents such as *"Rerum Novarum:* Encyclical of Pope Leo XIII on Capital and Labor, May 15, 1891," in *The Papal Encyclicals,* 5 vols., ed. Claudia Carlen (Raleigh, N.C.: McGrath Publishing Co., 1981), vol. 2, pp. 241–61. Pope Leo XIII addressed, among other issues, unacceptable working-class conditions of the Industrial Revolution. He argued that a natural social division exists between owners and workers, with mutual obligations. The state must play an active role, as well, in redressing economic wrongs by remedying the social evils of excessive working hours and poor working conditions. See also *"Quadragesimo Anno:* Encyclical of Pope Pius XI on Reconstruction of the Social Order, May 15, 1931," *The Papal Encyclicals,* vol. 3, pp. 415–43. Here Pope Pius XI attempted to clarify the thoughts of Leo in *Rerum Novarum.* He also wanted to restore a sense of social harmony as had existed in medieval Christendom. Consequently, he rejected both liberal or laissez-faire capitalism and collectivist socialism. Furthermore, Pius expressed in stronger language than that of Leo, a condemnation of the concentration of wealth in a few hands as not part of the natural order of class divisions intended by God. Cf. Ricardo Planas, *Liberation Theology: The Political Expression of Religion* (Kansas City, Mo.: Sheed & Ward, 1986), pp. 126–35.

34. Gutiérrez, *Theology of Liberation*, p. 87.

35. Ibid., p. 88.

36. See, for example, Roger Benjamin and Stephen L. Elkin, eds., *The Democratic State* (Lawrence: University of Kansas Press, 1985).

37. José Comblin, *The Church and the National Security State* (Maryknoll, N.Y.: Orbis Books, 1973), chap. 5.

38. Despite the cursory nature of Comblin's account, Congress has frequently been described as either unable or unwilling to assert itself more vigorously with regard to foreign policy in the last thirty-five years. For a discussion of this problem, see Theodore J. Lowi, *The End of Liberalism*, 2d ed. (New York: Norton, 1979), chap. 6. With regard to Congress's attempt to regain political authority through the "legislative veto," see Lawrence C. Dodd and Richard L. Schott, *Congress and the Administrative State* (New York: Wiley, 1973), pp. 229–35; cf. the recent Supreme Court decision that the legislative veto is unconstitutional under certain conditions, *Immigration and Naturalization Service* v. *Chadha*, 103 S. Ct. 2764 (1983).

39. Comblin, *Church and the National Security State*, p. 64.

40. Ibid., p. 65.

41. Ibid.

42. Comblin cites the late, former senator J. W. Fulbright concerning the fact that the national security ideology is taught at Washington's National War College at Fort McNair (ibid., note 2, p. 229).

43. Comblin refers to the following authors and their works: General Golbery do Couto e Silva, *Geopolítica do Brasil* (Rio de Janeiro: José Olympio, 1967); Jorge E. Atencio, *Qué és la geopolítica?* (Buenos Aires: Pleamer, 1965); Augusto Pinochet Ugarte, *Geopolítica* (Santiago de Chile: Andres Bello, 1974); Rudolf Kjellen, *The State as an Organism* (Uppsala, 1916); and José Alfredo Amaral Gurgel, *Segurança e Democracia* (Rio de Janeiro: José Olympio, 1975).

44. Comblin, *Church and the National Security State*, p. 67.

45. Ibid., p. 68. Comblin notes that this doctrine was taught at the Geopolitics Institute of Munich, which played a significant role in the rise of Nazism between 1923 and 1932.

46. Ibid., pp. 68–69.

47. Comblin notes that General Golbery, a writer on geopolitics and the primary theoretician of the military junta in Brazil (1964–84), devised a program whereby Brazil was to dominate not only all of South America, but all of the South Atlantic region itself. In light of Comblin's example, recall that during the Falklands crisis of late spring 1982, the Argentine military junta, also guided by the ideology of the national security state, frequently referred to the taking of the Malvinas (Falkland Islands) as a move in support of "Greater Argentina."

48. Comblin, *Church and the National Security State,* p. 70.

49. Ibid., pp. 70–71.

50. Ibid., p. 71.

51. For a graphic example of the breakdown of rule of law by government authorities in contemporary violence-torn El Salvador, see Richard Alan White, "Rule Without Law: El Salvador," *Human Rights Quarterly* 4 (Spring 1982): 149–53.

52. Comblin, *Church and the National Security State,* pp. 71–72.

53. Ibid., p. 72.

54. Ibid.

55. Ibid., pp. 72–73.

56. Ibid., p. 73.

57. Ibid.

58. At this point, the role of the media becomes crucial in shaping the wants and desires of the citizens. For one critical assessment of this role, see Herbert I. Schiller, *Communication and Cultural Domination* (White Plains, N.Y.: M. E. Sharpe, 1976).

59. The amount of sacrifice necessary involves crucial ethical questions; in this regard, see Peter L. Berger, *Pyramids of Sacrifice: Political Ethics and Social Change* (Garden City, N.Y. Anchor Books, 1976), chap. 5.

60. Comblin, *The Church and the National Security State,* p. 74; but for an alternative understanding of the relationship between security and liberty, see Margaret E. Crahan, "National Security Ideology and Human Rights," in *Human Rights and Basic Needs in the Americas,* ed. Crahan (Washington, D.C.: Georgetown University Press, 1982), pp. 100–127.

61. Ibid., pp. 74–77.

62. Ibid., p. 75.

63. Ibid., pp. 75–76.

64. Ibid., pp. 76–77.

65. Ibid., p. 77; cf. Penney Lernoux, *Cry of the People: The Struggle for Human Rights in Latin America—The Catholic Church in Conflict with U.S. Policy* (New York: Penguin Books, 1982), chap. 6.

66. Ibid.

67. Ibid., p. 78.

68. See, for example, Gutiérrez, *Theology of Liberation,* p. 48, and Dussel, *Ethics and the Theology of Liberation,* p. 43.

69. Comblin, *Church and the National Security State,* chap. 3.

70. See, for example, Ronald H. Chilcote, ed., *Dependency and Marxism: Toward a Resolution of the Debate* (Boulder, Colo.: Westview Press, 1982).

71. Míguez Bonino, *Doing Theology in a Revolutionary Situation,* pp. 38–40.

72. Ibid., p. 40.

73. Ibid., p. 41.

74. Ibid., p. 42; cf. chap. 3.

75. See, for example, Allan Buchanan, *Ethics, Efficiency, and the Market* (Totowa, N.J.: Rowman and Allanheld, 1985), chap. 2.

76. On the competency and inadequacies of market systems, see Charles E. Lindblom, *Politics and Markets: The World's Political-Economic Systems* (New York: Basic, 1977), chaps. 3, 6.

77. For a complete discussion of efficiency versus justice, see Scott Gordon, *Welfare, Justice, and Freedom* (New York: Columbia University Press, 1980).

78. See, for example, Lawrence C. Becker, "Property Rights and Social Welfare," in *Economic Justice: Private Rights and Public Responsibilities,* eds. Kenneth Kipnis and Diana T. Myers (Totowa, N.J.: Rowman & Allanheld, 1985), pp. 71–86.

79. For a recent theoretical discussion of Sandinismo, see José Luis Coraggio, *Nicaragua: Revolution and Democracy* (Boston: Allen & Unwin, 1986).

80. Cf. Sergio Ramírez, ed., *Augusto C. Sandino: el pensamiento vivo,* 2 vols. (Managua: Nueva Nicaragua, 1981), and Jamie Wheelock Román, *Imperialismo y dictadura* (Managua: Nueva Nicaragua, 1985).

81. And, they maintain, it is for this reason of undermining its position of domination vis-à-vis other Third World countries and *not* for reasons of "anticommunism," that the United States opposes the Sandinista influence in regional politics.

82. Norma Stoltz Chinchilla, "Women in Revolutionary Movements: The Case of Nicaragua," in *Revolution in Central America,* ed. by Stanford Central America Action Network (Boulder, Colo.: Westview Press, 1983), p. 432.

83. Hannah Arendt, *On Revolution* (New York: Penguin Books, 1965).

84. Carlos M. Vilas, *The Sandinista Revolution: National Liberation and Social Transformation in Central America* (New York: Monthly Review Press, 1986), chap. 7.

85. Cf. Alexis de Tocqueville, *Democracy in America* (1835), primarily vol. 1, and Jean-Jacques Rousseau, *Social Contract* (1762), bk. 1, chap. 9; and *A Discourse on the Origin of Inequality* (1755). Also cf. Aristotle, *Politics* (c. 345 B.C.) bks. 3–6.

86. Cf. Rousseau, *Social Contract,* bks. 2, 3, passim.

87. From personal conversation with Professor Luis Villavicencio, FSLN member of the National Assembly and coauthor of the new constitution, in Managua, 16 March 1987. Cf. Nicaraguan Constitution, Title VIII, chaps. 2 (legislative branch), 3 (executive branch), 5 (judicial branch), and 6 (electoral branch).

88. For one discussion among many on this topic, see Linda J. Medcalf and Kenneth M. Dolbeare, *Neopolitics: American Political Ideas in the 1980s* (New York: Random, 1985); cf. Robert A. Dahl, *A Preface to Economic Democracy* (Berkeley: University of California Press, 1985).

89. Coraggio, *Nicaragua,* p. 8.

90. Cf. Nicaraguan Constitution (1987): Article I, chap. 1, art. 5 (on pluralism and mixed economy); Article IV, chap. 1 (individual rights) and chap. 2 (political rights); and Article VI, chap. 1 (national economy), esp. art. 98ff.

91. Cf. Vilas, *Sandinista Revolution,* chap. 6.

92. For discussion of this problem, see Otto Maduro, *Religion and Social Conflicts* (Maryknoll, N.Y.: Orbis Books, 1982), pt. 3.

93. Assmann, *Theology for a Nomad Church,* pp. 92–94.

94. Gutiérrez, "Freedom and Salvation," p. 57.

95. Ibid., p. 59.

Chapter 5

1. Juan Luis Segundo, "Christianity and Violence in Latin America," *Christianity and Crisis* 4 (March 1968): 33.

2. See, for example, Hélder Câmara, *Revolution Through Peace* (New York: Harper, 1971); cf. Leonardo Boff, *O destino do homem e do mundo: ensaio sôbre a vocação humana* (Petrópolis: Editora Vozes, 1973).

3. Cf. official statements found in Joseph Gremillion, ed., *The Gospel of Peace and Justice: Catholic Social Teaching since Pope John* (Maryknoll, N.Y.: Orbis Books, 1976).

4. Raúl Vidales, "Methodological Issues in Liberation Theology," in *Frontiers of Theology in Latin America,* ed. Rosino Gibellini (Maryknoll, N.Y.: Orbis Books, 1979), p. 51.

5. Ibid., pp. 52–53.

6. An example of one justification for this dichotomy, although not the suffering resulting from those who employ this dichotomy, can be found in Reinhold Niebuhr, *Moral Man and Immoral Society: A Study in Ethics and Politics* (1932; reprint ed., New York: Scribner, 1960); and *The Children of Light*

Notes to Chapter 5

and the Children of Darkness: A Vindication of Democracy and a Critique of Its Traditional Defense (1944; reprint ed., New York: Scribner, 1972).

7. Vidales, "Methodological Issues," p. 53.

8. For an alternative understanding, cf. Robert C. Freysinger, "The Just Revolution of Modern Christian Radicalism," *Contemporary Crises* 4 (1980): 353–66; however, cf. Ignacio Ellacuría, "Human Rights in a Divided Society," in *Human Rights in the Americas: The Struggle for Consensus,* eds. Alfred Hennelly and John Langan (Washington, D.C.: Georgetown University Press, 1982), pp. 52–65; and John R. Pottenger, "Liberation Theology: Its Methodological Foundation for Violence," in *The Morality of Terrorism: Secular and Religious Justifications,* eds. David C. Rapoport and Yonah Alexander (New York: Pergamon Press, 1982), pp. 99–123. Also for a contrast of European political theology with Latin American liberation theology, see Jürgen Moltmann, *Theology of Hope: On the Ground and the Implications of a Christian Eschatology* (New York: Harper, 1967). A critical assessment of Moltmann's position can be found in Jon P. Gunnemann, *The Moral Meaning of Revolution* (New Haven: Yale University Press, 1979), chap. 5; however, Gunnemann confuses European political theology with Latin American liberation theology by mistakenly assuming their methodologies are identical.

9. José Comblin, *The Church and the National Security State* (Maryknoll, N.Y.: Orbis Books, 1979), p. 29.

10. Juan Luis Segundo, *The Liberation of Theology* (Maryknoll, N.Y.: Orbis Books, 1976), p. 116.

11. Ibid., pp. 104–5.

12. José Míguez Bonino, *Doing Theology in a Revolutionary Situation* (Philadelphia: Fortress Books, 1975), p. 88.

13. Segundo, *Liberation of Theology,* p. 176.

14. Ibid., pp. 176–78.

15. Míguez Bonino, *Doing Theology in a Revolutionary Situation,* p. 90.

16. Hugo Assmann, *Theology for a Nomad Church* (Maryknoll, N.Y.: Orbis Books, 1976), pp. 34–35.

17. Segundo, *Liberation of Theology,* p. 179.

18. Ibid., pp. 178–80.

19. Ibid., p. 110. (emphasis original)

20. Ibid., pp. 102, 105; see chap. 4 for the explanation of the relationship of faith to ideology; cf. Juan Luis Segundo, *Faith and Ideologies* (Maryknoll, N.Y.: Orbis Books, 1984), p. 16.

21. Assmann, *Theology for a Nomad Church,* p. 122. This deliberate and positive use of ideology may be the most characteristic feature of liberation theology; see J. Andrew Kirk, *Theology Encounters Revolution* (Downers Grove, Ill.: InterVarsity Press, 1980), p. 118.

Notes to Chapter 5

22. On insightful essays dealing with the rule of law, see Arthur L. Harding, ed., *The Rule of Law* (Dallas: Southern Methodist University Press, 1961).

23. Cf. Guillermo Cook, *The Expectation of the Poor: Latin American Basic Ecclesial Communities in Protestant Perspective* (Maryknoll, N.Y.: Orbis Books, 1985), chaps. 2–4.

24. "Conscientization" is the English transliteration of the Portuguese word *conscientização* coined by the Brazilian educator Paulo Freire. For a critique of "conscientization," see Peter L. Berger, *Pyramids of Sacrifice: Political Ethics and Social Change* (Garden City, N.Y.: Anchor Books, 1976), chap. 4.

25. Leonardo Boff, *Ecclesiogenesis: The Base Communities Reinvent the Church* (Maryknoll, N.Y.: Orbis Books, 1986), p. 4; cf. Joseph G. Healy, "Let the Base Christian Communities Speak: Some Pastoral Theology Reflections on Portezuelo and Beyond," *Missiology: An International Review* 11 (January 1983): 15–30.

26. Thomas C. Bruneau, "Basic Christian Communities in Latin America: Their Nature and Significance (esp. in Brazil)," in *Churches and Politics in Latin America,* ed. Daniel H. Levine (Beverly Hills: Sage Publications, 1980), pp. 225–37. Cf. Daniel H. Levine, "Assessing the Impacts of Liberation Theology in Latin America," *The Review of Politics* 50 (Spring 1988): 241–63.

27. Boff, *Ecclesiogenesis,* pp. 4–6, 32–33.

28. Gustavo Gutiérrez, "Latin America's Pain Is Bearing Fruit," in *A New Way of Being Church: Interviews and Testimonies from Latinamerica Press* (Lima, Peru: Noticias Aliadas, 1984), p. 3.

29. Cf. Gottfried Deelen, "The Church on Its Way to the People: Basic Christian Communities in Brazil," *Cross Currents* 30 (Winter 1980–81): 385–408.

30. See, for example, Penny Lernoux, *Cry of the People: The Struggle for Human Rights in Latin America—The Catholic Church in Conflict with U.S. Foreign Policy* (New York: Penguin Books, 1982), pt. 1; Tommie Sue Montgomery, *Revolution in El Salvador: Origins and Evolution* (Boulder, Colo.: Westview Press, 1982), chaps. 2, 6; Joan Didion, *Salvador* (New York: Pocket Books, 1983); and John A. Booth, *The End and the Beginning: The Nicaraguan Revolution* (Boulder, Colo.: Westview Press, 1982), chaps. 4, 5.

31. See, for example, Jean-Jacques Rousseau, *The Social Contract* (1762).

32. See, for example, James Madison, *Federalist Papers* (1787–88), esp. nos. 10, 51.

33. For a general discussion on this, see Phillip Berryman, *The Religious Roots of Rebellion: Christians in Central American Revolutions* (Maryknoll, N.Y.: Orbis Books, 1984), chaps. 2–8.

Notes to Chapter 5

34. Cf. Arthur F. McGovern, *Marxism: An American Christian Perspective* (Maryknoll, N.Y.: Orbis Books, 1980), p. 289; for a treatment of just war theory, see Paul Ramsey, *War and the Christian Conscience: How Shall Modern War Be Conducted Justly?* (Durham, N.C.: Duke University Press, 1961); cf. John Langan, "Violence and Injustice in Society: Recent Catholic Teaching," *Theological Studies* 46 (1985): 685–99.

35. Cf. Comblin, *Church and the National Security State*, p. 29.

36. Cf. Míguez Bonino, *Doing Theology in a Revolutionary Situation*, chap. 3, and Gutiérrez, *A Theology of Liberation: History, Politics and Salvation* (Maryknoll, N.Y.: Orbis Books, 1973), chap. 11. Also, cf. J. G. Davies, *Christians, Politics, and Violent Revolution* (Maryknoll, N.Y.: Orbis Books, 1976), pp. 100–6.

37. Comblin, *Church and the National Security State*, pp. 30–40.

38. Ibid., p. 36.

39. For a recent statement of the eight criteria necessary for the development of a just social revolution, see Neal Riemer, *Karl Marx and Prophetic Politics* (New York: Praeger, 1987), p. 109.

40. Segundo, "Christianity and Violence," pp. 33–34. Rare is the pacifist Christian. Consider the millions of Christians who fought in the Second World War on both sides with the blessings of their respective religious leaders. In fact, in the history of Christianity, rarely has violence ever been ruled out absolutely. For example, cf. Aquinas on the relationship between unjust law and violence; see *Summa Theologica*, question 96, art. 4.

41. Míguez Bonino, *Doing Theology in a Revolutionary Situation*, p. 115.

42. Segundo, *Liberation of Theology*, p. 157.

43. Ibid., p. 159. (emphasis original)

44. Ibid., p. 160.

45. Ibid.

46. Ibid., p. 157.

47. The "Medellín Documents" can be found in Gremillion, *Gospel of Peace and Justice;* see here p. 459.

48. Ibid., p. 460.

49. José Míguez Bonino, *Toward a Christian Political Ethics* (Philadelphia: Fortress Press, 1983), p. 27.

50. Cf. Louis Althusser, "Ideology and Ideological State Apparatuses," in *Lenin and Philosophy and Other Essays*, ed. Althusser (New York: Monthly Review Press, 1971), pp. 27–186.

51. "Medellín Documents," pp. 459–60, 462.

52. See, for example, Hélder Câmara, *The Spiral of Violence* (Denville, N.J.: Dimension Books, 1971).

Notes to Chapter 5

53. Oscar Arnulfo Romero and Arturo Rivera Damos [Rivera y Damas], "The Church, Political Organization and Violence," *Cross Currents* 29 (Winter 1979–80): 385–408.

54. Ibid., p. 403.

55. See, for example, Raymond Bonner, "The Agony of El Salvador," *The New York Times Magazine* (22 February 1981), pp. 26–46; Lernoux, *Cry of the People,* passim; Stewart W. Fisher, "Human Rights in El Salvador and U.S. Foreign Policy," *Human Rights Quarterly* 4 (Spring 1982): 1–38; and "Pain and Hope for Guatemalans," *LADOC* 10 (May-June 1980): 33–40.

56. Brian H. Smith, "Churches and Human Rights in Latin America: Recent Trends on the Subcontinent," *Churches and Politics in Latin America,* ed. Daniel H. Levine (Beverly Hills: Sage Publications, 1980), p. 184.

57. Romero and Rivera y Damas, "The Church, Political Organization and Violence," p. 404. (Reprinted with permission from *Cross Currents,* Mercy College, Dobbs Ferry, NY 10522.)

58. Gustavo Gutiérrez, *A Theology of Liberation: History, Politics and Salvation* (Maryknoll, N.Y.: Orbis Books, 1973), pp. 275–76.

59. Segundo, "Christianity and Violence," p. 32.

60. Idem., *Liberation of Theology,* p. 165; cf. Kirk, *Theology Encounters Revolution,* pp. 123–25.

61. Ibid., pp. 158–59, 162–65; cf. Ignacio Ellacuría, *Freedom Made Flesh: The Mission of Christ and His Church* (Maryknoll, N.Y.: Orbis Books, 1976), chaps. 2, 3.

62. Míguez Bonino, *Doing Theology in a Revolutionary Situation,* p. 117; Míguez Bonino, *Toward a Christian Political Ethics,* p. 109.

63. Ellacuría, *Freedom Made Flesh,* p. 196.

64. Míguez Bonino, *Doing Theology in a Revolutionary Situation,* pp. 118–20. For Segundo, the just society must be constructed upon a socialist foundation; see "Capitalism-Socialism: A Theological Crux," *The Mystical and Political Dimension of the Christian Faith,* eds. Claude Geffré and Gustavo Gutiérrez (New York: Herder and Herder, 1974), pp. 105–23.

65. Segundo, *Liberation of Theology,* p. 166.

66. Comblin, *Church and the National Security State,* p. 48.

67. Ellacuría, *Freedom Made Flesh,* p. 121.

68. Assmann, *Theology for a Nomad Church,* pp. 141–42. With regard to religious images for the revolutionary, see Regis Debray, *Revolution in the Revolution? Armed Struggle and Political Struggle in Latin America* (New York: Grove, 1967), pp. 112–13.

69. Assmann, *Theology for a Nomad Church,* p. 142.

70. Segundo, *Liberation of Theology,* pp. 224–25.

Notes to Chapter 5

71. Míguez Bonino, *Doing Theology in a Revolutionary Situation*, pp. 124–26 (emphasis original); cf. José Míguez Bonino, "Historical Praxis and Christian Identity," in *Frontiers of Theology in Latin America*, ed. Rosino Gibellini (Maryknoll, N.Y.: Orbis Books, 1979), pp. 260–83, and "Whose Human Rights? A Historical-Theological Meditation," *International Review of Mission* 66 (July 1977): 220–24. For an analysis on the different approaches in this regard, see Robert T. Osborn, "Some Problems of Liberation Theology: A Polanyian Perspective," *Journal of the American Academy of Religion* 51 (March 1983): 79–95.

72. See, for example, Alfonso López Trujillo, *Liberation or Revolution? An Examination of the Priest's Role in the Socioeconomic Class Struggle in Latin America* (Huntington, Ind.: Our Sunday Visitor, 1977).

73. Dino Bigongiari, ed., *The Political Writings of St. Augustine* (Chicago: Henry Regnery, 1962), pp. 164–83.

74. "Medellín Documents," p. 461.

75. Míguez Bonino, *Toward a Christian Political Ethics*, p. 107.

76. With regard to religion and politics, there have been several reports on the role of Christians in the revolution, such as those of Teofilo Cabestrero, *Revolutionaries for the Gospel: Testimonies of Fifteen Christians in the Nicaraguan Government* (Maryknoll, N.Y.: Orbis Books, 1986); Connor Cruise O'Brien, "God and Man in Nicaragua," *The Atlantic Monthly* 258 (August 1986): 50–72; Margaret Randall, *Christians in the Nicaraguan Revolution* (Seattle, Washington: Left Bank, 1984); and Joseph Collins, "What Difference Could a Revolution Make? Farming in the New Nicaragua," in *Revolution in Central America*, ed. Stanford Central America Action Network (Boulder, Colo.: Westview Press, 1983), pp. 461–62. Also, cf. Berryman, *The Religious Roots of Rebellion*, chaps. 7, 8; Booth, *The End and the Beginning*, pp. 120, 134–36; Jane Cary Peck, "The Church of the Poor: Church of Life," *Missiology: An International Review* 11 (January 1983): 31–46; and Henri Weber, *Nicaragua: The Sandinist Revolution* (London: Verso, 1981), pp. 33–34.

77. Berryman, *Religious Roots of Rebellion*, pp. 361–62; David Nolan, *The Ideology of the Sandinistas and the Nicaraguan Revolution* (Coral Gables, Fla.: Institute of Interamerican Studies, 1984), pp. 74–75.

78. Cf. Wayne H. Cowan, "Nicaragua: The Revolution Takes Hold," *Christianity and Crisis* 40 (12 May 1980): 137–40.

79. Cf. Ernesto Cardenal, *The Gospel of Solentiname*, 4 vols. (Maryknoll, N.Y.: Orbis Books, 1982).

80. Ernesto Cardenal, "Revolution and Peace: The Nicaraguan Road," *Journal of Peace Research* 18 (1982); 202–3; cf. Leonardo Boff, "Nicaragua/-Solidarity," *Christianity and Crisis* 47 (28 September, 1987): 309–11. For further discussion on Christianity and violence, see Robert McAfee Brown, *Religion and Violence: A Primer for White Americans* (Philadelphia: Westminster Press, 1973); and Davies, *Christians, Politics and Violent Revolution.*

Notes to Chapter 6

81. Ibid., pp. 202, 206. For a similar response from an American Catholic priest, see Blase Bonpane, *Guerrillas of Peace: Liberation Theology and the Central American Revolution* (Boston: South End Press, 1985).

82. Michael Dodson and T. S. Montgomery, "The Churches in the Nicaraguan Revolution," in *Nicaragua in Revolution,* ed. Thomas W. Walker (New York: Praeger, 1982), pp. 162, 164–65. Cf. James McGinnis, *Solidarity with the People of Nicaragua* (Maryknoll, N.Y.: Orbis Books, 1985). Important clergymen have included Father Miguel d'Escoto as minister of international relations; Father Edgar Parrales as minister of social welfare; Father Ernesto Cardenal as minister of culture; and Father Fernando Cardenal as director of the national literacy campaign and leader of the July 19 Sandinista Youth Movement. Cf. the statement by the DN of the FSLN, "The Role of Religion in the New Nicaragua," in *Sandinistas Speak,* Tomas Borge et al (New York: Pathfinder Press, 1982), pp. 105–11.

83. Omar Cabezas, *Fire from the Mountain: The Making of a Sandinista* (New York: New American Library, 1985), p. 121.

84. Ibid., p. 85.

Chapter 6

1. On modernity, see, for example, Leo Strauss, "Three Waves of Modernity," in *Political Philosophy: Six Essays,* ed. Hilail Gildin (Indianapolis: Pegasus, 1975); cf. E. K. Hunt, *Property and Prophets: The Evolution of Economic Institutions and Ideologies,* 4th ed. (New York: Harper, 1981).

2. See, for example, Roberto Mangabeira Unger, *Knowledge and Politics* (New York: Free Press, 1975).

3. See, for example, Jürgen Habermas, *Legitimation Crisis* (Boston: Beacon Press, 1975).

4. Hannah Arendt, *On Revolution* (New York: Penguin Books, 1965).

5. Cf. Harvie M. Conn, "The Mission of the Church," in *Evangelicals and Liberation,* ed. Carl E. Amerding (Grand Rapids: Presbyterian and Reformed Publishing Co., 1977), pp. 60–89.

6. See, for example, Harvey Brooks, "Technology, Evolution, and Purpose," in *Technology and Man's Future,* 3rd ed., ed. Albert H. Teich (New York: St. Martin's, 1981), pp. 294–320; cf. Langdon Winner, *Autonomous Technology: Technics-out-of-Control as a Theme in Political Thought* (Cambridge: MIT, 1977); and David Dickson, "Technology and the Construction of Social Reality," in *Radical Science Essays,* ed. Les Levidow (Atlantic Highlands, N.J.: Humanities Press International, 1986), pp. 15–37.

Notes to Chapter 6

7. See, for example, Barbara J. Shapiro, "The Universities and Science in Seventeenth Century England," *Journal of British History* 10 (1971): 47–82; Robert Merton, *Science, Technology and Society in Seventeenth Century England* (1938; reprint ed., Harper Torchbooks, 1970); and Thomas Kuhn, *The Copernican Revolution* (New York: Random, 1957).

8. Cf. Thomas L. Hankins, *Science and the Enlightenment* (Cambridge: Cambridge University Press, 1985); Christopher Hill, *Intellectual Origins of the English Revolution* (Oxford: Oxford University Press, 1965); and Michael Boretsky, "Trends in U.S. Technology: A Political Economist's View," in *Science, Technology, and National Policy*, eds. Thomas J. Kuehn and Alan L. Porter (Ithaca, N.Y.: Cornell University Press, 1981), pp. 161–88.

9. See, for example, Mordechai Feingold, *The Mathematician's Apprenticeship: Science, Universities and Society in England, 1560–1640* (Cambridge: Cambridge University Press, 1984); cf. Phyllis Allen, "Scientific Studies in the English Universities of the Seventeenth Century," *Journal of the History of Ideas* 10 (1949): 291–53.

10. Cf. Max Horkheimer, *Eclipse of Reason* (1947; reprint ed., New York: Continuum, 1974); and Max Horkheimer and Theodor W. Adorno, *Dialectic of Enlightenment* (1944; reprint ed., New York: continuum, 1972).

11. See, for example, Herbert Marcuse, "The Problem of Violence and the Radical Opposition," in *Five Lectures: Psychoanalysis, Politics, and Utopia,* ed. Marcuse (Boston: Beacon, 1970), pp. 83–108.

12. So within the political tradition of liberalism, there are defenders who rely on a particular conception of human nature as the foundation and justification for legitimating a particular political regime; see, for example, Thomas Hobbes, *Leviathan* (1651), pt. 1, chaps. 1–10; and John Locke, *Second Treatise of Government* (c. 1688), chap. 2. However, other contemporary defenders rely not on a conception of human nature to justify liberalism, but on a particular dialogic process in contradistinction to contractarian as well as utilitarian approaches; see, for example, Bruce A. Ackerman, *Social Justice in the Liberal State* (New Haven: Yale University Press, 1980), chap. 1.

13. J. Andrew Kirk, *Theology Encounters Revolution* (Downers Grove, Ill.: InterVarsity Press, 1980), p. 179.

14. For a good assessment of the ways institutions and policies affect citizen decision making, see Charles E. Lindblom, *Politics and Markets: The World's Political-Economic Systems* (New York: Basic, 1977).

15. Cf. Reinhold Niebuhr, *Moral Man and Immoral Society: A Study in Ethics and Politics* (New York: Scribner, 1932). However, consider arguments that politics is a natural and necessary condition of human existence; see, for example, Aristotle, *Politics* (c. 345 B.C.), bks. 1, 3.

16. Cf. William K. McElvaney, *Good News Is Bad News Is Good News* (Maryknoll, N.Y.: Orbis Books, 1980), pp. 117–23.

Notes to Chapter 6

17. Cf. Alfonso López Trujillo, *Liberation or Revolution? An Examination of the Priest's Role in the Socioeconomic Class Struggle in Latin America* (Huntington, Ind.: Our Sunday Visitor, 1977).

18. Brian L. Hebblethwaite, *The Problems of Theology* (Cambridge: Cambridge University Press, 1980), p. 45; cf. Hugo Assmann, *Theology for a Nomad Church* (Maryknoll, N.Y.: Orbis Books, 1976), p. 96.

19. In terms of *being*, consider the Platonic conception discussed in the *Republic* (c. 390 B.C.), 504d–505b, 507b–d, 510c–511d, cf. 507e–510a; *being* appropriates the good, the transcendent values of truth, the essence of existence. In regard to process, consider active participation in social life, the politics of conflict, the dialectic of social change, and evolution; cf. Delwin Brown, *To Set at Liberty: Christian Faith and Human Freedom* (Maryknoll, N.Y.: Orbis Books, 1981).

20. Charles Davis, *Theology and Political Society* (Cambridge: Cambridge University Press, 1980), p. 22; cf. Unger, *Knowledge and Politics*, p. 22.

21. Kirk, *Theology Encounters Revolution*, pp. 128–30.

22. See, for example, José Porfirio Miranda, *Marx and the Bible: A Critique of the Philosophy of Oppression* (Maryknoll, N.Y.: Orbis Books, 1974); and Jon Sobrino, *Christology at the Crossroads: A Latin American Approach* (Maryknoll, N.Y.: Orbis Books, 1978).

23. Recall the Marxist-Christian dialogues and debates of the 1930s and later of the 1960s; for representative samples, see H. Wilson Harris, ed., *Christianity and Communism* (Boston: Marshall Jones Co., 1937); and Herbert Aptheker, ed., *Marxism and Christianity: A Symposium* (New York: Humanities Press, 1968). Also, cf. John C. Raines and Thomas Dean, eds., *Marxism and Radical Religion: Essays Toward a Revolutionary Humanism* (Philadelphia: Temple University Press, 1970).

24. Robert T. Osborn, "Some Problems of Liberation Theology: A Polanyian Perspective," *Journal of the American Academy of Religion* 51 (March 1983): 79–95. Cf. Kirk's position that "theology's function is to relate the changeless gospel to changing situations, being careful not to confuse the two"; see *Theology Encounters Revolution*, p. 103.

25. Davis, *Theology and Political Society*, p. 11.

26. Ibid., p. 12. (emphasis added)

27. Jürgen Moltmann, "On Latin American Liberation Theology: An Open Letter to José Míguez Bonino," *Christianity and Crisis*, 29 March 1976, pp. 58–59.

28. Liberation theologians appear, however, to be aware of this problem; see, for example, Juan Luis Segundo, *The Liberation of Theology* (Maryknoll, N.Y.: Orbis Books, 1976), chap. 2.

Notes to Chapter 6

29. Francis P. Fiorenza, "Political Theology and Liberation Theology: An Inquiry into their Fundamental Meaning," in *Liberation, Revolution, and Freedom: Theological Perspectives,* ed. Thomas M. McFadden (New York: Seabury Press, 1975), pp. 3–29; cf. Johannes B. Metz, *Faith in History and Society* (New York: Seabury Press, 1980); Jürgen Moltmann, *Theology of Hope: On the Ground and the Implications of a Christian Eschatology* (New York: Harper, 1967); Wolfhart Pannenberg, *Theology and the Philosophy of Science* (Philadelphia: Westminister Press, 1976); and Dorothee Soelle, *Political Theology* (Philadelphia: Fortress Press, 1974).

30. Matthew L. Lamb, "The Challenge of Critical Theory," in *Sociology and Human Destiny: Essays on Sociology, Religion and Society,* ed. Gregory Baum (New York: Seabury Press, 1980), p. 208.

31. Alfredo Fierro, *The Militant Gospel: A Critical Introduction to Political Theologies* (Maryknoll, N.Y.: Orbis Books, 1977) p. 109.

32. Miranda, *Marx and the Bible,* chap. 5, passim.

33. Hugo Assmann, *Opresión-liberación: desafío a los cristianos* (Montevideo, Uruguay: 1971), pp. 19, 174ff; cf. Hugo Assmann, *Theology for a Nomad Church* (Maryknoll, N.Y.: Orbis Books, 1976), p. 79.

34. Segundo, *Liberation of Theology,* pp. 52–53.

35. Ibid., p. 207n21; cf. p. 220.

36. Leonardo Boff, "Theological Characteristics of a Grassroots Church," in *The Challenge of Basic Christian Communities: Papers from the International Ecumenical Congress of Theology, February 20–March 2, 1980, São Paulo, Brazil,* eds. Sergio Torres and John Eagleson (Maryknoll, N.Y.: Orbis Books, 1981), p. 128.

37. Gustavo Gutiérrez, *A Theology of Liberation: History, Politics and Salvation* (Maryknoll, N.Y.: Orbis Books, 1973), pp. 31–32, 233.

38. Ibid., p. 13.

39. A larger study is necessary to trace the transmission of ideas from critical theory to political theology to liberation theology.

40. For an introduction to the study of the sociology of religion, see Roland Robertson, ed., *Sociology of Religion: Selected Readings* (New York: Penguin Books, 1981). With regard to the relationship between ideas and institutions, see Peter L. Berger and Thomas Luckmann, *The Social Construction of Reality: Treatise in the Sociology of Knowledge* (Garden City, N.Y.: Anchor Books, 1967).

41. Hunt, *Property and Prophets,* chaps. 2–4; cf. Max Horkheimer, "Europe and Christianity," in *Dawn and Decline: Notes 1926–1931 and 1950–1969,* ed. Horkheimer (New York: Seabury Press, 1978), pp. 88–91.

42. Cf. Ralph Miliband, *The State in Capitalist Society* (New York: Basic, 1969).

Notes to Chapter 6

43. Cf. Louis Althusser, "Ideology and Ideological State Apparatuses" in *Lenin and Philosophy and other Essays* (New York: Monthly Review, 1971), pp. 127–86.

44. See Segundo, *Liberation of Theology,* chap. 1.

45. See Richard Quinney, *Social Existence: Metaphysics, Marxism, and the Social Sciences* (Beverly Hills: Sage Publications, 1982), p. 132; and Kees W. Bolle, "The Myth of Our Materialism," in *Religion and Politics in the Modern World,* eds. Peter H. Merkl and Ninian Smart (New York: New York University Press, 1983), pp. 253–54.

46. See Delos B. McKown, *Classical Marxist Critiques of Religion: Marx, Engels, Lenin, Kautsky* (The Hague: Martinus Nijhoff, 1975).

47. Alfred T. Hennelly, *Theologies in Conflict: The Challenge of Juan Luis Segundo* (Maryknoll, N.Y.: Orbis Books, 1979), pp. 157–60.

48. For historical examples, see Tommie Sue Montgomery, *Revolution in El Salvador: Origins and Evolution* (Boulder, Colo.: Westview Press, 1982), chap. 2, and John A. Booth, *The End and the Beginning: The Nicaraguan Revolution* (Boulder, Colo.: Westview Press, 1982), chap. 2.

49. For a good array of views on the Marxist-Christian dialogue of the 1960s, see Peter Hebblethwaite, *The Christian-Marxist Dialogue: Beginnings, Present Status, and Beyond* (New York: Paulist Press, 1977); and Arthur F. McGovern, *Marxism: An American Christian Perspective* (Maryknoll, N.Y.: Orbis Books, 1980).

50. See, for example, Assmann, *Theology for a Nomad Church,* pp. 141–42, and Segundo, *Liberation of Theology,* pp. 55, 224–25; cf. John R. Pottenger, "Liberation Theology: Its Methodological Foundation for Violence," in *The Morality of Terrorism: Religious and Secular Justifications,* eds. David C. Rapoport and Yonah Alexander (New York: Pergamon Press, 1982), pp. 99–123.

51. Particularly useful assessments of the history and methodologies of critical theory can be found in Martin Jay, *The Dialectical Imagination: A History of the Frankfurt School and the Institute of Social Research, 1923–1950* (Boston: Little, Brown, 1973); and David Held, *An Introduction to Critical Theory: Horkheimer to Habermas* (Berkeley: University of California Press, 1980).

52. Max Horkheimer, "Thoughts on Religion," in *Critical Theory: Selected Essays,* ed. Horkheimer (New York: Herder and Herder, 1972), pp. 129–31.

53. Habermas, *Legitimation Crisis,* p. 121.

54. Ibid., pp. 96–100, 190; cf. Jürgen Habermas, *Toward a Rational Society: Student Protests, Science, and Politics* (Boston: Beacon, 1970).

55. Gutiérrez, *Theology of Liberation,* pp. 69–72; on this same point from an Asian liberation theology perspective, see Raimundo Panikkar,

Notes to Chapter 6

"Religion or Politics: The Western Dilemma," in *Religion and Politics in the Modern World,* pp. 44–60.

56. Habermas, *Legitimation Crisis,* pp. 103, 105; cf. Jürgen Habermas, *Reason and the Rationalization of Society,* vol. 1 of *The Theory of Communicative Action* (Boston: Beacon, 1981); and *Lifeworld and System: A Critique of Functionalist Reason,* vol. 2 of *The Theory of Communicative Action* (Boston: Beacon, 1987).

57. Habermas, *Lifeworld and System,* p. 193.

58. Cf. Dennis P. McCann, "Political Ideologies and Practical Theology: Is There a Difference?" *Union Seminary Quarterly Review* 36 (Summer 1981): 252–53.

59. Ibid., p. 252.

60. Cf. Dietrich Weiderkehr, *Belief in Redemption: Concepts of Salvation from the New Testament to the Present Time* (Atlanta: John Knox Press, 1979), chap. 6, and Hebblethwaite, *The Christian-Marxist Dialogue,* chaps. 1, 2.

61. Although virtually all liberation theologians deal with praxis, see Gutiérrez, *Theology of Liberation,* pp. 6–19.

62. Lamb, "The Challenge of Critical Theory," p. 187; cf. Max Horkheimer, "Theism and Atheism," in *Critique of Instrumental Reason,* ed. Horkheimer (New York: Seabury Press, 1974), pp. 34–50; and "Atheism and Religion," in *Dawn and Decline,* pp. 65–66.

63. Cf. Juan Luis Segundo, "Capitalism-Socialism: A Theological Crux," in *The Mystical and Political Dimension of the Christian Faith,* eds. Claude Geffré and Gustavo Gutiérrez (New York: Herder and Herder, 1974), pp. 105–23.

64. See Otto Maduro, *Religion and Social Conflicts* (Maryknoll, N.Y.: Orbis Books, 1982), chaps. 25, 33–35. Curiously, liberation theology is increasingly being recognized as a permanent and legitimate political ideology; see, for example, Roy C. Macridis, *Contemporary Political Ideologies: Movements and Regimes,* 3rd ed. (Boston: Little, Brown and Company, 1986), chap. 14: "Liberation Theology—The Voice of the Church and the Poor"; and H. Mark Roelofs, "Liberation Theology: The Recovery of Biblical Radicalism," *American Political Science Review* 82 (June 1988): 549–66.

65. In this sense, a theoretical framework is understood as any attempt to order reality to provide explanations of how and why it appears as it does. For one of the first modern, generally comprehensive explanations of how the world of appearance is given rational ordering by the mind in its attempt to understand the world as it really is, see Immanuel Kant, *Critique of Pure Reason* (1787).

66. Cf. Leo Strauss, "Political Philosphy and History," in *What Is Political Philosophy? and other Studies* (Glencoe, Ill.: Free Press, 1959), pp. 56–57.

Notes to Chapter 6

67. Locke, *Two Treatises of Government,* passim; John Stuart Mill, *Essay on Liberty* (1859); Robert Nozick, *Anarchy, State and Utopia* (New York: Basic, 1974); Isaiah Berlin, "Two Concepts of Liberty," in *Four Essays on Liberty,* Berlin (London: Oxford University Press, 1969), pp. 118–72; L. T. Hobhouse, *Liberalism* (1911; reprint ed., London: Oxford University Press, 1964).

68. Jean-Jacques Rousseau, *The Social Contract* (1762), *The Second Discourse* (1754); C. B. Macpherson, *The Real World of Democracy* (New York: Oxford University Press, 1966); Robert Dahl, *After the Revolution? Authority in a Good Society* (New Haven: Yale University Press, 1970); Robert Paul Wolff, *In Defense of Anarchism* (New York: Harper, 1970).

69. Karl Marx, *Economic and Philosophic Manuscripts of 1844, Capital* (1867), vol. 1; Althusser, *Lenin and Philosophy and other Essays,* passim; Georg Lukács, *History and Class Consciousness: Studies in Marxist Dialectics* (Cambridge: MIT, 1971); Eugene Kamenka, *Marxism and Ethics* (London: Macmillan, 1969).

70. Hobbes, *Leviathan;* cf. Norman Frolich and Joe A. Oppenheimer, *Modern Political Economy* (Englewood Cliffs, N.J: Prentice-Hall, 1978).

71. It is this issue over the logic of explanation—modern symbolic logic versus dialectical logic—which has been one of the distinguishing characteristics that has separated logical positivists from Marxists, according to Rudolf Carnap; see his article, "Intellectual Autobiography," in *The Philosophy of Rudolf Carnap,* ed. Paul Arthur Schilpp (London: Cambridge University Press, 1963), p. 24.

72. A. J. Ayer, *Language, Truth and Logic* (1946; reprint ed., New York: Dover Publications, 1952), chap. 1; cf. Rudolf Carnap, "The Elimination of Metaphysics through Logical Analyses of Language," in *Logical Positivism,* ed. A. J. Ayer (New York: Free Press, 1959), pp. 60–80.

73. Karl Popper, *Conjectures and Refutations: The Growth of Scientific Knowledge* (New York: Harper, 1963), chaps. 10, 11.

74. Cf. Habermas, *Legitimation Crisis,* and Herbert Marcuse, *One-Dimensional Man: Studies in the Ideology of Advanced Industrial Society* (Boston: Beacon, 1964).

75. For an insightful criticism of Karl Popper, see Willi Oelmüller, "The Limitations of Social Theories," in *Religion and Political Society,* Jürgen Moltmann et al (New York: Harper, 1974), pp. 121–69.

76. For a critique of behavioral social science, see Leo Strauss, "An Epilogue," in *Essays on the Scientific Study of Politics,* ed. Herbert J. Storing (New York: Holt, 1962), pp. 305–27.

77. Cf. David B. Burrell, "Religious Belief and Rationality," in *Rationality and Religious Belief,* ed. C. F. Delaney (Notre Dame: University of Notre Dame Press, 1979), pp. 84–115.

Bibliography

The bibliography consists of references cited in this book. However, to facilitate identification, the references have been grouped according to the most likely subject matter. And the subject matter has been classified under two general categories.

The first category classifies those references dealing directly with the topic of liberation theology, according to the following subject matter groupings: primary sources (p.231) and secondary sources (p.234).

The second category classifies those references dealing with topics related to the study of the political theory of liberation theology, according to the following subject matter groupings: economic, political, and intellectual conditions in Latin America (p.237); political theory, economic theory, and moral philosophy (p.239); Marxism and Christianity (p.244); religion and politics (p.245); theology (p.247); and history and philosophy of science (p.248).

Liberation Theology

Primary Sources

Assmann, Hugo. "Democracy and the Debt Crisis." *This World* (Spring-Summer 1986): 83–103.

_____. *Opresión-liberación: desafío a los cristianos.* Montevideo: Uruguay, 1971.

_____. *Theology for a Nomad Church.* Maryknoll, N.Y.: Orbis Books, 1976.

Bibliography

Barreiro, Alvaro. *Basic Ecclesial Communities: The Evangelization of the Poor.* Maryknoll, N.Y.: Orbis Books, 1982.

Boff, Leonardo. "Christians Called to Transform Marxism into Tool for Liberation." In *A New Way of Being Church: Interviews and Testimonies,* pp. 7–8. Lima: Latinamerica Press, 1984.

_____. *Ecclesiogenesis: The Base Communities Reinvent the Church.* Maryknoll, N.Y.: Orbis Books, 1986.

_____. *O destino do homem e do mundo: ensaio sôbre a vocação humana.* Petrópolis, Brazil: Editora Vozes, 1973.

_____. "The Need for Political Saints: From a Spirituality of Liberation to the Practice of Liberation." *Cross Currents* 30 (Winter 1980–81): 369–76, 384.

_____. "Nicaragua/Solidarity." *Christianity and Crisis* 47 (28 September 1987): 309–11.

_____. "Theological Characteristics of a Grassroots Church." In *The Challenge of Basic Christian Communities: Papers from the International Ecumenical Congress of Theology, February 20–March 2, 1980, São Paulo, Brazil,* edited by Sergio Torres and John Eagleson, pp. 124–44. Maryknoll, N.Y.: Orbis Books, 1981.

Boff, Leonardo, and Boff, Clodovis. *Introducting Liberation Theology.* Maryknoll, N.Y.: Orbis Books, 1986.

Comblin, José. *The Church and the National Security State.* Maryknoll, N.Y.: Orbis Books, 1979.

Croatto, J. Severino. "Biblical Hermeneutics in the Theologies of Liberation." In *Irruption of the Third World: Challenge to Theology,* edited by Virginia Fabella and Sergio Torres, pp. 140–68. Maryknoll, N.Y.: Orbis Books, 1983.

_____. *Exodus: A Hermeneutics of Freedom.* Maryknoll, N.Y.: Orbis Books, 1981.

Dussel, Enrique. "Domination-Liberation: A New Approach." In *The Mystical and Political Dimension of the Christian Faith,* edited by Claude Geffré and Gustavo Gutiérrez, pp. 34–56. New York: Herder and Herder, 1974.

_____. *Ethics and the Theology of Liberation.* Maryknoll, N.Y.: Orbis Books, 1978.

_____. "Historical and Philosophical Presuppositions for Latin American Theology." In *Frontiers of Theology in Latin America,* edited by Rosino Gibellini, pp. 184–212. Maryknoll, N.Y.: Orbis Books, 1979.

_____. *Philosophy of Liberation.* Maryknoll, N.Y.: Orbis Books, 1985.

Bibliography

Ellacuría, Ignacio. *Freedom Made Flesh: The Mission of Christ and His Church.* Maryknoll, N.Y.: Orbis Books, 1976.

―――. "Human Rights in a Divided Society." In *Human Rights in the Americas: The Struggle for Consensus,* edited by Alfred Hennelly and John Langan, pp. 52–65. Washington, D.C.: Georgetown University Press, 1982.

Gutiérrez, Gustavo. "Freedom and Salvation: A Political Problem." In *Liberation and Change,* edited by Ronald H. Stone, pp. 3–94. Atlanta: John Knox Press, 1977.

―――. "Latin America's Pain Is Bearing Fruit." In *A New Way of Being Church: Interviews and Testimonies,* pp. 3–5. Lima: Latinamerica Press, 1984.

―――. "Liberation Praxis and Christian Faith." In *Frontiers of Theology in Latin America,* edited by Rosino Gibellini, pp. 1–33. Maryknoll, N.Y.: Orbis Books, 1979.

―――. "Liberation Theology and Proclamation." In *The Mystical and Political Dimension of the Christian Faith,* edited by Claude Geffré and Gustavo Gutiérrez, pp. 57–77. New York: Herder and Herder, 1974.

―――. *The Power of the Poor in History.* Maryknoll, N.Y.: Orbis Books, 1983.

―――. "Talking About God." *Sojourners* 12 (February 1983): 26–29.

―――. *A Theology of Liberation: History, Politics and Salvation.* Maryknoll, N.Y.: Orbis Books, 1973.

Mesters, Carlos. "The Use of the Bible in Christian Communities of the Common People." In *The Challenge of Basic Christian Communities: Papers from the International Ecumenical Congress of Theology, February 20–March 2, 1980, São Paulo, Brazil,* edited by Sergio Torres and John Eagleson, pp. 197–210. Maryknoll, N.Y.: Orbis Books, 1981.

Míguez Bonino, José. *Christians and Marxists: The Mutual Challenge to Revolution.* Grand Rapids, Mich.: William B. Eerdmans Publishing Co., 1976.

―――. *Doing Theology in a Revolutionary Situation.* Philadelphia: Fortress Press, 1975.

―――. "Historical Praxis and Christian Identity." In *Frontiers of Theology in Latin America,* edited by Rosino Gibellini, pp. 260–83. Maryknoll, N.Y.: Orbis Books, 1979.

―――. "Popular Piety in Latin America." In *The Mystical and Political Dimension of the Christian Faith,* edited by Claude Geffré and Gustavo Gutiérrez, pp. 148–57. New York: Herder and Herder, 1974.

_____. *Toward a Christian Political Ethics.* Philadelphia: Fortress Press, 1983.

_____. "Whose Human Rights? A Historico-Theological Meditation." *International Review of Mission* 66 (July 1977): 220–4.

Miranda, José Porfirio. *Communism in the Bible.* Maryknoll, N.Y.: Orbis Books, 1982.

_____. *Marx Against the Marxists: The Christian Humanism of Karl Marx.* Maryknoll, N.Y.: Orbis Books, 1980.

_____. *Marx and the Bible: A Critique of the Philosophy of Oppression.* Maryknoll, N.Y.: Orbis Books, 1974.

Santa Ana, Julio de. *Goods News to the Poor: The Challenge of the Poor in the History of the Church.* Maryknoll, N.Y.: Orbis Books, 1979.

Segundo, Juan Luis. "Capitalism-Socialism: A Theological Crux." In *The Mystical and Political Dimension of the Christian Faith,* edited by Claude Geffré and Gustavo Gutiérrez, pp. 105–23. New York: Herder and Herder, 1974.

_____. "Christianity and Violence in Latin America." *Christianity and Crisis* 4 (March 1968): 32–35.

_____. *Faith and Ideologies.* Maryknoll, N.Y.: Orbis Books, 1984.

_____. *The Liberation of Theology.* Maryknoll, N.Y.: Orbis Books, 1976.

_____. *Theology and the Church: A Response to Cardinal Ratzinger and a Warning to the Whole Church.* Minneapolis: Winston Press, 1985.

Sobrino, Jon. *Christianity at the Crossroads: A Latin American Approach.* Maryknoll, N.Y.: Orbis Books, 1978.

Vidales, Raúl. "Methodological Issues in Liberation Theology." In *Frontiers of Theology in Latin America,* edited by Rosino Gibellini, pp. 34–57. Maryknoll, N.Y.: Orbis Books, 1979.

Secondary Sources

Berryman, Phillip. *Liberation Theology: The Essential Facts About the Revolutionary Movement in Latin America and Beyond.* Oak Park, Ill.: Meyer, Stone Books, 1987.

Bonpane, Blase. *Guerrillas of Peace: Liberation Theology and the Central American Revolution,* 2nd ed. Boston: South End Press, 1987.

Brown, Robert McAfee. *Gustavo Gutiérrez.* Atlanta: John Knox Press, 1980.

_____. *Theology in a New Key: Responding to Liberation Themes.* Philadelphia: Westminster Press, 1978.

Congregation for the Doctrine of the Faith. "Instruction on Christian Freedom and Liberation." *Origins: NC Documentary Service* 15 (17 April 1986): 713, 715–28.

Conn, Harvie M. "The Mission of the Church." In *Evangelicals and Liberation,* edited by Carl E. Amerding, pp. 60–89. Grand Rapids: Presbyterian and Reformed Publishing Co., 1977.

Dodson, Michael. "Liberation Theology and Christian Radicalism in Contemporary Latin America." *Journal of Latin American Studies* 2 (May 1979): 203–22.

_____. "Prophetic Politics and Political Theory in Latin America." *Polity* 12 (Spring 1980): 388–408.

Eagleson, John, and Scharper, Philip, eds. *Puebla and Beyond: Documentation and Commentary.* Maryknoll, N.Y.: Orbis Books, 1979.

Fierro, Alfredo. *The Militant Gospel: A Critical Introduction to Political Theologies.* Maryknoll, N.Y.: Orbis Books, 1977.

Fiorenza, Francis P. "Political Theology and Liberation Theology: An Inquiry into their Fundamental Meaning." In *Liberation, Revolution, and Freedom: Theological Perspectives,* edited by Thomas M. McFadden, pp. 3–29. New York: The Seabury Press, 1975.

Freysinger, Robert C. "The Just Revolution of Modern Christian Radicalism." *Contemporary Crisis* 4 (1980): 353–66.

Goulet, Denis. *A New Moral Order: Development Ethics and Liberation Theology.* Maryknoll, N.Y.: Orbis Books, 1974.

Gutiérrez Gonzalez, Juan. *The New Libertarian Gospel: Pitfalls of the Theology of Liberation.* Chicago: Franciscan Herald Press, 1977.

Hennelly, Alfred T. *Theologies in Conflict: The Challenge of Juan Luis Segundo.* Maryknoll, N.Y.: Orbis Books, 1979.

Kirk, J. Andrew. *Theology Encounters Revolution.* Downers Grove, Ill.: InterVarsity Press, 1980.

Kroger, Joseph. "Prophetic-Critical and Practical-Strategic Tasks of Theology: Habermas and Liberation Theology." *Theological Studies* 46 (March 1985): 3–20.

Laurentine, René. *Liberation, Development and Salvation.* Maryknoll, N.Y.: Orbis Books, 1972.

Lernoux, Penny. "The Long Path to Puebla." In *Puebla and Beyond: Documentation and Commentary,* edited by John Eagleson and Philip Scharper, pp. 3–27. Maryknoll, N.Y.: Orbis Books, 1979.

Levine, Daniel H. "Assessing the Impacts of Liberation Theology in Latin America." *The Review of Politics* 50 (Spring 1988): 241–63.

Bibliography

López Trujillo, Alfonso. *Liberation or Revolution? An Examination of the Priest's Role in the Socioeconomic Class Struggle in Latin America.* Huntington, Ind.: Our Sunday Visitor, 1977.

McCann, Dennis P. *Christian Realism and Liberation Theology: Practical Theologies in Conflict.* Maryknoll, N.Y.: Orbis Books, 1981.

McElvaney, William K. *Good News Is Bad News Is Good News.* Maryknoll, N.Y.: Orbis Books, 1980.

McGovern, Arthur F. "Latin America and Dependency Theory." *This World* (Spring-Summer 1986): 104–23.

Macridis, Roy C. *Contemporary Political Ideologies: Movements and Regimes,* 3rd ed. Boston: Little, Brown and Company, 1986, chap. 14.

Moltmann, Jürgen. "On Latin American Liberation Theology: An Open Letter to José Míguez Bonino." *Christianity and Crisis* 36 (29 March 1976): 57–63.

Novak, Michael. "The Case Against Liberation Theology." *New York Times Sunday Magazine,* 21 October 1984, pp. 51, 82–87, 93–95.

————. *Will It Liberate? Questions about Liberation Theology.* Mahwah, N.J.: Paulist Press, 1987.

————, ed. *Liberation South, Liberation North.* Washington, D.C.: American Enterprise Institute, 1981.

Osborn, Robert T. "Some Problems of Liberation Theology: A Polanyian Perspective." *Journal of the American Academy of Religion* 51 (March 1983): 79–95.

Planas, Ricardo. *Liberation Theology: The Political Expression of Religion.* Kansas City: Sheed & Ward, 1986.

Pottenger, John R. "Liberation Theology: Its Methodological Foundation for Violence." In *The Morality of Terrorism: Religious and Secular Justifications,* edited by David C. Rapoport and Yonah Alexander, pp. 99–123. New York: Pergamon Press, 1982.

Roelofs, H. Mark. "Liberation Theology: The Recovery of Biblical Radicalism." *American Political Science Review* 82 (June 1988): 549–66.

Sagrada Congregação para a Doutrina da Fé. *Instrução sobre alguns aspectos da "teologia da libertação,"* edited by Joseph Cardinal Ratzinger. São Paulo, Brazil: Edições Paulinas, 1984.

Sanks, T. Howland, and Smith, Brian H. "Liberation Ecclesiology: Praxis, Theory, Praxis." *Theological Studies* 38 (March 1977): 3–38.

Sturm, Douglas. "Praxis and Promise: On the Ethics of Political Theology." *Ethics* 92 (July 1982): 733–50.

Vekemans, Roger. *Caesar and God: The Priesthood and Politics.* Maryknoll, N.Y.: Orbis Books, 1972.

Related Topics

Economic, Political, and Intellectual Conditions in Latin America

Bonner, Raymond. "The Agony of El Salvador." *The New York Times Magazine,* 22 February 1981, pp. 26–46.

Booth, John A. *The End and the Beginning: The Nicaraguan Revolution.* Boulder, Colo.: Westview Press, 1982.

Cabestrero, Teofilo. *Revolutionaries for the Gospel: Testimonies of Fifteen Christians in the Nicaraguan Government.* Maryknoll, N.Y.: Orbis Books, 1986.

Cardoso, Fernando Henrique, and Faletto, Enzo. *Dependency and Development in Latin America.* Berkeley: University of California Press, 1979.

Chinchilla, Norma Stoltz. "Women in Revolutionary Movements: The Case of Nicaragua." In *Revolution in Central America,* edited by the Stanford Central America Action Network, pp. 422–34. Boulder, Colo.: Westview Press, 1983.

Collier, David, and Collier, Ruth Berins. "Who Does What to Whom, and How: Toward a Comparative Analysis of Latin American Corporatism." In *Authoritarianism and Corporatism in Latin America,* edited by James M. Malloy, pp. 489–512. Pittsburgh: University of Pittsburgh Press, 1977.

Collins, Joseph. "What Difference Could a Revolution Make? Farming in the New Nicaragua." In *Revolution in Central America,* edited by the Stanford Central America Action Network, pp. 458–65. Boulder, Colo.: Westview Press, 1983.

Coraggio, José Luis. *Nicaragua: Revolution and Democracy.* Boston: Allen & Unwin, 1986.

Cowan, Wayne H. "Nicaragua: The Revolution Takes Hold." *Christianity and Crisis* 40 (12 May 1980): 137–40.

Crahan, Margaret E. "National Security Ideology and Human Rights." In *Human Rights and Basic Needs in the Americas,* edited by Crahan, pp. 100–127. Washington, D.C.: Georgetown University Press, 1982.

de Janvry, Alain. *The Agrarian Question and Reformism in Latin America.* Baltimore: The Johns Hopkins University Press, 1981.

Bibliography

DeWitt, Peter, and Petras, James F. "The Political Economy of International Debt." In *Class, State and Power in the Third World: With Case Studies on Class Conflict in Latin America,* edited by Petras, pp. 96–117. Montclair, N.J.: Allanheld, Osmun, 1981.

Didion, Joan. *Salvador.* New York: Pocket Books, 1983.

Dore, Elizabeth, and Weeks, John F. "Economic Performance and Basic Needs: The Examples of Brazil, Chile, Mexico, Nicaragua, Peru, and Venezuela." In *Human Rights and Basic Needs in the Americas,* edited by Margaret E. Crahan, pp. 150–89. Washington, D.C.: Georgetown University Press, 1982.

Fisher, Stewart W. "Human Rights in El Salvador and U.S. Foreign Policy." *Human Rights Quarterly* 4 (Spring 1982): 1–38.

Huntington, Samuel P. *Political Order in Changing Societies.* New Haven: Yale University Press, 1968.

Matthews, Herbert L. *Revolution in Cuba: An Essay in Understanding.* New York: Charles Scribner's Sons, 1975.

Montgomery, Tommie Sue. *Revolution in El Salvador: Origins and Evolution.* Boulder, Colo.: Westview Press, 1982.

Nolan, David. *The Ideology of the Sandinistas and the Nicaraguan Revolution.* Coral Gables, Fla.: Institute of Interamerican Studies, 1984.

O'Donnell, Guillermo. *Modernization and Bureaucratic-Authoritarianism Studies in South American Politics.* Berkeley: Institute for International Studies, 1973.

"Pain and Hope for Guatemalans." *LADOC* 10 (May–June 1980): 33–40.

Political Constitution. National Assembly of the Republic of Nicaragua. Managua, Nicaragua: 9 January 1987.

Ramírez, Sergio, ed. *Augusto C. Sandino: el pensamiento vivo.* 2 vols. Managua: Nueva Nicaragua, 1981.

Schoultz, Lars. "U.S. Foreign Policy and Human Rights in Latin America: A Comparative Analysis of Foreign Aid Distribution." In *Revolution in Central America,* edited by the Stanford Central America Action Network, pp. 271–79. Boulder, Colo.: Westview Press, 1983.

Stavrianos, L. S. *Global Rift: The Third World Comes of Age.* New York: William Morrow and Company, 1981.

Summers, Robert, and Heston, Alan. "Improved International Comparisons of Real Product and Its Composition: 1950–1980." *The Review of Income and Wealth* 30 (June 1984): 207–62.

Vilas, Carlos M. *The Sandinista Revolution: National Liberation and Social Transformation in Central America.* New York: Monthly Review Press, 1986.

Weber, Henri. *Nicaragua: The Sandinist Revolution.* London: Verso, 1981.

Wheelock Román, Jaime. *Imperialismo y dictadura.* Managua: Nueva Nicaragua, 1985.

White, Richard Alan. "Rule Without Law: El Salvador." *Human Rights Quarterly* 4 (Spring 1982): 149–53.

Zea, Leopoldo. *The Latin American Mind.* Norman: University of Oklahoma Press, 1963.

Political Theory, Economic Theory, and Moral Philosophy

Ackerman, Bruce A. *Social Justice in the Liberal State.* New Haven: Yale University Press, 1980.

Alfarabi. "The Political Regime." In *Medieval Political Philosophy: A Sourcebook,* edited by Ralph Lerner and Muhsin Mahdi, pp. 31–57. Ithaca, N.Y.: Cornell University Press, 1963.

Arendt, Hannah. *On Revolution.* New York: Penguin Books, 1965.

Aristotle. *Politics.* c. 345 B.C.

Avicenna. "Healing: Metaphysics X." In *Medieval Political Philosophy: A Sourcebook,* edited by Ralph Lerner and Muhsin Mahdi, pp. 98–111. Ithaca, N.Y.: Cornell University Press, 1963.

Becker, Lawrence C. "Property Rights and Social Welfare." In *Economic Justice: Private Rights and Public Responsibilities,* edited by Kenneth Kipnis and Diana T. Meyers, pp. 71–86. Totowa, N.J.: Rowman & Allanheld, 1985.

Benjamin, Roger, and Elkin, Stephen L., eds. *The Democratic State.* Lawrence: University of Kansas Press, 1985.

Berger, Peter L. *Pyramids of Sacrifice: Political Ethics and Social Change.* Garden City, N.Y.: Anchor Books, 1976.

_____, and Luckmann, Thomas. *The Social Construction of Reality: A Treatise in the Sociology of Knowledge.* Garden City, N.Y.: Anchor Books, 1967.

Berlin, Isaiah. "Two Concepts of Liberty." In *Four Essays on Liberty,* edited by Berlin, pp. 118–72. London: Oxford University Press, 1977.

Bernstein, Richard. *The Restructuring of Social and Political Theory.* Philadelphia: University of Pennsylvania Press, 1978.

Bibliography

Bigongari, Dino, ed. *The Political Writings of St. Augustine.* Chicago: Henry Regnery 1962.

Brown, Robert McAfee. *Religion and Violence: A Primer for White Americans.* Philadelphia: Westminster Press, 1973.

Buchanan, Allen. *Ethics, Efficiency, and the Market.* Totowa, N.J.: Rowman & Allanheld, 1985.

Chilcote, Ronald H., ed. *Dependency and Marxism: Toward a Resolution of the Debate.* Boulder, Colo.: Westview Press, 1982.

Cicero. *On the Commonwealth,* trans. George H. Sabine and Stanley B. Smith. Indianapolis: The Bobbs-Merrill Co., 1976.

Coleman, Frank. *Hobbes and America: Exploring the Constitutional Foundations.* Toronto: University of Toronto Press, 1977.

Dahl, Robert. *After the Revolution? Authority in a Good Society.* New Haven: Yale University Press, 1970.

_____. *Dilemmas of Pluralist Democracy: Authority vs. Control.* New Haven: Yale University Press, 1982.

_____. *A Preface to Economic Democracy.* Berkeley: University of California Press, 1985.

Davies, J. G. *Christians, Politics and Violent Revolution.* Maryknoll, N.Y.: Orbis Books, 1976.

Debray, Regis. *Revolution in the Revolution? Armed Struggle and Political Struggle in Latin America.* New York: Grove Press, 1967.

Dietz, Mary. "Trapping the Prince: Machiavelli and the Political Regime." *American Political Science Review* 80 (September 1986): 777–99.

DiQuattro, Arthur. "Rawls and Left Criticism." *Political Theory* 11 (February 1983): 53–78.

Dodd, Lawrence C., and Schott, Richard L. *Congress and the Administrative State.* New York: John Wiley & Sons, 1973.

Euben, J. Peter. "The Battle of Salamis and the Origins of Political Theory." *Political Theory* 14 (August 1986): 359–90.

Frankena, William E. "The Naturalistic Fallacy." In *Perspectives on Morality: Essays of William K. Frankena,* edited by Kenneth K. Goodpaster, pp. 1–11. Notre Dame: University of Notre Dame Press, 1976.

Freire, Paulo. *Pedagogy of the Oppressed.* New York: Seabury Press, 1970.

Frolich, Norman, and Oppenhiemer, Joe A., *Modern Political Economy.* Englewood Cliffs, N.J.: Prentice-Hall, 1978.

Gebhardt, Jürgen. "The Origins of Politics in Ancient Hellas: Old Interpretations and New Perspectives." In *Sophia and Praxis: The*

Boundaries of Politics, edited by J. M. Porter, pp. 1–31. Chatham, N.J.: Chatham House, 1984.

Gerassi, John, ed. *Revolutionary Priest: The Complete Writings and Messages of Camilo Torres.* New Haven: Yale University Press, 1979.

Gordon, Scott. *Welfare, Justice, and Freedom.* New York: Columbia University Press, 1980.

Gunnemann, Jon P. *The Moral Meaning of Revolution.* New Haven: Yale University Press, 1979.

Habermas, Jürgen. *Legitimation Crisis.* Boston: Beacon Press, 1975.

_____. *Lifeworld and System: A Critique of Functionalist Reason,* vol. 2, *The Theory of Communicative Action.* Boston: Beacon Press, 1987.

_____. *Reason and the Rationalization of Society,* vol. 1, *The Theory of Communicative Action.* Boston: Beacon Press, 1981.

_____. *Toward a Rational Society: Student Protest, Science, and Politics.* Boston: Beacon Press, 1970.

Harding, Arthur L., ed. *The Rule of Law.* Dallas: Southern Methodist University Press, 1961.

Held, David. *Introduction to Critical Theory: Horkheimer to Habermas.* Berkeley. University of California Press, 1980.

Herson, Lawrence J. R. *The Politics of Ideas: Political Theory and American Public Policy.* Homewood, Ill.: Dorsey Press, 1984.

Hobbes, Thomas. *Leviathan.* 1651.

Hobhouse, L. T. *Liberalism.* 1911. Reprint. London: Oxford University Press, 1964.

Horkheimer, Max. "Atheism and Religion." In *Dawn and Decline: Notes 1926–1931 and 1950–1969,* edited by Horkheimer, pp. 65–66. New York: Seabury Press, 1978.

_____. *Eclipse of Reason.* 1947. Reprint. New York: Continuum, 1974.

_____. "Europe and Christianity." In *Dawn and Decline: Notes 1926–1931 and 1950–1969,* edited by Horkheimer, pp. 88–91. New York: Seabury Press, 1978.

_____. "Theism and Atheism." In *Critique of Instrumental Reason,* edited by Horkheimer, pp. 34–50. New York: Seabury Press, 1974.

_____. "Thoughts on Religion." In *Critical Theory: Selected Essays,* edited by Horkheimer, pp. 129–31. New York: Herder and Herder, 1972.

Horkheimer, Max, and Adorno, Theodor W. *Dialectic of Enlightenment.* 1944. Reprint. New York: Continuum, 1972.

Hunt, E. K. *Property and Prophets: The Evolution of Economic Institutions and Ideologies,* 4th ed. New York: Harper and Row Publishers, 1981.

Bibliography

Jay, Martin. *The Dialectical Imagination: A History of the Frankfurt School and the Institute of Social Research, 1923–1950.* Boston: Little, Brown and Company, 1973.

Kant, Immanuel. *Critique of Pure Reason.* 1787.

Lerner, Ralph, and Mahdi, Muhsin, eds. *Medieval Political Philosophy: A Sourcebook.* Ithaca, N.Y.: Cornell University Press, 1963.

Lindblom, Charles E. *Politics and Markets: The World's Political-Economic Systems.* New York: Basic Books, 1977.

Locke, John. *Two Treatises of Government.* c. 1688.

Lowi, Theodore J. *The End of Liberalism,* 2nd ed. New York: W. W. Norton & Company, 1979.

MacIntyre, Alasdair. *After Virtue: A Study in Moral Theory.* Notre Dame: University of Notre Dame Press, 1981.

Macpherson, C. B. *The Political Theory of Possessive Individualism: Hobbes to Locke.* London: Oxford University Press, 1962.

_____. *The Real World of Democracy.* New York: Oxford University Press, 1966.

Madison, James. *The Federalist Papers,* nos. 10, 51. 1787–88.

Machiavelli, Niccolò. *The Prince.* 1513.

Marcuse, Herbert. *One-Dimensional Man: Studies in the Ideology of Advanced Industrial Society.* Boston: Beacon Press, 1964.

_____. "The Problem of Violence and the Radical Opposition." In *Five Lectures: Psychoanalysis, Politics, and Utopia,* edited by Marcuse, pp. 83–108. Boston: Beacon Press, 1970.

Margolis, Michael. *Viable Democracy.* New York: Penguin Books, 1979.

Medcalf, Linda, and Dolbeare, Kenneth M. *Neopolitics: American Political Ideas in the 1980s.* New York: Random House, 1985.

Mill, John Stuart. *Essay on Liberty.* 1859.

_____. *Principles of Political Economy.* 1848.

Nash, Ronald H. *Poverty and Wealth: The Christian Debate Over Capitalism.* Westchester, Ill.: Crossway Books, 1986.

Niebuhr, Reinhold. *The Children of Light and the Children of Darkness: A Vindication of Democracy and a Critique of Its Traditional Defense.* New York: Charles Scribner's Sons, 1972.

_____. *Moral Man and Immoral Society: A Study in Ethics and Politics.* New York: Charles Scribner's Sons, 1960.

Nielson, Kai. "Capitalism, Socialism and Justice." In *And Justice For All: New Introductory Essays in Ethics and Public Policy,* edited by Tom Regan and Donald VanDeVeer, pp. 264–86. Totowa, N.J.: Rowman and Littlefield, 1982.

Nozick, Robert. *Anarchy, State and Utopia.* New York: Basic Books, 1974.

Oelmüller, Willi. "The Limitations of Social Theories." In *Religion and Political Society,* edited by Jürgen Moltmann, Herbert W. Richardson, Johann Baptist Metz, Willi Oelmüller, and M. Darrol Bryant, pp. 121–69. New York: Harper & Row, 1974.

Piven, Francis Cox, and Cloward, Richard A. *The New Class War.* New York: Pantheon Books, 1982.

Plato. *Republic.* c. 390 B.C.

Rawls, John. *A Theory of Justice.* Cambridge: Harvard University Press, 1971.

Rostow, W. W., ed. *The Economics of Take-Off into Sustained Growth.* New York: St. Martin's Press, 1963.

Rousseau, Jean-Jacques. *A Discourse on the Origins of Inequality.* 1755.

_____. *The Social Contract.* 1762.

Sartre, Jean-Paul. *Anti-Semite and Jew.* New York: Schocken, 1965.

Schiller, Herbert I. *Communication and Cultural Domination.* White Plains, N.Y.: M. E. Sharpe, 1976.

Shue, Henry *Basic Rights: Subsistence, Affluence, and U.S. Foreign Policy.* Princeton: Princeton University Press, 1980.

Smith, Adam. *Wealth of Nations.* 1776.

Strauss, Leo. "An Epilogue." In *Essays on the Scientific Study of Politics,* edited by Herbert J. Storing, pp. 305–27. New York: Holt, Rinehart and Winston, 1962.

_____. *Jerusalem and Athens.* New York: The City College, 1967.

_____. "Political Philosophy and History." In *What Is Political Philosophy? and other Studies,* edited by Strauss, pp. 56–77. Glencoe, Ill.: The Free Press, 1959.

_____. "Three Waves of Modernity." In *Political Philosophy: Six Essays,* edited by Hilail Gildin, pp. 81–98. Indianapolis: Pegasus, 1975.

Tocqueville, Alexis de. *Democracy in America.* 1835.

Unger, Roberto Mangabeira. *Knowledge and Politics.* New York: The Free Press, 1975.

Warren, Scott. *The Emergence of Dialectical Theory: Philosophy and Political Inquiry.* Chicago: University of Chicago Press, 1984.

Wilhelmsen, Frederick D. *Christianity and Political Philosophy.* Athens: The University of Georgia Press, 1978.

Wolff, Robert Paul. *In Defense of Anarchism.* New York: Harper & Row, 1970.

Bibliography

Marxism and Christianity

Althusser, Louis. "Ideological and Ideological State Apparatuses." In *Lenin and Philosophy and other Essays,* edited by Althusser, pp. 127–86. New York: Monthly Review Press, 1971.

Aptheker, Herbert. *The Urgency of Marxist-Christian Dialogue.* New York: Harper & Row, 1970.

_____, ed. *Marxism and Christianity: A Symposium.* New York: Humanities Press, 1968.

Engels, Friedrich. Letter to Joseph Bloch, 21–22 September 1890. In *The Marx-Engels Reader,* edited by Robert C. Tucker, pp. 640–42. New York: W. W. Norton, 1972.

Garaudy, Roger. *The Alternative Future: A Vision of Christian Marxism.* New York: Simon & Schuster, 1974.

_____. *From Anathema to Dialogue: A Marxist Challenge to the Christian Churches.* New York: Vintage Books, 1968.

Girardi, Giulio. *Marxism and Christianity.* New York: Macmillan Publishing Co., 1968.

Harris, H. Wilson, ed. *Christianity and Communism.* Boston: Marshall Jones Co., 1937.

Hebblethwaite, Peter. *The Christian-Marxist Dialogue: Beginnings, Present Status, and Beyond.* New York: Paulist Press, 1977.

Kamenka, Eugene. *Marxism and Ethics.* London: Macmillan, 1969.

Lukács, Georg. *History and Class Consciousness: Studies in Marxist Dialectics.* Cambridge: The MIT Press, 1971.

MacIntyre, Alasdair. *Marxism and Christianity.* New York: Schocken Books, 1968.

McGovern, Arthur F. *Marxism: An American Christian Perspective.* Maryknoll, N.Y.: Orbis Books, 1980.

McKown, Delos B. *Classical Marxist Critiques of Religion: Marx, Engels, Lenin, Kautsky.* The Hague: Martinus Nijhoff, 1975.

Marx, Karl. *Capital.* 3 vols. 1867.

_____. *Economic and Philosophical Manuscripts.* 1844.

_____. "Introduction to the Contribution to the Critique of Hegel's Philosophy of Right." In *Karl Marx: Early Writings,* edited by T. B. Bottomore, pp. 43–49. New York: McGraw-Hill Book Company, 1964.

_____. "On the Jewish Question." In *Karl Marx: Early Writings,* edited by T. B. Bottomore, pp. 1–40. New York: McGraw-Hill Book Company, 1964.

Miliband, Ralph. *The State in Capitalist Society.* New York: Basic Books, 1969.

Niebuhr, Reinhold. "Social Justice." In *Christianity and Communism,* edited by H. Wilson Harris, pp. 62–69. Boston: Marshall Jones Co., 1937.

Oestreicher, Paul. *The Christian Marxist Dialogue: An International Symposium.* London: Collier-Macmillan, 1969.

Piediscalzi, Nicholas, and Thobaben, Robert G., eds. *From Hope to Liberation: Towards a New Marxist-Christian Dialogue.* Philadelphia: Fortress Press, 1974.

Quinney, Richard. *Social Existence: Metaphysics, Marxism, and the Social Sciences.* Beverly Hills: Sage Publications, 1982.

Raines, John C., and Dean, Thomas, eds. *Marxism and Radical Religion: Essays Toward a Revolutionary Humanism.* Philadelphia: Temple University Press, 1970.

Religion and Politics

Berryman, Phillip. *The Religious Roots of Rebellion: Christians in Central American Revolutions.* Maryknoll, N.Y.: Orbis Books, 1984.

Bolle, Kees W. "The Myth of Our Materialism." In *Religion and Politics in the Modern World,* edited by Peter H. Merkl and Ninian Smart, pp. 249–66. New York: New York University Press, 1983.

Bruneau, Thomas C. "Basic Christian Communities in Latin America: Their Nature and Significance (especially in Brazil)." In *Churches and Politics in Latin America,* edited by Daniel H. Levine, pp. 225–37. Beverly Hills: Sage Publications, 1980.

Cabezas, Omar. *Fire from the Mountain: The Making of a Sandinista.* New York: New American Library, 1985.

Câmara, Hélder. *Revolution through Peace.* New York: Harper & Row, 1970.

_____. *The Spiral of Violence.* Denville, N.J.: Dimension Books, 1971.

Cardenal, Ernesto. *The Gospel of Solentiname.* 4 vols. Maryknoll, N.Y.: Orbis Books, 1982.

_____. "Revolution and Peace: The Nicaraguan Road." *Journal of Peace Research* 18 (1981): 201–7.

Cook, Guillermo. *The Expectation of the Poor: Latin American Basic Ecclesial Communities in Protestant Perspective.* Maryknoll, N.Y.: Orbis Books, 1985.

Deelen, Gottfried. "The Church on Its Way to the People: Basic Christian Communities in Brazil." *Cross Currents* 30 (Winter 1980–81): 385–408.

Bibliography

Dodson, Michael, and Montgomery, T. S. "The Churches in the Nicaraguan Revolution." In *Nicaragua in Revolution*, edited by Thomas W. Walker, pp. 161–80. New York: Praeger Publishers, 1982.

Guevara, Ernesto Ché. Citation from *Cristo vivo en Cuba*, p. 27. By Sergio Arce Martínez. San Jose: DEI, 1978.

Healy, Joseph G. "Let the Base Christian Communities Speak: Some Pastoral Theology Reflections on Portequelo and Beyond." *Missiology: An International Review* 11 (January 1983): 15–30.

Joint Directorate of the Sandinista National Liberation Front (DN-FSLN). "The Role of Religion in the New Nicaragua." In *Sandinistas Speak*, edited by Thomas Borge et al., pp. 105–11. New York: Pathfinder Press, 1982.

Lernoux, Penney. *Cry of the People: The Struggle for Human Rights in Latin America—The Catholic Church in Conflict with U.S. Policy*. New York: Penguin Books, 1982.

Levine, Daniel H. *Religion and Politics in Latin America: The Catholic Church in Venezuela and Colombia*. Princeton: Princeton University Press, 1981.

McGinnis, James. *Solidarity with the People of Nicaragua*. Maryknoll, N.Y.: Orbis Books, 1985.

Maduro, Otto. *Religion and Social Conflicts*. Maryknoll, N.Y.: Orbis Books, 1982.

O'Brien, Connor Cruise. "God and Man in Nicaragua." *The Atlantic Monthly*, August 1986, pp. 50–72.

Panikkar, Raimundo. "Religion or Politics: The Western Dilemma." In *Religion and Politics in the Modern World*, edited by Peter H. Merkl and Ninian Smart, pp. 44–60. New York: New York University Press, 1983.

Peck, Jane Cary. "The Church of the Poor: Church of Life." *Missiology: An International Review* 11 (January 1983): 31–46.

Randall, Margaret. *Christians in the Nicaraguan Revolution*. Seattle, Washington: Left Bank, 1984.

Robertson, Roland, ed. *Sociology of Religion: Selected Readings*. New York: Penguin Books, 1981.

Romero, Oscar Arnulfo, and Rivera Damos [Rivera y Damas], Arturo. "The Church, Political Organization and Violence." *Cross Currents* 29 (Winter 1979–80): 385–408.

Rossi, Cardinal Agnelo. Interview with J. A. Dias Lopes. "A política destrói a igreja," *Veja* (São Paulo), no. 664 (27 May 1981), pp. 5–8.

Smith, Brian H. *Church and Politics in Chile: Challenges to Modern Catholicism*. Princeton: Princeton University Press, 1982.

Bibliography

_____. "Churches and Human Rights in Latin America: Recent Trends on the Subcontinent." In *Churches and Politics in Latin America*, edited by Daniel H. Levine, pp. 155–93. Beverly Hills: Sage Publications, 1980.

Weber, Max. *The Protestant Ethic and the Spirit of Capitalism*. New York: Charles Scribner's Sons, 1958.

Theology

Aquinas. *Summa Theologica*. 1265.

Augustine. *The City of God*. 412–26.

Brown, Delwin. *To Set at Liberty: Christian Faith and Human Freedom*. Maryknoll, N.Y.: Orbis Books, 1981.

Burrell, David B. "Religious Belief and Rationality." In *Rationality and Religious Belief*, edited by C. F. Delaney, pp. 84–115. Notre Dame: University of Notre Dame Press, 1979.

Carlen, Claudia, ed. *The Papal Encyclicals*. 5 vols. Raleigh, N.C.: McGrath Publishing Co., 1981.

Cobb, John B., Jr. *Process Theology as Political Theology*. Philadelphia: Westminster Press, 1982.

_____, and Griffin, David Ray *Process Theology: An Introductory Exposition*. Philadelphia: Westminster Press, 1976.

_____, and Schroeder, W. Widick, eds. *Process Philosophy and Social Thought*. Chicago: Center for the Scientific Study of Religion, 1981.

Cone, James. *God of the Oppressed*. New York: Seabury Press, 1975.

Cox, Harvey. *Religion in the Secular City: Toward a Postmodern Theology*. New York: Simon & Schuster, 1984.

Davis, Charles. *Theology and Political Society*. New York: Cambridge University Press, 1980.

Dorr, Donal. *Option for the Poor: A Hundred Years of Vatican Social Teaching*. Maryknoll, N.Y.: Orbis Books, 1982.

Flannery, Austin, ed. *Vatican Council II: The Conciliar and Post Conciliar Documents*. Northport, N.Y.: Costello Publishing Co., 1975.

Gottwald, Norman K., ed. *The Bible and Liberation: Political and Social Hermeneutics*. Maryknoll, N.Y.: Orbis Books, 1983.

Gremillion, Joseph, ed. *The Gospel of Peace and Justice: Catholic Social Teaching since Pope John*. Maryknoll, N.Y.: Orbis Books, 1976.

Gudorf, Christine E. *Catholic Social Teaching on Liberation Themes*. Lanham, Md.: University Press of America, 1980.

Bibliography

Hebblethwaite, Brian L. *The Problems of Theology.* Cambridge: Cambridge University Press, 1980.

Lamb, Matthew L. "The Challenge of Critical Theory." In *Sociology and Human Destiny: Essays on Sociology, Religion and Society,* edited by Gregory Baum, pp. 183–213. New York: Seabury Press, 1980.

Langan, John. "Violence and Injustice in Society: Recent Catholic Teaching." *Theological Studies* 46 (1985): 685–99.

McCann, Dennis P. "Political Ideologies and Practical Theology: Is There a Difference?" *Union Seminary Quarterly Review* 36 (Summer 1981): 243–57.

Metz, Johannes B. *Faith in History and Society.* New York: Seabury Press, 1980.

Moltmann, Jürgen. *Theology of Hope: On the Ground and the Implications of a Christian Eschatology.* New York: Harper & Row, 1967.

_____. "The Cross and Civil Religion." In *Religion and Political Society,* edited by Moltmann et al., pp. 9–47. New York: Harper & Row, 1974.

Pannenberg, Wolfhart. *Theology and the Philosophy of Science.* Philadelphia: Westminster Press, 1976.

Rahner, Karl. *Foundations of Christian Faith.* New York: Seabury Press, 1978.

Ramsey, Paul. *War and the Christian Conscience: How Shall Modern War Be Conducted Justly?* Durham, N.C.: Duke University Press, 1961.

Soelle, Dorothee. *Political Theology.* Philadelphia: Fortress Press, 1974.

Suelzer, Alexa. "Modern Old Testament Criticism." In *The Jerome Biblical Commentary,* vol. 2, edited by Joseph A. Fitzmyer and Raymond E. Brown, pp. 590–604. Englewood Cliffs, N.J.: Prentice-Hall, 1968.

Tracy, David. *Blessed Rage for Order: The New Pluralism in Theology.* New York: Seabury Press, 1975.

History and Philosophy of Science

Allen, Phyllis. "Scientific Studies in the English Universities of the Seventeenth Century." *Journal of the History of Ideas* 10 (1949): 219–53.

Ashton, T. S. *The Industrial Revolution: 1760–1830.* London: Oxford University Press, 1948.

Ayer, A. J. *Language, Truth and Logic.* New York: Dover, 1952.

Bibliography

_____, ed. *Logical Positivism.* New York: The Free Press, 1959.

Bacon, Francis. *Novum Organum.* 1620.

Barbour, Ian G. *Issues in Science and Religion.* New York: Harper Torchbooks, 1966.

Boretsky, Michael. "Trends in U.S. Technology: A Political Economist's View." In *Science, Technology, and National Policy,* edited by Thomas J. Kuehn and Alan L. Porter, pp. 161–88. Ithaca, N.Y.: Cornell University Press, 1981.

Brooks, Harvey. "Technology, Evolution, and Purposes." In *Technology and Man's Future,* 3rd ed., edited by Albert H. Teich, pp. 294–320. New York: St. Martin's Press, 1981.

Butterfield, Herbert. *The Origins of Modern Science,* rev. ed. New York: The Free Press, 1965.

Carnap, Rudolf. "Intellectual Autobiography." In *The Philosophy of Rudolf Carnap,* edited by Paul Arthur Schilpp, pp. 3–84. London: Cambridge University Press, 1963.

_____. "The Elimination of Metaphysics through Logical Analyses of Language." In *Logical Positivism,* edited by A. J. Ayer, pp. 60–80. New York: The Free Press, 1959

Dickson, David. "Technology and the Construction of Social Reality." In *Radical Science Essays,* edited by Les Levidow, pp. 15–37. Atlantic Highlands, N.J.: Humanities Press International, 1986.

Feingold, Mordechai. *The Mathematician's Apprenticeship: Science, Universities and Society in England, 1560–1640.* Cambridge: Cambridge University Press, 1984.

Greene, John C. *Science, Ideology, and World View: Essays in the History of Evolutionary Ideas.* Berkeley: University of California Press, 1981.

Hankins, Thomas L. *Science and the Enlightenment.* Cambridge: Cambridge University Press, 1985.

Hill, Christopher. *Intellectual Origins of the English Revolution.* Oxford: Oxford University Press, 1965.

Kuhn, Thomas. *The Copernican Revolution.* New York: Random House, 1957.

Merton, Robert. *Science, Technology and Society in Seventeenth Century England.* New York: Harper Torchbooks, 1970; originally 1938.

Popper, Karl. *Conjectures and Refutations: and the Growth of Scientific Knowledge.* New York: Harper & Row, 1963.

Shapiro, Barbara J. "The Universities and Science in Seventeenth Century England." *Journal of British History* 10 (1971): 47–82.

Bibliography

Turner, D. M. *The Book of Scientific Discovery: How Science Has Aided Human Welfare*. New York: Barnes & Noble Books, 1933.

Winner, Langdon. *Autonomous Technology: Technics-out-of-Control as a Theme in Political Thought*. Cambridge: The MIT Press, 1977.

Index

Absolutes, 42, 180–81
Absolutization, 136–37
Academic theology, theologians,
36–37, 54, 59, 133, 180; and
exegesis, 47; and revelation, 46;
and search for essence of
Christianity, 44; critical analysis
by, 42–43; critique of 38–44;
interpretation, 40; methodology
of, 53. *See also* Theology
Act of will (first step of
hermeneutic circle), 59–60, 89.
See also Hermeneutic circle;
Hermeneutics; Segundo, Juan Luis
Agnosticism, 26
Alfarabi, 24
Alienation, 82, 85, 178; use of, in
language of pope, 81
Aquinas, Thomas, 24, 201n.2,
221n.40; philosophy and
Christian theology of, 42
Arendt, Hannah, 125, 162
Argentina, 109, 111, 142, 151,
215n.47
Aristotle, 24, 42, 125, 201n.2,
208n.26
Aristotelian categories, 42
Aristotelianism, 78
Arns, Paulo Cardinal, 32

Assmann, Hugo: and critique of
Marxism, 92–94; and faith and
politics, 136–37; and Frankfurt
School, 173–74; and language of
liberation, 213n.4; and Marcuse,
174; and Marxist social
analysis, 87; and political
theology, 128; and revolution,
92–94, 154–55; biography of, 190
Atheism, 83, 96–97; and
conservative critics, 80; and
Marxism, 74–75, 80–81; and
Ratzinger, 74–75, 78; and
Second Vatican Council, 14
Augustine, 50, 155, 201n.2
Authoritarianism, 125, 149
Autonomy: and religion and
revolution, 82, 90; individual,
184; religious, 88, 128–29, 177,
179; state, 110
Avicenna, 24
Ayer, A. J., 185

Bauer, Bruno, 83
Becoming, 82
Being, 226n.19
Berlin, Isaiah, 34, 201n.1
Bible, 60, 67, 202n.16; and biblical
criticism, 38; and early Church,

251

Index

41; and Gustavo Gutiérrez, 41; and hermeneutics, 57; study of, 10–11, 53, 202n.16; themes in, 60; *See also* Hermeneutic circle; Hermeneutics; Interpretation
Bloch, Joseph, 90
Boff, Clodovis: biography of, 191
Boff, Leonardo: and CEBs, 139–40; and Frankfurt School, 173–74; and Gramsci, 174; and Marxist social analysis, 87; biography of, 191; on Christianity and Marxism, 94
Bolivia, 111
Bonino, José Míguez. *See* Míguez Bonino, José
Brazil, 138–42, 109, 111, 151, 215n.47; and Bible study, 10–11; and CEBs, 2; and human rights, 32; and liberation theology, 1

Câmara, Dom Hélder, 32
Capitalism, 13, 68, 96, 100, 120, 123, 163, 177, 197–98n.37; and Catholic social teachings, 16, 214n.33; and modernity, 160; dependent, 124; international, 107; logic of, 180; merchant, 101; monopoly, 60; United States, 29. *See also* Dependency theory; Development, economic; Developmentalism; Modern era
Cardenal, Father Ernesto, 157, 224n.82
Cardenal, Father Fernando, 224n.82
Carnap, Rudolf, 230n.71
Casaldáliga, Bishop Dom Pedro, 10
Castro, Fidel, 12
Catholic Action, 138–39
Catholic church, Catholicism, Catholics, 2, 30, 138–39; and development, 32; and human rights, 32; and Marxism, 205n.3; social teachings of, 6, 16;

thinkers, 14. *See also* Religion; Theology
CEBs (*as comunidades eclesiais de base*), 9, 62, 138–43; and conscientization, 157; and Habermas, 181; and liberation theology, 6; and national security state, 141–43; and revolution, 141, 157–58; in Brazil, 2; in Nicaragua, 157; Medellín documents, 18
CELAM (*Consejo Episcopal Latinoamericano*), 12–13, 19–20, 64, 198n.45; and liberation theology, 15; and human rights, 32; and property, 149; and violence, 151. *See also* Medellín documents
Center-periphery, 104–6. *See also* Dependency theory
Certitudes, 45; absolute, 7, 53, 59, 119, 144, 182; problem of, 44–45; propositional, 43, 68, 136; theological, 47, 61, 99, 133, 203n.39; universal, 45, 48–50. *See also* Truth
Chile, 1, 111, 142, 151
Christian base communities. *See* CEBs
Christian theology, 41, 75, 155. *See also* Theology
Christianity, Christians, 3, 180; and economic morality, 108; and fundamentalist sects, 188; and historical-materialist theory, 91; and love, 152–53; and pacifism, 221n.40; and philosophy, 35; beliefs and traditions, 72, 83, 92, 188; essence of, 38–39; evolution of, 40; Iberian, 108; mainstream, 150, 178; traditional, 132, 150
Church, 14, 41, 65; and CELAM, 20; and ideological

Index

Index

totalities, 71; as Bible, 57; as method of academic theology, 38, 40–41; of Christian theology, 155; of Christianity and violence, 221n.40; prophetic character of, 57. *See also* Academic theology; Comblin, José

Hobbes, Thomas, 25–26, 184–85

Hope, 96–97

Horkheimer, Max, 180

Human nature, 165–67

Human rights, 33, 55, 109, 119, 123, 164, 172; and Medellín documents, 18; and state violence, 151–52. *See also* Medellín documents; Rights

Humanism, 67, 69–70, 93

Hyperpluralism, 26

Ideological suspicion (second step of hermeneutic circle), 60–62, 66, 89, 177. *See also* Hermeneutic circle

Ideology, ideologies, 111, 115, 135, 137, 182, 195n.12, 197n.37; and CELAM, 20; and faith, 20; and liberation theology, 219n.21; and religion, 77, 88; and Marxism, 73, 80–81; and social analysis, 73; and theology, 37; as public philosophy, 101; authoritarian, 92; of national security state, 114–18, 152; political, 7

Individualism, 101, 159–60, 184; ethical, 33, 188; radical, 26, 28. *See also* Modern era; Rights

Industrial Revolution, 28–29, 89, 101, 108, 160, 200n.70, 214n.33

Industrialization, 16, 164

Institutionalized violence, 16, 19, 20–21, 149, 151–52. *See also* Violence

Interpretation, 155; *aktuelles Verstehen*, 167; and hermeneutics, 11, 15; and scholarship, 44; biblical, 6; *erklärendes Verstehen*, 167; of facts, 172; of Marx, 121; of Scripture, 11, 15, 135; theological, 49. *See also* Hermeneutic circle; Hermeneutics

Imperialism, 69, 100, 106, 121, 164; and Medellín documents, 15; theoretical, 169. *See also* Medellín documents

Jesus, 178; and Pharisees, 47–48; and prophetic tradition, 67; and revolution, 157; and violence, 153, 155–56; evangelization of, 132

John the Baptist, 156

John XXIII, 195–96n.12

Judaism, 85–86, 210n.76. *See also* Marx, critique of religion

Just revolution, 133–34, 143–45. *See also* Revolution

Just war, 13, 133–34, 143–44. *See also* War

Kant, Immanuel, 160, 201n.1, 208n.26

Kirk, J. Andrew, 22, 56, 165–66, 170–71, 202n.16

Kjellen, Rudolf, 112

Knowledge, 72, 187. *See also* Epistemology

Kroger, Joseph, 81–82

Lamb, Matthew L., 173, 182

Language, 213n.4; and conscientization, 139; and revolution, 145; Church use of, 57, 204n.64; God and poverty, 52; of liberation theology,

Index

Marx, Karl, 13, 96, 121, 208 n.26; and economic determinism, 211n.91; and emancipation, 83–85; and hermeneutic circle, 88–91; and historical materialism, 77, 90; and labor theory of value, 186; and ontological dualism, 181–82; and property, 83–84; and revolutionary potential of religion, 91, 128, 178; critique of religion, 83–88; on Judaism, 84–86, 210n.76; writings of, 67, 74, 80, 82–83, 184–85. *See also* Segundo, Juan Luis

Marxism, 80, 95, 158, 208n.31; and Christianity, 72–73, 92, 154: and death, 93–94; and existentialism, 70; and faith, 68; and Hegelian thought, 82; and hermeneutic circle, 7; and historical materialism, 87, 90; and interpretation, 92; and liberation, 97, 174; and methodology of liberation theology, 162, 169–72, 178; and metaphysics, 81; and religion, 87; and social justice, 66; and socialism, 206n.3; and Western thought, 69; and dialectics and theology, 68; flexible, 182; orthodox, 3, 173, 179

Marxist philosophy, frameworks, 5, 80, 172; analytical categories of, 72; and Christianity, 83; and Juan Gutiérrez, 79; and liberation theology, 6; and López Trujillo, 76–78; and Ratzinger, 74–76; as tradition, 72; explanations of, 62–63; perspectives of, 167; project of 97

Marxist social analysis, 5, 8, 206n.3; and Christianity, 65, 94–95; and class analysis, 5, 7, 67, 88, 97, 99; and dialectical

thinking, 71; and Dussel, 105–6; and hermeneutic circle, 66, 179; and liberation theology, 72, 92, 131, 149, 154, 161, 172; and religion, 83, 87, 169, 174–75; and revolution, 177; and sociology, 8, 96, 213n.4; and tension, 73; and theology, 9, 82, 165

Marxist social science, 63, 66, 68, 72–73, 154; and López Trujillo, 77; and Ratzinger, 75; liberation of, 172, 178–83

Marxist-Christians: alliance of, 7, 72, 76; dialogue by, 67, 76, 96, tension of, 63, 88, 92–94

Marxists, 87, 116–18, 230n.71

Mass organizations, 126–27. See also Nicaragua

Mater et Magistra, 195–96n.12

Materialism, 74, 96–97

Medellín documents, 11–23, 196n.13; and CELAM, 12; and human rights, 32; and liberation theology, 15; and López Trujillo, 76; and property, 149; and revolution, 197n.30; and violence, 151. *See also* CELAM

Medieval era, 24, 101, 159, 162

Medieval thought, 27

Methodology, 36, 40; of academic theology, 45, 94; of liberation theology, 33, 53, 59, 65, 88, 92, 98, 119, 131, 144, 153, 158, 161–62, 170, 177, 187; of science, 90; social scientific, 36, 167, 186

Mexico, 1, 206n.3

Middle Ages, 23

Míguez Bonino, José, 38; and class struggle, 154; and historical project, 119–22; and lack of market analysis, 123; and Marxist social analysis, 87;

Index

Ontological dualism, 16, 54, 132, 134, 145, 180–81
Organic intellectual, 174
Orthodox theology, 133. *See also* Theology
Orthodoxy, 40–41, 52, 65, 140
Orthopraxis, 52, 140, 171
Osborn, Robert T., 171

Pacem in Terris, 195–96n.12
Pacifism, 131
Paraguay, 142
Parrales, Father Edgar, 224n.82
Paul VI, 19, 197–98n.37, 206n.3
Pharisees, 47–48
Phenomenological analysis, 45–47
Philosophy of science, 4
Philosophy, Cartesian, 86
Pius XI, 205–6n.3, 214n.33
Piven, Francis Fox, 24
Plato, 24, 34, 41, 184, 226n.19
Pluralism, 60, 116, 124
Political theology, 4, 128; and CELAM, 19; and liberation theology, 7, 229n.64; and Marxism, 92, 208n.26; and political philosophy, 23; and social science, 168; European, 171, 173, 180–81; Latin American, 21. *See also* Theology
Popper, Karl, 185
Populorum Progressio, 19, 197n.37
Positivism, positivists, 91, 185, 230n.71
Post-Enlightenment, 160. *See also* Enlightenment; Modern era; Modernity
Praxis, 7, 52, 173, 182; and critique of Gustavo Gutiérrez, 79; and Dussel, 106; and ethics, 168–69; and hermeneutics, 58; and liberation theology, 53–56, 131, 133; and Marx, 96; and Marxist ideology, 75; and Ratzinger, 75; and scriptural

interpretation, 61; and theory, 136. *See also* Vidales, Raúl
Process, 49–50, 168
Property: and Catholic social teachings, 14, 16; and liberal state, 85; and Medellín documents, 149; and United States, 29; private, 25, 67, 142, 197–98n.37; rights of, 24, 27, 30–31, 123, 126. *See also* Modern era; Modernity; Rights
Prophetic denunciation, 15, 22
Prophetic function, 136–37, 174
Prophetic movement, 183
Prophetic tradition, 55, 67, 72, 133
Propositions, 187. *See also* Certitudes; Truth
Protestant Reformation, 25, 30, 101, 159
Protestantism, Protestants, 2, 14, 30

Quadragesimo Anno, 205n.3, 214n.33
Quietism, 132, 188

Rationality, 42, 37; capitalist, 149, 180; egoistic, 165; scientific, 77, 164, 177; state and, 176; technological, 163–64, 177. *See also* Reason
Ratzinger, Joseph Cardinal, 73–78, 81, 208n.31
Rawls, John, 92, 160
Reason, 23, 25, 41, 58, 176
Reform, 137, 158; and CEBs, 143; and Frankfurt School, 173–74; and Medellín documents, 150–51; and religion, 127–29; nonviolent, 131; political, 9, 13–14
Relativism, 49, 57
Religion: and liberation 86–87, 175–77; and politics, 35; and rationality, 43; and revolution,